Kierkegaard and Postmodernism

GENERAL EDITOR
Mark C. Taylor, williams college

ASSOCIATE EDITORS
E. F. Kaelin, florida state university
Louis Mackey, the university of texas at austin

POINTS OF VIEW
READINGS OF KIERKEGAARD

Louis Mackey

University Presses of Florida
FLORIDA STATE UNIVERSITY PRESS/TALLAHASSEE

University Presses of Florida is the central agency for scholarly publishing of the State of Florida's university system, producing books selected for publication by the faculty editorial committees of Florida's nine public universities. Orders for books published by all member presses of University Presses of Florida should be addressed to University Presses of Florida, 15 NW 15th Street, Gainesville, FL 32603.

Library of Congress Cataloging-in-Publication Data

Mackey, Louis.
   Points of view.

   Bibliography: p.
   Includes index.
   1. Kierkegaard, Søren, 1813–1855.   I. Title.
B4377.M27 1986   198'.9   85–22713
ISBN 0-8130-0824-7

Copyright 1986 by the Board of Regents of the State of Florida
Printed in the U.S.A. on acid-free paper.
Typesetting by G&S Typesetters, Austin, Texas

FOR
> STEPHEN LOUIS,
> THOMAS ADAM,
> JACOB LOUIS,
>   AND
> EVA MARIA

Contents

Foreword by Mark C. Taylor	ix
Preface	xv
1. Starting from Scratch: Kierkegaard Unfair to Hegel	1
2. The Analysis of the Good in Kierkegaard's *Purity of Heart*	23
3. The View from Pisgah: A Reading of *Fear and Trembling*	40
4. Once More with Feeling: Kierkegaard's *Repetition*	68
5. A Ram in the Afternoon: Kierkegaard's Discourse of the Other	102
6. The Loss of the World in Kierkegaard's Ethics	141
7. Points of View for His Work as an Author: A Report from History	160
Bibliography	193
Index	199

Foreword

Points of View: Readings of Kierkegaard is not a book. One might well say of this text what Jacques Derrida has written of his own work, *Dissemination*:

> This (therefore) will not have been a book.
> Still less, despite appearances, will it have been a collection of [seven] "essays" whose itinerary it would be time, after the fact, to recognize; whose continuity and underlying laws could be pointed out; indeed, whose overall concept or meaning could at last, with all the insistence required on such occasions, be squarely set forth. (3)

Written over a period of twenty-two years (1960–82), the essays that comprise this volume display no overall coherence and do not unfold a strictly consistent interpretation of Kierkegaard. As his title indicates, Louis Mackey presents *"points* of view" and *"readings* of Kierkegaard." Despite the lack of any continuous thread of development, it is possible to group the points of view represented in these readings (and rereadings) under the general headings "early" and "late." In the middle of the volume, there is a hole or a gap; a ten-year silence separates the earlier and later essays. During this decade of silence, Mackey rethinks Kierkegaard (and one suspects much else) from A to Z. Between the writing of "The Analysis of the Good in Kierkegaard's *Purity of Heart*," "The View from Pisgah: A Reading of *Fear and Trembling*," and "The Loss of the World in Kierkegaard's Ethics," and the writing of "Starting from Scratch: Kierkegaard Unfair to Hegel," "Once More with Feeling: Kierkegaard's *Repetition*," "A Ram in the Afternoon: Kierkegaard's Discourse of the Other," and "Points of View for His Work as an Author: A Report from History," Mackey's preoccupations shift. A different style and a new language invade his text. Strange terms displace familiar categories: absence, absurdity, beginning, boundary, castration, closure, crypt, desire, discontinuity, dissemination, double bind, excess, expenditure, exteriority, farce, fault, gender, gift, humor, hymen, irony, iteration, jest, jouissance, kenosis, kinesis, logocentrism, madness, margin, mime, naming, negativity, neuter, other, paradox, phallogocentrism, quotation, repetition, representation, rupture, sacrifice, signature, signification, silence, text, truth, unknowing, uncanny, ventriloquism, violence, virginity, wit, woman, writing, *x*, yearning, zero. What are we to make of this shift?

Mackey presents something that approximates an answer to this question in the preface to the essays. But his remarks are not unequivocal, for he recognizes that prefaces are irreducibly duplicitous. Gazing both outward toward the reader and inward toward the text, the preface remains double-faced. Derrida's insight again is helpful.

> Prefaces, along with forewords [N.B.], introductions, preludes, preliminaries, preambles, prologues, and prolegomena, have always been written, it seems, in view of their own self-effacement. Upon reaching the end of the *pre-* (which presents and precedes, or rather forestalls, the presentative production, and, in order to put before the reader's eyes what is not yet visible, is obliged to speak, predict, and predicate), the route which has been covered must cancel itself out. But this subtraction leaves a mark of

erasure, a *reminder* which is added to the subsequent text and which cannot be completely summed up within it. Such an operation thus appears contradictory, and the same is true of the interest one takes in it.

But does a preface exist? (*Dissemination*, 3)

Mackey subtly erases his preface in the very act of inscribing it. He begins by confessing: "I would be the last to argue that their [the essays'] chronological sequence is matched by a succession of refinements in my understanding of Kierkegaard. For that reason, among others, they are not here arrayed in order of composition." Throughout the preface, Mackey resists the temptation to impose an order on his writings or to retrace the complex course his thinking has followed. He never tries to close the gaps in his work or to break the silence that pervades his "book." To the contrary, Mackey's crafty foreplay actually serves to deepen the enigma of his text. What he gives with one hand, he repeatedly takes away with the other: *fort . . . da, fort . . . da. . . .* Left empty-handed, the reader begins to suspect that the hors d'oeuvre is neither simply inside nor outside the work it is supposed to frame. This suspicion grows when one turns from the preface to the text "proper."

In his opening essay, Mackey explains: "The problem is: beginning. And equivalently: repetition." Mackey's beginning is, in fact, a repetition—a repetition of Kierkegaard's beginning. Like Kierkegaard, Mackey begins with irony. The significance of this beginning does not become apparent until the end of the text. Mackey's ending is also a repetition—a repetition of Kierkegaard's (premature) ending. *Points of View* begins by examining Kierkegaard's *The Concept of Irony* and ends by rereading *The Point of View for My Work as an Author: A Report to History.* In ending, Mackey insists that one must always be suspicious of ironists.

There is perhaps never good reason (even in the "normal" case) to identify the "writer" with the "actual" person whose name he signs, though it is natural to do so. But in the latter the course of nature is blocked by the flagrant interposition of artifice. The irruption of artifice introduces the distinction between art and nature. The proliferation of artifice makes the distinction undecidable and the identity of the natural indeterminable. When a man fabricates as many masks to hide behind as Kierkegaard does, one cannot trust his (purportedly) direct asseverations. And when he signs his own name, it no longer has the effects of the signature.

(Søren Kierkegaard was one of his own pseudonyms. Or perhaps all of them are God's pseudonyms. That is what Søren would have us believe.)

What, then, are we to make of Louis Mackey or "Louis Mackey"? Can we take *him* at his word? Can we trust the preface that is his own (premature) "report to history"? In a manner reminiscent of Victor Eremita's preface to *Either/Or*, Mackey appears in "his own" preface as both editor and author. In his (pre)liminary remarks, Mackey, as editor, surveys the points of view of Mackey, as author. Appearances to the contrary notwithstanding, the editor enjoys no "Archimedean point" from which to survey the writings and draw definite conclusions. The editor, of course, is also an author who represents yet another point of view that is no more and no less definitive than the perspective of every other author "he" already has been. Louis, like his subject Søren, is an ironist. The reader, therefore, "cannot trust his (purportedly) direct asseverations. And when he signs his own name,

Louis Mackey
Austin, Texas
December 9, 1982

it no longer has the effects of the signature." Or it has the effects of a signature suspended between quotation marks. When Louis Mackey is read as "Louis Mackey," author becomes text. Rewriting "Louis's" words about "Søren," we might conclude (if conclusions still could be drawn) that "the actuality of [Louis Mackey] is his texts. He is a discourse. Everything—[Mackey], his fictions, and his fictions' fictions—is language." In this play of signs (which might or might not be significant), author disappears in text.

With the effacement of author in work, the reader is free to enter the labyrinthian text. The tangled lines of *Points of View: Readings of Kierkegaard* repeatedly return to questions that bear on the possibility and impossibility of language. "How," asks one of the authors, "can language, *being* language, undercut itself *as* language? Can language ever do more than repeat itself, even if not especially when it tries to deny itself? Is literary language a special case, an exception, or is it not rather a distillation of the 'essence' of language: to question meaning by multiplying meanings and to fold the referentiality of discourse back on itself. Human language, as Climacus observes, is rooted in self-love. Its extravagant fascination with itself is not a perversion of language but a singularly pellucid manifestation of its nature." Endlessly playing with itself, the language of literature nonetheless points to, though never properly reveals, an "other" that language can never comprehend. If *Points of View* could be said to have a theme (which it really does not), this theme might be defined as "alterity" or, more precisely, "the very alterity of the other-than-discourse." Like *Philosophical Fragments*, *Points of View* "is obsessed with alterity. In particular with the question, how can language give expression to that which is wholly other than language?"

> Is it possible that Something Else has invaded language, foisting upon it both an interpretation and a meaning, dissolving its autonomy, enslaving it to a sense and committing it to a referent—all of which, as language, it must and will be free of? Is it possible that there is Something that can make language speak what cannot be spoken? Possible. But scarcely thinkable. And surely unspeakable.

In the hands of the authors of *Points of View*, this unaskable question and unthinkable thought appear, disappear, and reappear in their elusive complexity. Problems traditionally assumed to be theological and philosophical return as questions of language and literature. And questions of language and literature inevitably spill over into theological and philosophical puzzles and aporia. The readings of Kierkegaard presented (or re-presented) in *Points of View* resituate Kierkegaard's works. Writers like Nietzsche, Derrida, Agacinski, and Lacan now join an interminable analysis that Kierkegaard long ago began with

Hegel. In the course of this exchange, it becomes clear that "the discourse of the other" makes every system incomplete and

> [There *is* an other-than-all-that-is which is beyond recuperation by the dialectic. There is something—namely, nothing—that falls outside the system. Irony, which is the *no* to everything that exists, *is*. Is: the possibility of an escape that eludes recapture, of irrecoverable loss, and of self-expenditure without reserve.
>
> In terms of terms: it is possible not only to say one thing while meaning something determinately other than what one says. It is also possible—and irony is the motive for the exploration of this possibility—to say something in such a way as to negate indeterminately what is said and at the same time negate the saying. It is possible to say, and to mean, nothing.]

(ironically) makes every book impossible.

Like the works it explores, *Points of View* is open to many readings. On one level, it records the wanderings of one of Kierkegaard's most creative and imaginative readers. The grace and wit of Louis Mackey's styles and arguments delight and illuminate. On another level, this nonbook reflects changes in the intellectual climate during the past several decades that have made it necessary to rethink some of our most important critical assumptions: What is an author? What is a book? What is a text? What is writing? What is reading? How is interpretation to be interpreted? Are books and/or texts meaningful? Can writings speak? Do texts communicate? By approaching Kierkegaard's writings with questions such as these in mind, Louis Mackey shows (albeit indirectly) the extent to which Kierkegaard anticipated some of the most seminal insights of contemporary philosophers and literary theorists. Kierkegaard, we are learning, was more than modern; he was (always) already postmodern.

"Mark C. Taylor"
Mark C. Taylor

Preface

> There is, then, always already a preface between two hands holding open a book. And the "prefacer," of the same or another proper name as the "author," need not apologize for "repeating" the text.
>
> Gayatri Chakravorty Spivak

The earliest essay in this collection was written in 1960, the latest in 1982. I would be the last to argue that their chronological sequence is matched by a succession of refinements in my understanding of Kierkegaard. For that reason, among others, they are not here arrayed in order of composition.

Nevertheless, one is tempted (especially in the irresponsible sanctuary of a preface) to repeat oneself—with variations. As one always betters one's exploits in the recounting and thereby continually recasts and recants one's identity. The author of "The Analysis of the Good," written in 1960, is an earnest young man whom I scarcely recognize at this distance. To his excesses I am still in debt, though his gravity now oppresses (read: embarrasses) me. I am pleased to note that just a year later, in "The Loss of the World," he knows how serious he is and therefore no longer takes himself quite so seriously. But he was, in the long run, undone by his self-consciousness. The person who (a few years on) writes "The View from Pisgah" thinks himself a very clever fellow indeed. He has learned a few tricks from the New

Critics, and he has obviously been boning up on medieval exegesis. I am willing to admit that he has turned his ingenuity, occasionally, to good account. Unfortunately, he seems to feel that he has at last comprehended Kierkegaard, irony and all, so that the final solemnity is worse than the first. The successor who, after a silence of ten years, produces the rest of the essays in this volume is a thoroughly corrupt and unreliable sort. Philosophically speaking (at least), little more than a dirty old man.

But a preface is not a valediction, and I should not (ab)use it (even without apology) to disown the many other people I have not been. It is time to get down to the serious business of repeating myself. One is tempted.

One is tempted, for example, to rewrite "The Loss of the World" so as to insinuate the suspicion that Kierkegaardian freedom is nothing but the masturbatory gesture of a perfectly isolate and uncommunicating subject: the fruitless intercourse of the *nihil* with itself. The inscription of this impropriety, already so blatantly unwritten in the text of 1961, would make unnecessary (and impossible) the desperate protests on behalf of abstractions like "reality" and "community" that intervene so noisily in the text as it stands. It would also give the irony at the end of the piece a somewhat apocalyptic tone: the vacuous Kierkegaardian subjectivity could function tacitly as (it could not be *called*) the inverse sign of grace: the Other which (if I understand Kierkegaard) we cannot construct for ourselves or incorporate in the construction of ourselves, for which we can only prepare ourselves de-constructively, to which we are (possibly) exposed and by which we are (necessarily if at all) moved when we put ourselves under erasure. Kierkegaard's text would then be the linguistic performance of this sign of the cross (*kreuzweise Durchstreichung*) by which we cross ourselves/are crossed out.

One is tempted (again) to improve "The Analysis of the Good" in much the same way. If this earnestly direct report of a purportedly direct communication were reinscribed under the sign of irony, the infinite(simal) circle of Kierkegaardian "purity"—taut and void—would re-present itself as the deconstructive moment in the constitution of a subject always already invaded by its absolute Other and decentered in advance by its ultimate Author. The "office of confession"—a verbal recitation of sins—would become thereby the experience of human insufficiency: "what neither a man's burning wish nor his determined resolution may attain to." And Kierkegaard's "spiritual preparation" for this office would be the enactment *by language* of the impossibility of this penance: language, rooted in self-love and the agency of human self-assertion, cannot confess its own incompetence or consent to its own annihilation. It might also be the realization *in language* that "the sorrowing of repentance" is already the trace—the absent presence—of Him who gives both "the beginning and the completion . . . victory in the day of need" (*Purity of Heart*, 3, 32, 219). So easily is the *sermo humilis* of irony inflated by the warmer rhetoric of solemn divinity.

It would be more challenging—at least as much challenge as temptation—to revise "The View from Pisgah." More challenging because the piece is already fully aware of Kierkegaard's irony, and to some extent contaminated by it. The challenge would be to finish the job. To sharpen the irony by which Kierkegaard makes an Old Testament patriarch the figure of the Christian believer. To incorporate in this text and the one that follows it some indicative of the relationships between the two father-figures—Job and Abraham—and the two books—*Fear and Trembling* and *Repetition*—which appeared on the same day in 1843 and which their authors' author clearly intended (*une façon de parler*) as companions. And (most challenging of all, perhaps impossible) to submit the deployment of typological theory in "Pisgah" to the scrutiny of that irony which, as it stands, the text presumes to elude or (maybe even) transcend. For all its sensitivity to Kierkegaard's indirection, the essay *takes itself* quite seriously and by so doing surreptitiously pretends to have *appropriated* Kierkegaard's book. If it were made to examine its methodological assumptions—or at least to leave them ironically suspended—its own figural reading of Kierkegaard might (ironically) *be taken* more seriously and Kierkegaard's text *liberated* to play out its (im)proper effect in uncontained fear and trembling. In his own way the new-critical author of "The View from Pisgah" claims to have "gone beyond" faith. He should back off or take the consequences.

So might the grave young father of these early essays be corrupted by the feckless old scribbler who succeeds him.

But this is not yet serious, scarcely even a repetition. A propos: there is, in this country and in these days, a group of writers—mostly young, mostly philosophers—determined (as I think they might put it) to "take Kierkegaard seriously as a philosopher." What this means, operationally, is to produce tidied up versions (repetitions) of Kierkegaard's doctrine. It is always already supercilient[1] to talk without blushing about Kierkegaardian "doctrine." And it is as sad as it is inevitable that the serious philosopher Kierkegaard becomes when thus emended a dreary academic who couldn't possibly have scandalized the Copenhagen literati of the 1840s, much less disturbed the subsequent history of philosophy and theology.

And now it seems I *am* getting serious. As I reread these things I (one or another of us) have written, I do think I discern a certain family resemblance. One or two motifs (I don't want to run with the metaphor of paternity) appear, variously varied, in all of these essays.[2] In the earlier pieces it is mostly implicit. Virtually there, but not yet ex-sisting its causes, it remains a mere *an sich*. In the later papers it is allowed to trouble the surface of the argument. If anything, it is in these (this) text(s) too often and too stridently insisted on.

Matters of tone aside,[3] the burden of all these essays comes to something like this. (1) Kierkegaard's writings are absolutely antiphilosophical and resolutely antitheological. (2) Because the paleonymic predicament requires him to deconstruct philosophy and theology in the terms of traditional religion and reflection, the antiphilosopher Kierkegaard becomes the Torquemada of discourse, his works a merciless in/disquisition on/of (the problem of) language. *Avant la lettre*, and with apocalyptic vengeance,[4] he argues (ironically): philosophy and theology are signed with the mark of undecidability and thrust into endless closure. And he blames it all (ironically?) on . . . Christianity.

If this is the case, then the way to "take Kierkegaard seriously" as a philosopher (or a theologian) is not to domesticate him but

---

1. There *ought* to be such a word: a present active participial form of "supercilious," meaning "eyebrow-raising."

2. And for that matter, even in my book, *Kierkegaard: A Kind of Poet*.

3. On the question of tone, cf. Jacques Derrida, "Of an Apocalyptic Tone Recently Adopted in Philosophy."

4. On "apocalypse," cf. ibid.

rather to magnify, as much as the case allows, the essential perversity of his texts. "Thoughts that wound from behind" (*Christian Discourses*, pt. 3), their literary form barely masks (because it incarnates) their profound offensiveness to the normal and normative modes of philosophical and religious discourse.

In defense of my own methods I am tempted to claim (what few will deny) that the essays here collected become increasingly offensive as they grow more and more frivolous. Like most interpretive theses, this one is at least true of the interpreter, whatever the fate of his victim-text.

It has been argued forcefully that Kierkegaard did not really understand Hegel and that he remained, therefore, trapped within the "System" he thought to oppose. It has been asserted, with equal vehemence if not with equal force, that he escapes the jaws of the dialectic and therefore occupies the Archimedean standpoint from which to dislodge and disperse the whole Hegelian enterprise. I want to stay out of this fight. The field is bloody enough as it is and the contest probably undecidable. But I do think that, whether or not he understood Hegel, he did understand what it would take to challenge him successfully. Whether or not he himself took possession of the *poū stō*,[5] he knew where to look for it.

According to Hegel the Absolute Spirit (*an sich*) produces (itself in) history by first going outside itself (*für sich*) and then recalling itself (*an und für sich*) out of this self-imposed exile. Subject and Substance are one: the Absolute is its own estrangement and its own recuperation. The effect of this (thoroughly dialectical) point of view is to transform every objection *to* itself into an expression *of* itself. The system is all-encompassing, and the Hegelian philosophy of Absolute Knowledge is so designed that it has no outside. Whether implicitly or explicitly, everything one says *about* it has already been said *by* it.

The Hegelian dialectic is a sequence of positions and negations, each sublated into its own opposite *ad* (*bonum*) *infinitum*. It will preempt or co-opt every attack mounted against it, *unless* one can discover an *undialectical position*—an other that is not

---

5. Attributed to Archimedes: "Give me a place to stand (*poū stō*) and I will move the earth." Cf. Pappus Alexandrinus, *Collectio*, bk. 8, prop. 10, sec. 11.

just a clever disguise of the same, a difference that cannot be resumed into identity—and a *radical negation*—a flat-out *no* that is not just a cunning preliminary gesture of renunciation empowering a subsequent and culminating affirmation. The discontinuity between these two—undialectical position and radical negation—would be *unmediatable*. As such, it would *stand outside* the supposed totality of absolute knowledge, and by so outstanding it detotalize it and frustrate its autoteleology.

But where do you go to look for a difference that eludes the dialectic and a negation that does not nourish it? Kierkegaard characteristically locates the wholly other in/as *God*: the God who speaks exclusively in/as a revelation incomprehensible to men and who is available to human reason only as/in the inconceivable concept of the unknown. Radical negation he identifies as freedom [*at kunne* (*Concept of Anxiety*, 44), indeterminate possibility]: the counteressential essence of the human individual, definitively expressed in the infinitely indeterminate and indeterminable nay-saying of irony. His texts regularly and insistently explore aspects of the discontinuity between indefeasible irony and unimaginable apocalypse. Any relationship between God and man will thus (for Kierkegaard) take the form not of absolute knowledge but of *absolute surprise*: the overtaking and taking over of the most perfectly prepared *nil admirari* by the (nevertheless) utterly unexpected.

There is a subject more intimate than the Absolute Subject and a substance more remote than the Absolute Substance: an irreconcilable diversity of s/Spirit(s) uncontained within the Absolute Spirit, which reduces the Hegelian philosophy to hubristic presumption or ludicrous pretension.

It was, Kierkegaard believes, not human reason (certainly not his) but *Christianity* that discovered (in God) the wholly other and (in sin) abysmal freedom. "Eye hath not seen, nor ear heard, neither have entered into the heart of man, the things which God hath prepared" (1 Cor. 2:9).[6] By locating the undialectical positive and the radical negative, Christianity *brought into the world* the *difference* that undoes philosophy. Christianity has once and

---

6. Cf. Kierkegaard's sermon on this text in *Johannes Climacus or, De omnibus dubitandum est*, 159–73.

for all and in the fullness of time pronounced irrevocable doom on (not just Hegel but) the whole philosophical project of comprehending being in thought.

The Christian revelation, which opens an immeasurable gap between God and man and proposes (absurdly) that it is closed by the God-man, is the death of philosophy. This would be the sense in which Kierkegaard is implacably antiphilosophical. It would also seem to be the subject matter of Christian theology. Unfortunately, Christian theology, as distinct from apostolic proclamation, has only human words and human thoughts in which to formulate its content of revelation: the language and the logic of philosophy. There is no other. Therefore, the construction of a systematic theology would be an act of treason: a revisionary exposition of the gospel that would, by representing it, disown it and subvert it. Necessarily, by the linguistic and conceptual conditions of its possibility, theology is dropped into the vortex that endlessly engulfs philosophy. The address of God to men (the God-man) disrupts and dismisses every discourse of man, including if not especially discourse about God. Irreconcilably antiphilosophical, Kierkegaard is thereby also—necessarily and in principle—set against theology.

In the *Concluding Unscientific Postscript*, Johannes Climacus declares that it will be his purpose "to discover where the misunderstanding lies between speculative philosophy [including theology] and Christianity" (216). But as Climacus himself is aware, it is easier to make a resolve than to keep it. Who begins as critic ends as accomplice. To denounce speculation in the name of Christianity and to explicate the grounds of the incommensurability between revelation and the discourse of man would imply that one had measured the incommensurable and closed the irreparable breach. And yet, to this end, one would necessarily have recourse to the language (this side of the breach) that one proposed to discount. There is no other. The act by which one effected this abyssing of philosophy and theology would amount (in effect) to a reappropriation of the absolutely improper: the irreducible position of the other, the "infinite absolute negativity" of the subject (*Concept of Irony*, 63, 271), and the unmediatable and unimmediate difference between them. The project would, in fact and at once, self-destruct. The text that announced the end of philosophy would be a philosophical text, and the proposition that closed down theology would be a theological proposition.

Therefore, whatever its other (ethical and religious) grounds, Kierkegaard's theory and practice of "indirect communication" is occasioned by the (insoluble) problem of paleonymy, founded on the abyss of a perfectly suspensive irony,[7] and opened (this is the hope) to the intrusion of the inconceivable and unimaginable gift: the meaning it cannot give itself and for which it can only prepare itself kenotically. Failure is all the success there is: the oblique purpose of the Kierkegaardian text is to take itself out of the way and thereby facilitate its displacement and replacement by the discourse of the Other. The unique self-consciousness of the Kierkegaardian text is the knowledge that if it accomplishes this purpose, it does so not by its own power but "by virtue of the absurd" (*Fear and Trembling* [1968], 38–64 passim).

Once it is recognized that Kierkegaard's writings are not to be arrayed under the rubrics of philosophy and theology, it is not sufficient (as some of us used to think) to call them "literary." Not only because literary discourse is continuous with the discourse of philosophy and theology, caught in the same paleonymic predicament and subject to the same critique (though it is), but also because (for that reason) no "literature," no matter how indirect and devious, could unconditionally propose its own deconstruction, much less its own reconstitution by grace. Kierkegaard's works so audaciously attempt both that their ambiguity is almost perfectly illegible. "To bring defense and attack together in such a unity that no one can say directly whether one is attacking or defending . . . here is an example of indirect communication" (*Training in Christianity*, 133).

This characterization of Kierkegaard's "literary" impasse would explain his persistent preoccupation with the problem of communication, his insistence on the "aesthetic" character of his works, and the mystification practiced in everything he wrote. The same clutch of circumstance would account for the dominant tone of his texts. To double business bound, their tone is

---

7. On suspensive irony, cf. Alan Wilde, *Horizons of Assent*, intro. and pt. 3.

just as ambivalent as their purpose is devious and their method duplicitous. On the one hand, they are all—clearly enough—the work of an *ironic* subject who lurks behind a barricade of pseudonyms (including "Søren Kierkegaard") and withholds *himself* absolutely. The "communicator" is "nobody, an absentee . . . null, a no man, an objective something" (*Training in Christianity*, 133). By virtue of his authorial self-restraint, his texts exhibit an almost complete abstention from determinate meaning and an almost perfect recalcitrance to interpretation. Like poetry, they "resist the intelligence almost successfully" (Stevens, *Opus Posthumous*, 171). And yet at the same time, aloof and elusive as they are, Kierkegaard's texts swell with a portentousness that can only be called *apocalyptic*. There is, haunting the margins of every page, a sense of impending revelation: the imminence of "the direct epileptic Word, the cry that might abolish the night" (Pynchon, *The Crying of Lot 49*, 87). But the saving truth is never displayed, the "Operational Word" never spoken (Pynchon, *Gravity's Rainbow*, 510). Or what's worse, the suspicion is implanted—unwriteable and unreadable—that the Word has already (been) spoken and resounds unheard down all the unexplored corridors of thought and in all the redundant catastrophes of history.

It is this combination of irony and apocalypse—ironic apocalypse or apocalyptic irony—that is the unwritten message of Kierkegaard's works. Unwritten and—in view of the circumstances that produced them—unwriteable. Unreadable forever, and irresistibly compelling endless interpretation.

As witness the essays here assembled, which repeat in their own way the ambiguity and the ambivalence of their subject.

"This sounds almost as if I were in earnest" (*Concluding Unscientific Postscript*, 210; cf. 163). From serious to tedious is not far, and from tiresome to self-important is no way at all. Therefore: no more rumination.

It is a simpler and more agreeable task to say (without ambivalence) thank you. Some of these essays have already appeared in print. I am grateful to the following editors and publishers for permission to reprint them here.

Chapter 2 was originally published in a *Festschrift* for Professor Paul Weiss, *Experience, Existence, and the Good*, edited by

I.C. Lieb and copyrighted by Southern Illinois University Press in 1961. It appears here by permission of the original publishers.

Chapters 3 and 6 were included in *Kierkegaard: A Collection of Critical Essays*, edited by Josiah Thompson and published by Doubleday and Company, Incorporated, in 1972. They are reprinted here (with a few very slight revisions) by permission of the first copyright holder, Josiah Thompson.

Chapter 4 appeared in *Kierkegaard and Literature: Irony, Repetition, and Criticism*, edited by Ronald Schleifer and Robert Markley and published by the University of Oklahoma Press in 1984. It is reprinted here with the permission of the publisher.

Chapter 5 was my contribution to *Psychiatry and the Humanities*, volume 5, edited by Joseph H. Smith, M.D., and entitled *Kierkegaard's Truth: The Disclosure of the Self* (1981). It is reprinted here by permission of the editor and of the Forum on Psychiatry and the Humanities of the Washington School of Psychiatry, holders of the copyright.

The labor of assembling this volume, along with part of the actual writing, was done in the fall semester of 1982. To this end I was granted a leave of absence by the Department of Philosophy of the University of Texas at Austin and supported by a Faculty Research Assignment from the University Research Institute of the University of Texas. U.R.I. has also awarded me special research grants to pay for the typing and indexing of this manuscript. I am grateful to my department and to U.R.I. for the opportunity to complete this work.

Professor Mark C. Taylor, general editor of "Kierkegaard and Postmodernism," first proposed that I put together a collection of my essays for this series. For activating an impulse that had long lain dormant in the back of my brain, and for his judicious help in selecting and arranging these materials—not to mention the enlightenment offered by his own work on Kierkegaard—I thank him. I am also greatly in debt to the staff of the Florida State University Press, and especially to its director, Jeanne Ruppert. Her editorial expertise and generosity (far in excess of my merits as a scribbler) are matched only by her personal goodwill and congeniality. I have enjoyed our association. I am also grateful to the editors at University Presses of Florida for the good-humored solicitude with which they guarded the already fragile integrity of this text as they saw it through production.

Finally, I want to thank Gail Cohen for her fine job of typing the manuscript and Patrick Bigelow for the care and thoroughness with which he has prepared the index.

To the four people named in the dedication I owe the greatest debt of all. By making outrageous unliterary demands and by providing me with unimaginable extratextual satisfactions, they have seen to it, and continue to see to it, that I do not disappear entirely into my pseudonyms. Not even the dread *nom du père*. For that I am more than grateful.

Louis Mackey
Austin, Texas
December 9, 1982

1.
STARTING FROM SCRATCH:
KIERKEGAARD UNFAIR TO HEGEL

> A: But I love my irony.
> Q: Does it give you pleasure?
> A: A poor . . . A rather unsatisfactory. . . .
> Q (aside): He has given away his gaiety, and now has nothing.
>
> Donald Barthelme

The five professors appointed to evaluate Kierkegaard's master's thesis didn't know what to make of it. It was obviously the work of a brilliant mind, but the author's style was outrageous and his manners incorrigible. A sixth reader was drafted. He concurred in the majority opinion: accept the essay for its substantive merit, and leave the author's manners and morals to heaven (translator's introduction, *Concept of Irony*, 8–13).

So Kierkegaard became Magister Artium. But the little academic tempest over the form of his thesis was no accident. *The Concept of Irony*, written in Hegelianese, is anti-Hegelian. But it is impossible to write Hegel's language without writing Hegel's philosophy. In order to attack Hegel, therefore, Kierkegaard's essay on irony has to undercut itself. Ironically.

I

In mid-nineteenth-century Denmark, Latin was still the official language of the schools. Although university lectures were given in the vernacular, dissertations were expected to be in Latin. Therefore, when Kierkegaard wanted to write his master's thesis—*On the Concept of Irony with Constant Reference to Socrates*—in Danish, he was obliged to make formal petition to the King for permission to do so. In the course of his petition, and by way of justifying his request, he wrote that "the concept of irony, to be sure, belongs in a sense to antiquity, but it really [*egentlig*] belongs to it only insofar as the modern age takes its beginning from irony, so that the apprehension of this concept must in the strictest sense be claimed by modernity" (*Concept of Irony*, 350; hereinafter cited in this essay as CI).[1] The sense in which irony belongs to antiquity—namely, that in the strict sense it belongs to modernity—is decidedly Pickwickian. For in spite of the constant reference to Socrates, and notwithstanding the fact that he is credited with discovering the principle of irony, the concept of irony is distinctively modern. It is in fact the originating concept of the modern age.

(It is already ironic to speak of irony as an originating concept. Of origins and of irony and of ironic origins there will be more to say in the end.)

Appended to Kierkegaard's essay are fifteen Latin theses which the candidate promised to sustain in public oral defense. The last of these reads: "As philosophy begins with doubt, so also the life that is worthy to be called human begins with irony" (CI, 349).[2] That "philosophy begins with doubt" may be an eternal truth. (Or it may not. The fragment *Johannes Climacus, or de omnibus dubitandum est*[3] makes it doubtful whether the proposition means anything at all.) But it is a truth (*sic*, for the time being) that first comes to light at the beginning of the modern age. We

---

1. For the Danish I have consulted *Søren Kierkegaard: Samlede Værker*. I am indebted throughout this essay to Sylviane Agacinski, *Aparté: Conceptions et Morts de Søren Kierkegaard*, 7–57.

2. In Kierkegaard's Latin: *Ut a dubitatione philosophia sic ab ironia vita digna, quae humana vocetur, incipit* (CI, 348).

3. In connection with this essay, and on the problem of "beginning", cf. the following: *Johannes Climacus or, de omnibus dubitandum est*; *Concluding Unscientific Postscript*, on the "dialectic of the beginning," 101–6; Louis Mackey, *Kierkegaard: A Kind of Poet*, 137–50.

might say that in the meditations of René Descartes the eternal truth that philosophy begins with doubt is the truth that originates modern philosophy.

(Ironic as it is to speak of irony as an originating concept, it is at least no less so to speak of original doubt, or of doubt as an originating truth—or, for that matter, of an eternal truth that originates [v.t.] or originates [v.i.].)

It is true at the very least, if it is true at all, that philosophy in the modern age begins with (Descartes') doubt. But the modern age also begins with irony. Therefore (perhaps) doubt equals irony and irony equals doubt.

On top of that, the only life worthy to be called human begins with irony, that is, with doubt. The beginning of philosophy is the beginning of modernity is the beginning of humanity equals irony equals doubt. The beginning begins with Socrates as well as with Descartes—and perhaps with the eternal. One of Kierkegaard's examiners objected to his fifteenth thesis on the grounds that it would be difficult to discuss in Latin (CI, 13).

Difficult in any language. All of Kierkegaard's beginnings are difficult, this one not the least. *The beginning* is difficult, as we shall see once we manage to begin. Doing what comes naturally, we begin with the beginning of Kierkegaard's essay on irony. That at least is a true beginning. In the English translation it begins on page 47 (page 69 in the last Danish edition), just after the translator's historical introduction—which, in spite of the consecutive pagination, is not a true beginning but a preface to the beginning, composed some 120 years later. Over a century after the publication of *The Concept of Irony*, which came just before the first of the books designated by Kierkegaard as his "literature." Very shortly before the tragic and untimely end of Mr. Capel.

To begin (then) with the beginning of this beginning:

I

In the first paragraph of his introduction, Kierkegaard says that the phenomenon, to which modern philosophy is laudably attentive, is feminine—as opposed to the Idea, which is masculine and (therefore) stronger (CI, 47).[4] As the knight of the Idea, the philosopher should be enthusiastic and courtly. Though he all too often jangles his spurs and plays lord and master, the philosopher should be a lover. As eroticist, he should use his superior strength to assist the phenomenon toward self-manifestation. The phenomenon itself should remain inviolate (*sic*), so that the (masculine) concept is seen (or seems) to come into existence by and through the (feminine) phenomenon.

The concept [*Begreb*] or Idea [*Idee*]—in a word, the logos—is to come into being, or seem to, from an intemerate phenomenon. But the concept is the *truth* of the phenomenon. Truth is the masculine fulfillment/lover/perfect gentle master of the feminine phenomenon, from which it makes itself be born without violating the lady.

It is difficult not to think of the passage with which, some forty years later, Nietzsche opened the preface to *Beyond Good and Evil*:

> Supposing truth is a woman—what then? Are there not grounds for the suspicion that all philosophers, insofar as they were dogmatists, have been very inexpert about women? That the gruesome seriousness, the clumsy obtrusiveness with which they have usually approached truth so far have been awkward and very improper methods for winning a woman's heart? What is certain is that she has not allowed herself to be won. (2)

And this, from later on in the same book:

> Even now truth finds it necessary to stifle her yawns when she is expected to give answers. In the end she is a woman: she should not be violated. (148–49)

---

4. Kierkegaard says that it is "seemly" [*sømmer det*] for the phenomenon, which is always *foeminini generis*, to submit itself to the stronger because of its feminine nature [*paa Grund af sin qvindelige Natur at hengive sig til den Staerkere*] (*Samlede Værker*, 1: 69). In a preliminary sketch of this passage he wrote "because of its feminine nature, to submit itself to the stronger sex" [*paa Grund af sin qvindelige Natur at hengive sig til det staerkere Kjøn*]. Cf. *Søren Kierkegaards Papirer*, III B 12.

Here it is truth who is feminine and should be left inviolate, who at least will not be possessed or even impressed by the dogmatic posturings and pantings of masculine philosophers. She is in fact bored.

In Kierkegaard truth emerges from the inviolate phenomenon by a kind of virgin birth. In Nietzsche truth is the object of a clumsily managed and unsuccessful attempt at seduction—and in that sense inviolate.

The point of all this heterosexual play will be sharpened later. For the moment the operative word is "inviolate." What is inviolate is untouched. It remains impenetrably other. The notion of the other—the irreducibly alien—is crucial to Kierkegaard's understanding of the concept of irony.

For example, consider the relationship between philosophy and history. In an early draft of the opening paragraph of *The Concept of Irony* (which he did not use) Kierkegaard wrote (the sexual metaphor appears also in this version):

> In opposition to what has so often been remarked, that the observer ought to submit himself [*hengive sig*, devote himself sc. to the phenomenon], one should also, and with right, recall that it [sc. submission] is if anything incumbent on [*paaligger*, literally "lies on"] the phenomenon. And we will say that history, so to speak, rejoices in this embrace.
>
> However dry history is, its embrace is nevertheless fruitful. . . . In the arms of philosophy history is restored to divine youth. (*Søren Kierkegaards Papirer*, III B 12)

In a footnote to *The Concept of Irony* Kierkegaard remarks that philosophy, as the eternal, is older than history, which is concerned only with the temporal (48n.). Many an old man has found his lost youth (or his second childhood) in the arms of a younger woman, but Kierkegaard apparently had some trouble deciding who rejuvenates whom. In his final rescension an infinitely old philosophy fructifies history . . . by leaving her intact. In not quite the way that Søren, who had never been young (*Point of View*, 80–81), left Regine intact . . . and made himself fruitful.

Be that as it may. In *The Concept of Irony* we get this:

> Philosophy relates to history as a confessor to the penitent, and, like a confessor, it ought to have a supple and searching ear for the penitent's secrets, but after having listened to a full account of his confession, it must then be able to make this appear to the penitent as an other [*som et Andet*]. . . . History can then experience the pleasant surprise that while at first it would almost disown its philosophic counterpart, it afterwards identifies itself with [*lever sig ind i*] this conception of philosophy to such a degree that, finally, it would regard this as the essential truth, the other [*det Andet*] as mere appearance. (48)

The confessor gets the penitent to confront her sins by detaching them from the inner life of the soul and objectifying them. As the confessor alienates sin, so philosophy "others" the revelations of history. The philosopher as alienist displaces temporal fact into the eternal Idea. The result is that history, at first resentful of her conceptual translation, comes to identify with ("live herself into") her philosophical other. In the end she regards the Idea as her own truth and reality and demotes herself (the temporal phenomenon) to the level of appearance. So history participates in her own alienation, which she then re-appropriates as her essence.

That (save the feminine pronouns) sounds just like Hegel. Well, almost. For while history may identify with her philosophical transfiguration, the alienation of Idea and phenomenon is not quite overcome:

> The whole sum of historical existence is still not the absolutely adequate medium of the Idea, since it is the temporality and fragmentariness of the Idea . . . , which longs for what issues from consciousness. (CI, 49)

All this by way of introducing the historical Socrates as the phenomenon (the temporal appearance) who brought the concept of irony (its eternal philosophical Idea) into the world. For "it is in Socrates that the concept of irony has its inception in the world" (CI, 47).

How he brought this off is an essential part not only of the history of the concept of irony but also of the concept itself. In this connection another passage, from the end of Kierkegaard's beginning:

> He was not like a philosopher lecturing upon his views, wherein the very lecture itself constitutes the presence of the Idea; on the contrary, what Socrates said meant something 'other' [*noget Andet*]. The outer and the inner did not form a harmonious unity, for the outer was in opposition to the inner, and only through this angle of refraction is he to be apprehended. . . . If we say next that the substantial aspect of Socrates' existence was irony (this is indeed a contradiction, but also meant as one), and if we postulate further that irony is a negative concept, then one easily sees how difficult it becomes to secure an image of him, yes, that it seems impossible, or at least as baffling as trying to depict an elf wearing a hat that makes him invisible. (CI, 50)

These words look ahead to chapter 3 of the *Philosophical Fragments*, in which prolepsis they tell us that irony is the nondialectical opposite of the Hegelian union of thought and being (subject and object, word and thing, signifier and signified . . .).[5] As saying one thing but meaning another (we've known all along what irony is), irony is the alienating discourse that guarantees the objectivity, the irreducible reality, and the very alterity of the other-than-discourse. Irony is a device of the inner (of thought and language) by which the outer (being, the object) is locked in its externality.

> Essence is the negation of appearance, though not its absolute negation, for then essence would essentially have vanished. Now to a certain extent this is irony: it negates the phenomenal, not in order to posit anything by means of this negation, but negates the phenomenal altogether. It

---

5. Cf. the essay, "A Ram in the Afternoon: Kierkegaard's Discourse of the Other," chapter 5 in this volume.

flees back into itself instead of going out of itself, it is not in the phenomenon but seeks to deceive by means of the phenomenon, the phenomenon is not in order to manifest essence but to conceal essence. (CI, 234–35n.)

Thanks to irony, the relation of phenomenon and essence (object and subject, outer and inner, what is said and what is meant, etc.) is one of invincible diremption.

The concept of irony is contradictory. The beginning of/with irony is a negation of the possibility of beginning, since irony itself is the alienation by which the eternal is irreparably sundered from every temporal origin. It is only ironically, therefore, that irony may be said to begin with Socrates. And it is only in an ironical sense that this introduction is the beginning of Magister Kierkegaard's thesis on the concept of irony. For that matter, what is the relation of essence and phenomenon in this essay? How ironical is *The Concept of Irony*?

If there is to be any issue out of all this travail, it will have to be a miraculous birth from an undefiled virgin. The (original) Virgin Birth, from which the eternal Truth took its temporal beginning, was not the least of the ironies of history.

I

The beginning is nothing. Not quite and no longer the Hegelian nothing, but a nothing which is given a local habitation and a name in Socrates. The founder and finder of irony, Socrates is described in contradictions that echo and repel the paradoxes of Hegelian metaphysics. He is said to be the nothing from which one begins, nonexistent for immediate conception, and the negation of substantial immediacy. But he exists for thought in the form of infinite negativity. To which Kierkegaard appends the most ironic understatement (we've known all along what irony means) as a conclusion: "To this extent the form of his existence in history is not a perfectly adequate image [*billedlig Betegnelse*] of his intellectual [*aandelige = geistliche*] significance" (CI, 222). For what it's worth, Kierkegaard thinks the Aristophanic Socrates closer to historical fact than Plato (who adds to the truth) and Xenophon (who subtracts) (CI, 349).

The Sophists, to whom Socrates responds in the intellectual

milieu of fifth-century Greece, discovered finite reflection and the finite subjectivity that is the condition of its possibility. To nature [*physis*] they opposed convention [*thesis* or *nomos*]. As against the supposedly substantial foundation of Greek ethics they posited the principle that the individual man is the measure of all things. Relativizing everything, the Sophists boasted that they could defend or, with equal force, refute any proposition whatever. On their view every proposition is true and, equivalently, every proposition is false. Nothing is univocally true or firmly real; everything is a matter of opinion, private perceptions, man-made rules, or social convention. Their position is—relatively and finitely—both positive and negative, and therefore neither.

Socrates seizes the Sophists' discovery—reflection—and takes it to the end of the line. Wholly negative, Socrates knows nothing and questions everything. He is silence itself. Unlike sophistic reflection, which is finite, Socratic reflection is infinite: the capacity of subjectivity to refuse every objective determination and to deny every proposition. Without limit. "What we see in Socrates is the infinitely exuberant freedom of subjectivity, that is, irony" (CI, 233). There we have Magister Kierkegaard's definition of irony: the infinite freedom of the abstract subject. Negativity in and for itself.

The Sophist can refute all propositions, but only serially. His reflection being finite, to refute one proposition he must assume another. Likewise he can negate all things, but only one at a time. A finite power of abstraction must stand on something in order to demolish something else. But Socrates' irony is infinite. Therefore, he can deny all possible propositions without affirming any and negate existence as such and as a whole without standing on anything but his own freedom to do so.

Between the first immediacy, which it annihilates, and the second, which it does nothing to produce, irony is the intermediate state. Disdaining reality, irony demands the ideal; it loses the finite in the infinite. Never a means merely, irony becomes in Socrates the one and only end: infinite negation is his position. From the vantage of the idea, irony renders negative judgment on existence as such.

Irony is also—here we go again—a beginning. The beginning of the reconciliation of the actual and the ideal: the recovery of actuality for the ideal and of ideality for the actual. But it is only the beginning and not the reconciliation itself. Irony is the end of immediacy and the beginning, the mere beginning, the bare possibility of . . . everything. As one of Kierkegaard's pseudonyms says, freedom is simply *to be able* [*at kunne*] (*Concept of Anxiety*, 44): indeterminate possibility or the possibility of the indeterminate.

> Socrates was completely negative in his relation to the existent [*Bestaaende*]. . . . He hovered in ironic satisfaction above all the determinations of substantial life. . . . His entire standpoint, therefore, culminates in infinite negativity, for it exhibits itself as negative both in relation to the past development and the subsequent development, though in another sense it is positive in both instances, that is to say, it is infinitely ambiguous. (CI, 240)

Like the nothing that propels the Hegelian system (is it?), irony is an ever-elusive and indefinitely postponed origin.

Irony is a way of getting into orbit. It generates the escape velocity by which the spirit is enabled to pull away from (while it remains ambiguously and indecisively bound by) the gravitational pull of actuality. A means of escape and only that, irony is not a technique of reentry. Reentry was always a problem for Kierkegaard. If your escape velocity is infinite, how can you ever return? If. There is always gravity's rainbow. But repetition's end is as difficult to conceive as irony's beginning.

Socrates' death, which is not followed by resurrection, is his consummate irony. As he himself once put it (ironically?), philosophy is learning how to die (*Phaedo*, 64a passim).

> Socrates ferried the individual from reality over to ideality, and the ideal infinity, as infinite negativity, was the nothingness in which he allowed the whole manifold of reality to disappear. . . . He therefore had the absolute in the form of nothingness. *Reality*, by means of the absolute, *became nothingness*, but *the absolute* in turn *was nothingness*. (CI, 255)

The whole Socratic discourse (and therewith the whole philosophy of Socrates) is a *mise en abîme* by which he drops existence—

as such and in totality—into the bottomless pit of nonbeing. That is: irony.

This negative is the Socratic positivity. Knowing no way to reconcile reality and reflection without relativizing (violating) both, it safeguards the substantiality of the former by infinitizing the latter. The actual is affirmed by its denial. Reality is the other-than-reflection, and the alterity of this other is protected by its unreserved unconceiving in/as irony. The real is the rational and the rational is the real, but only insofar as the extremest act of reason is to alienate (unviolate) reality. Thought lays hold on being only when and insofar as it lets it alone.

That, ironically, is the radical anti-Hegelian polemic inscribed in this most Hegelian of Kierkegaardian texts.

I

In part 2 of *The Concept of Irony*, entitled "The Concept of Irony," Kierkegaard turns from the ancient history of irony to the concept itself. That is: irony in the modern age. The introduction to part 2 recalls the introduction to part 1. In the first paragraph of this second beginning—the real and conceptual beginning—we are told, "In the previous part of this essay I have not so much presupposed the concept as I have allowed it to come into existence, since I sought to orient myself in the phenomenon" (259; cf. 47). With this sentence Kierkegaard claims to be the ideal lover (the eroticist) who, in the foregoing, has helped the phenomenon (Socrates) give birth to the concept of irony. The true Alcibiades at last! But a strange fate for Socrates, who was barren and content to be no more than a midwife. Has he remained intact?

The concept together with the phenomenon—the two parts of this text taken in tandem—produce a kind of incarnation, for "the phenomenal appearance of the concept will accompany this discussion as a pervasive possibility of dwelling among us [*at tage Bolig iblandt os*]" (CI, 259; cf. John 1: 14). "*Similitudo Christum inter et Socratem in dissimilitudine praecipue est posita*" (CI, 348).[6]

---

6. In English (349): "The similarity between Christ and Socrates consists essentially in dissimilarity."

Necessarily, because it is a determination of subjectivity, irony makes two appearances in the world. First, subjectivity as such asserts itself in the irony of Socrates. But Socrates did not affirm irony. He simply *was* irony. Here we have the extremely ironical notion of an irony *an sich*. Then subjectivity becomes conscious of itself—a subjectivity of subjectivity, a reflection on reflection, and a self-consciousness of self-consciousness. This is modern (post-Kantian) irony, an irony *an und für sich* which has (ironically) reflected itself out of and back into unity with itself. With what?

In Socrates irony makes its debut on the stage of world history. In modern times, showing itself in its essential truth and reality, irony is clearly and consciously affirmed by subjectivity *as its standpoint*. So it says. How shall we take this sincere and straightforward self-assertion of the ironic consciousness? Shall we trust it? Not without further ado. For upon this, its second incarnation, irony is met and mastered (read: *aufgehoben*)[7] by Hegel.

Who? Immediately after his tribute to Hegel, Kierkegaard writes: "At the point in his system where one would expect to find an explanation of irony, we find it merely talked about instead" (CI, 261). After more of this sort of thing, he ends with:

> Hegel . . . has absolute significance through his positive total view whereby he conquers that polemical prudishness, which, like the virginity of Queen Brunhilde, required a more than average man, a Siegfried, in order to be subdued. (262)

The Hegel here portrayed does not sound like the ideal eroticist demanded by the first introduction. Too much spur-jangling and phallus-rattling. Doubtless Hegel's "mastery" of irony is to be understood ironically. (The second time is farce.) Hegel combats irony and destroys it, sublates it, conquers its polemical prudishness, and subdues its virginity. That is, quite seriously and with consummate irony, his absolute significance. Whereas

---

7. Kierkegaard's word, *ophaevet*, which Capel translates "abrogated" (260), is the Danish cognate of *aufgehoben*. For the Danish, cf. *Samlede Værker*, 1: 260.

Kierkegaard, who allowed himself to be called Master of Irony, permits the inviolate phenomenon to achieve self-realization (= self-alienation) in the concept of irony and in *The Concept of Irony*.

This title, the title of the whole work, is repeated as the title of the second part of the whole. The device is not uncommon in Kierkegaard. Notably, the title of *Repetition* is repeated as the title ("Repetition") of the second part of the book. What is the purport of these double ironies and repeated repetitions of repetitions? (Second time as farce?) Perhaps: the repetition, if one can (first) achieve it and (second) prevent it from iterating itself, is the true beginning. Therefore, once again. . . .

I

For orientation (which in the case of irony would have to mean disorientation) we are reminded of the ordinary meaning of irony. Irony in the ordinary sense is (as we have always known) a figure of speech in which what is said is the opposite of what is meant. The essence (thought or meaning) is not the phenomenon (language) but its opposite. These two—essence (meaning) and phenomenon (word) or, briefly, signified and signifier—are necessary to all thought and discourse. Thought without words is not thought, and words without thought are not words.

Truth (we're still riding Hegel's masterful coattails) is the identity of signifier and signified, and the positive freedom of the speaker. Bound by what he says and to what he means, he who speaks the truth coincides with himself and communes directly with his auditors. But the ironist dissociates signifier and signified. His freedom—in relation to his utterance, to others, and to himself—is wholly negative. He is answerable for nothing to no one (CI, 264-65).

However, irony in the ordinary sense (what is said is the opposite of what is meant) is only a special case of allegory. The extreme case. He who speaks ironically in this sense (what Wayne Booth calls "stable irony" [*A Rhetoric of Irony*, esp. pt. 1]) presupposes that he is understood in spite of the deviousness of his manner. Ordinary irony is a form of communication, albeit indirect, by means of which an elite assure themselves of their own solidarity and exclude the vulgar from their circle. As Kierkegaard says, the "figure of speech cancels itself" (CI, 265).

But irony (in principle) is not a form of communication. It is a technique of concealment that isolates the speaker (in principle) absolutely. For the "principle" of irony is unlimited negative subjective freedom, the always available (and necessarily abstract) possibility of a radical breach with "previous conditions." The opportunity, always at hand for subjectivity, to suspend all prior determinations and start from scratch. The "truth" of irony, so understood, is the discrepancy between (on the one hand) existence [*Tilvaerelse*] and personality and (on the other) actuality [*Virkelighed*]. The distinction between appearance and reality. More pointedly, the difference between mere existence, whether subjective or objective, and the existence that is identical with its essence (CI, 270).

Irony "in the eminent sense"—irony which is in fact what it is in principle—"differs qualitatively" from irony in the ordinary sense. Unlike the latter, which brackets existence in particular and *seriatim*, irony *sensu eminentiori* suspends existence as a whole and as such. It is, as Hegel rightly says, "infinite absolute negativity" (CI, 271).

Irony as a figure of speech—the stable irony that says one thing and means the opposite—is not an infinite but only a finite negation. It is therefore immediately reducible to its implied affirmation. But irony in the eminent sense, when it expresses itself in speech, negates itself infinitely. That is to say, indeterminately. Absolutely unstable, the perfectly ironic utterance cannot be reduced to any determinate meaning. Signifier and signified exist only in relation to each other, so that by negating indeterminately what it *means*, ironic discourse also negates what it *says*. As indeterminate negation, irony allows both word and meaning to drop into the abyss of "infinite absolute negativity." When Socrates says that he is the wisest man in Athens because he is the only man in Athens who knows that he is ignorant, no one knows or can know what he means. Or what he has said.

True irony has the autotelic character of art. It is its own end, insofar as the purpose of the ironist is just to insist upon that negative freedom which is the "substance" of his irony. His aim is to seem incalculably other than he is, and to the extent that he succeeds he disappears into the vast inane while his speech vibrates in the void from which he has vanished (CI, 273). Irony is thus the sheer being-for-itself of subjectivity. As distinct from philosophical doubt, which clears away the phenomena so as to get at their essence, and as distinct from religious devotion, which abjures the world and all things temporal in favor of God and things eternal, irony subverts everything in order to enjoy its own negative capability. Playing on the word "*spøger*," which means both "to joke" and "to haunt," Kierkegaard says that the ironic nothingness is a deathly stillness in which irony returns to inhabit the subject as a spectral jest: the apophrades of the spirit (CI, 275).

Having delivered himself of these necessary but somewhat tedious discriminations, Kierkegaard returns to his constant point of reference. Within the second part of *The Concept of Irony*, itself a repetition of the whole, we have a repetition of Socrates. The Socratic irony is here reconceived under the newly achieved rubric: infinite absolute negativity. Socrates appears in this discussion attired in his "world historical validity" (CI, 276).

Existence as a whole is alien to the ironic consciousness, which in turn is estranged from existence. Phenomenal existents (which of course still exist) have no validity—no weight, no value, no legitimacy: no truth and reality—for the ironic subject.

> Thus we here have irony as infinite absolute negativity. It is negativity because it only negates; it is infinite because it negates not this or that phenomenon; and it is absolute because it negates by virtue of a higher which is not. (CI, 278)

As a historical moment, irony is the Hegelian negative. It negates what is (that is, what has been) and evacuates the present (that is, the past). But it neither announces nor establishes a future. It merely negates, and that by virtue of a nonexistent superiority. Negatively free, the ironic consciousness swings about existence in perpetual orbit, intoxicated by infinite possibility and in the name of possibility enthusiastic for destruction (CI, 279). Irony is the vacuous infinitesimal present and the moment—equally vain—in which subjectivity is fully present to itself.

It is Socrates' world historical mission to instantiate this abstract subjectivity (CI, 281). His irony is expressed in his ignorance and his maieutic practice. Not to mention his death, which is the consummate ironic comment both on the Athenian state and on the fate to which it consigned him. His irony cannot express itself as a thesis: hence Socrates' abstention from doctrine. Irony, as infinite absolute negativity, cannot be affirmed in the finite propositions and relations of human discourse. It is, but it cannot assert, the nothingness of all things. Irony is not serious about nothing. It only plays with it. But insofar as there is no something about which the ironist is serious, to that extent his play with nothingness is absolutely serious. Wholly negative, ironic discourse cannot affirm anything. Nor can it negate, since every negation implies a corresponding affirmation as surely as every determination is also a negation. Unable to say what it is, irony can only *be* the nonbeing of abstract and indeterminate freedom that defines the essence of subjectivity (CI, 285–88).

It is this nonbeing that Kierkegaard says is the origin of modernity . . . and of authentic humanity. It is impossible not to wonder how it is possible to begin from this beginning. How could anything determinate be built on indeterminate negation? How can the standpoint of irony recuperate the being of which it is the alienation? A crucial moment in Kierkegaard's polemic against Hegel (how can you begin with nothing?), the problem seems to be defined in such a way that no solution is even conceivable. In the concluding section of his thesis the Master of Irony triumphantly pulls the rasher out of the coals.

Or seems to. With an ironist you can never be sure.

III

The problem is: beginning. And equivalently: repetition. Every repetition is a new beginning, and every beginning already a repetition: the recovery, for the first time, of an origin always already lost. Kierkegaard approaches the problem from the standpoint of poetics. Irony, he says, "renders both the poem and the poet free" (CI, 366). By which he means that irony detaches the subject (the poet in his radical freedom) from the object (the poem in its radical alterity). Poetry is the aesthetic manifestation of the ironic diremption of essence and phenomenon.

The mastery of irony (recall the opprobrium attached to the

notion of mastery in the introduction to his book) is the negation of the negation: the objectivity alienated by irony is now resumed by subjectivity, as a content of freedom rather than a constraining given. The unity of form and content in the poem is attainable only on the other side of the prior sundering effected by irony. Negative capability, of which ironic subjectivity is the perfection, is the necessary (but not yet sufficient) condition of poetic production. Together, irony and the mastery of irony make up the necessary and sufficient conditions of poetry.

By the same logic they define the possibility of authentic human existence. Irony is the baptism of the spirit (CI, 338–39): the infinite reflection through which a person must pass in order to appropriate her proper reality. Authentic existence is actuality actualized: one's given phenomenal objectivity, which one must first renounce (as merely given) in order to regain it as a postulate of freedom. Irony is thus the way to a recovery—that is, a first appropriation—of one's distinctively human being.

It may be difficult to understand how irony can constitute the possibility of authenticity in any but a negative sense. How can irony—infinite absolute negativity—make possible a reentry into and a repossession of that reality from which it is (only and in principle) the departure? As the Master of Irony points out, irony is never a result (CI, 339–40). It is hard to see how it could have any. Kierkegaard's penultimate words are full of ambiguity:

> The content of life must become a true and meaningful moment in the higher actuality whose fullness the soul desires. Actuality in this way acquires its validity [a validity which irony denies it] . . . as a history wherein consciousness successively lives itself out, though in such a way that happiness consists not in forgetting all this but remains present in it. (CI, 341)

Actuality appropriated by freedom through the mediation of irony becomes history. A history in which consciousness repeatedly "lives itself out" moment by moment. Kierkegaard's word *udleve* (literally "out-live") means to exhaust one's powers and so use up one's life. Its participle, *udlevet*, means "decrepit" or "effete."[8] Yet the consciousness that dies by inches in this way does not forget what it leaves behind but rather abides there and is beatified by its presence in its own past.

It should not be altogether surprising that a master of irony doesn't quite know what to do with that sequence of beginnings and repetitions and repeated beginnings called history. The history which during the gestation of this work was said to rejuvenate philosophy, which in the book itself is fructified by her elder and better, who as her confessor also reconciles her to herself—at the end of all this ambivalence history is proposed as the fruit of the intercourse of irony with itself. The monstrous progeny of an unnaturally autotelic sexuality.

Be that as it may. In a statement like this, clogged with contradictions, the essay on irony, which has corrupted everyone and everything it touched, at last subverts itself. The ironic negation of Hegel has to negate itself, else it plays right into his hand. Irony mastered remains unreconciled, and the actuality recuperated by mastered irony remains elusive. Authentic human life becomes—that paradoxical junction of time and eternity—history. That is: a reality from which consciousness is at every moment escaping and in which it is at the same time perpetually and happily present. It is hardly possible to read Kierkegaard's "positive" conclusion as anything but an ironic representation, doubly deceptive in form, of the same old thing: alienation. More than that: irony is now, in this moment of truth and mastery, an indefinitely self-iterating alienation. As "man shall not put asunder what God has joined together, so neither shall man join together what God has put asunder, for such a sickly longing is simply an attempt to have the perfect before its time" (CI, 341). The words are directed against romantic aspirations toward

---

8. The verb *udleve* means to use up one's life, to exhaust one's powers, so that one becomes decrepit or effete. Capel's version, generally unexceptionable, simply transliterates *udleve* as "outlive." But "outlive" means "survive" (Danish *overleve*), and "to survive oneself" is the opposite of *at udleve sig*. My own translation, "lives itself out," is no stroke of genius, but it's the best I could come up with short of an awkward paraphrasis. In the last phrase of this passage, *bliver praesent deri*, *bliver* can mean either "become" or "remain". Capel opts for "become", but I think the context favors "remain".

the infinite. But they come from the Scriptures and the marriage service, and they appear to rule out the historical union of time and eternity envisioned only a few lines earlier as the happy ending of mastered irony. Four years after *The Concept of Irony*, Johannes the Seducer noted that a woman's husband should not be her seducer and vice versa, although (he added) she needs both (*Stages on Life's Way*, 87). He spoke, transparently, in his own interest. But even Magister Kierkegaard could not, it appears, join together the two—eroticist and master, lover and husband—whom God had put asunder.

What is perfection? And when is its time? One thing seems clear: it will not come from irony. For irony is the endlessly iterated origin from which necessarily nothing can originate.

"So much for the practical" (CI, 341). The theoretical gets even shorter shrift, and the essay concludes with a portentous prolepsis toward humor. Humor is (on the authority of the Master of Irony) both more deeply skeptical and more deeply positive than irony, for "it does not find repose in making man human, but in making man God-Man" (CI, 342).

Of all things.

II

On the negative side the purpose of Kierkegaard's analysis of irony is to mount an attack on two important Hegelian concepts. The concept of the *nothing* (= bare being) from which the Hegelian system is alleged to begin; and the *negation* that is alleged to move the dialectic and thereby provide the Idea with the repeated new beginnings essential to its unfolding and fulfillment in history. Over against both of these notions Kierkegaard sets the concept of irony. Irony, which Hegel himself characterizes as "infinite absolute negativity" (CI, 271),[9] Kierkegaard describes at length as the capacity of subjectivity, abstractly and as such, to detach itself absolutely and indeterminately from all and every actuality.

---

9. Cf. J. Glenn Gray, ed., *G. W. F. Hegel On Art, Religion, Philosophy*, 102. Gray reprints, slightly emended, Bernard Bosanquet's translation of the introduction to Hegel's *Vorlesungen über die Aesthetik*.

In *The Concept of Irony* Kierkegaard attempts the impossible (from a philosophical point of view) task of sundering subject and object so as to prevent the synthesis of absolute knowledge. Abstract subjectivity, realized as irony, and being, in its undialectical alterity, repose in mutual incomprehension. The task *is* (philosophically) impossible: Kierkegaard unfair to Hegel. *The Concept of Irony* must be understood retroproleptically from the point of view of (is undertaken for the sake of) the reflective translation of Christianity essayed in the *Fragments* and the *Postscript*, from which we learn that Christianity first and for all precluded philosophical synthesis by declaring itself the discourse of the Absolute Other addressed to that (human freedom) which is absolutely other than the Absolute Other. This patently is something it could not have entered the heart of man to conceive, so that if Kierkegaard brings it off he does so by virtue of the absurd. For which reason the thesis on irony must be not a self-deconstructing discourse but a discourse both deconstructed and made possible in advance by its object and its aim. Outrageous as it is, that is Kierkegaard's preposterous project.

The anti-Hegelian point of all this can be summed up in the (not so) simple tautology: negation is really negation. From nothing—real nothing—nothing can begin. Certainly not *das absolut Wissen*. And if irony be conceived as possibility, it must also be conceived as *mere* possibility—the negation of the actual in toto and in principle—which can never inaugurate a repetition.

There *is* an other-than-all-that-is which is beyond recuperation by the dialectic. There is something—namely, nothing—that falls outside the system. Irony, which is the *no* to everything that exists, *is*. Is: the possibility of an escape that eludes recapture, of irrecoverable loss, and of self-expenditure without reserve.

In terms of terms: it is possible not only to say one thing while meaning something determinately other than what one says. It is also possible—and irony is the motive for the exploration of this possibility—to say something in such a way as to negate indeterminately what is said and at the same time negate the saying. It is possible to say, and to mean, nothing.

Socrates isolates the principle underlying sophistic practice and takes it to the point of no return. As Socrates is to the Sophists, so Kierkegaard (not Hegel) is to the Romantic ironists he reviews in part 2 of his master's thesis. Both Socrates and Kierkegaard are dead ends. Socrates, who wrote not a word, ironically terminated and consummated his philosophizing with his death. Even more ironically, Søren Kierkegaard, who wrote volumes, prefaced his corpus by denying the possibility of beginning and of continuation . . . by beginning with irony.

Nevertheless, scattered throughout *The Concept of Irony* there are promises of beginning and of repetition. The work concludes reassuringly with an epilogue which says that irony is the beginning of authentic human existence and the condition of the possibility of that repetition by which the human individual acquires a personal history. However, the epilogue itself, if it is not to lapse into the Hegelian dialectic and become an *aufgehoben* moment in the system it meant to destroy, must erase itself. It does. Ironically. And that—apparently—is no more than the last spasm of an organism already dead. Irony is the bottomless abyss. There is no return—apparently—from the infinite.

That is the—apparently—insoluble problem, at once philosophical and linguistic, to which the Kierkegaardian canon is addressed. To which, indirectly and preposterously, it offers a solution: an impossible solution, befitting an insoluble problem.

Irony, however, is only the problem. It is not a result, not even a negative result. The ironic consciousness' alienation from immediacy, which evacuates the subject as thoroughly as it devalues the object, and the self-cancellation of ironic discourse, which abysses signification, create a situation in which it is impossible to find repose. Not even the cheap repose of skepticism or the even cheaper consolations of nihilism. The situation inhabited by irony demands a new departure just as surely as it seems to prohibit it. Ironically, the ironic negation is no more negative than it is positive. Irony is not a destination, it is only a way. But to what?

Kierkegaard's treatise on irony does not undertake a critique of Hegel, nor does it offer a new solution to Hegel's problem. Taking Hegel's problem (infinitely) more seriously than he himself did, it creates the need for what Kierkegaard (who liked to associate himself with the Greeks) called a *metabasis eis allo genos*. Not a new solution, but a new kind of solution: a solution which, if Hegel be taken to have brought Western philosophy to an end, will no longer be able to be called philosophical.

Something (Kierkegaard wants us to think) is slouching toward Bethlehem, something "as yet unnameable which is proclaiming itself and which can do so . . . only under the species of the non-species, in the formless, mute, infant, and terrifying form of monstrosity" (Derrida, "Structure, Sign and Play," 293).

Of all things.

2.
THE ANALYSIS OF THE GOOD IN KIERKEGAARD'S *PURITY OF HEART*

Kierkegaard's views on ethics are conditioned by his interest in the relation between ethics and religion. He believes that the attempt to understand life in ethical terms cannot succeed in practice, and that this impasse of ethics discloses the relevance of the religious view of life. In this respect he is opposed to Kant, who defines the dignity and destiny of man in exclusively ethical terms, and whose "practical faith" is a claim which the moral man is entitled to lay on the universe.

In *Purity of Heart* Kierkegaard argues that the only adequate understanding of the Good is religious: the Good is really known only when it is experienced as God. The power of the Good (= God) is effective for a human individual in the situation of remorse and the act of penitence. In remorse and penitence a man acknowledges his impotence to comprehend and attain the Good. The only "purity of heart" is the penitent confession of one's own irrefragable *impurity*. But it is in the consciousness of his impurity and impotence that a man is opened to a realization of the goodness and the power of God.

It is this argument which I shall analyze in the present essay. Before I proceed, however, I must insert a cautionary word about method. Philosophers have commonly believed that the Good may be defined and its possibility in general demonstrated with no more than illustrative reference to the existential predicament of the individual who is trying to do the Good. Kierkegaard's explicit rejection of this conviction makes his discussions of ethical problems virtually unique. He is persuaded that the Good cannot be known nor its possibility apprehended except by *individuals*, each in the context of his personal exigence. Therefore, his ethical writings take one of two forms: the form of indirect communication, in which (by devices such as humor, irony, polemic, narrative, and lyric) existential possibilities are presented which demand but in no way enforce a decision on the part of the reader; or the form of direct discourse, in which a speaker, out of his own existential situation, addresses himself persuasively and immediately to every other individual in *his* situation. *Purity of Heart*, described on its title page as "spiritual preparation for the office of confession," is written in the latter form. My own essay, which is second-intentional with respect to Kierkegaard's book, will be a philosophical abstract of his argument. This means that I shall present as matter for contemplation what Kierkegaard presents as a need for action. However, it will be necessary to recall at every point the existential reference of the argument, without which it loses both rigor and significance. The logic of existential address has its own validity in situation, a validity which can only be indicated indirectly in a philosophical discussion.

I shall refer frequently to Kant's ethics. For in spite of his extensive indebtedness to the *bête noire* Hegel, and perhaps because of his fundamental opposition to Kant, Kierkegaard's views are most clearly seen (in a philosophical regard) against the background of the *Foundations* and the second *Critique*.

With this in mind, let us proceed to the argument itself, first to Kierkegaard's examination of the experience of remorse. He writes: "When remorse calls to a man it is always late. . . . The inner agitation of the heart understands what remorse insists upon, that the eleventh hour has come" (*Purity of Heart*, 40; hereinafter cited in this essay as PH). The moral task of man, according to Kierkegaard, is defined by the reality of the Eternal and its presence to the human consciousness. Because the Eternal is, there is something which shall "have no time," that is, shall not be simply one among the many things a man does, but which demands the whole of time, that is, must infuse and direct whatever he does. There is something which shall always be done (PH, 37). And that which shall always be done is: a man shall always *will one thing*. He shall always have *purity of heart*, an undivided commitment to the Good.

Regarded as the starting point of an argument, this is either a *petitio principii* (if specific meanings of "Eternal" and "Good" are tacitly assumed) or extremely vague (if no such meanings are assumed). I suggest that it is deliberately vague, and that all Kierkegaard means to describe here is the structure of the moral consciousness in general. The demand of the Eternal for purity of heart may be specified in various ways. One may think Socratically of the integrity of the soul constrained by the vision of the Good, or in Kantian terms of the moral disposition singly and simply intent on its duty. In any case no particular definition of "Good" or of "Eternal" is at issue here. Kierkegaard is not interested in offering a theory of values, especially not a delineation of the "supreme value," the Good. As we shall see, the problem of the apprehension of the Good is not a problem of values at all for Kierkegaard, but an existential and religious problem of *being*. At present he only proposes to recall the necessity, in any moral system, of rooting categorical obligation in a transcendent ground. What Kierkegaard does assume, therefore, is that any serious ethics expresses the demand for absolute integrity of motive, however the origin and the content of this demand are specified.

Kierkegaard continues: "Alas, and when this [purity of heart] is not done, then once again, there is something (*or more correctly, it is the same thing*, that reappears, changed, *but not changed in its essence*) which should at all times be done. There is something which in no temporal sense shall have its time. *There must be repentence and remorse*" (PH, 38, my emphasis). The *essential* moral task is: to will the Good with purity of heart. But in actuality the consciousness of this task arises only after the condition of its fulfillment has been lost. "When remorse calls to a man it is always late" (PH, 40). The human individual, whatever his *essential* nature, never *exists* as an unsullied potentiality for moral action, but always finds himself already entangled inextricably in a web of actual evil.

Kant thought that the basic moral phenomenon was the consciousness of categorical obligation, the consciousness of a discrepancy between a law which I recognize as objectively incumbent upon me, and my will, which is not necessarily subjectively disposed to obey that law. But the consciousness so described is the consciousness of a will suspended in self-contemplation, a will which is only potentially good or potentially evil. The actual moral self-consciousness is the self-consciousness of a human being who has *already enacted* and *even now enacts* his potentialities for good and evil. Elsewhere Kierkegaard writes that "freedom is never in *abstracto*. If one would grant freedom an instant to make a choice between good and evil, without being itself in either of the two positions, then precisely at that instant freedom is not freedom but a meaningless reflection. . . . In case (*sit venia verbo*) freedom remains in the good, it knows nothing at all of the evil" (*Concept of Dread*, 99n.).

The fundamental moral phenomenon is the consciousness of guilt, and this consciousness of guilt is the existential meaning of the consciousness of obligation. "Guilt" does not refer to specific sins of commission or omission, nor to my failure to achieve certain values. The consciousness of guilt is the consciousness of the *actual* discrepancy between the *being* that I am and the *being* I am morally required to be. Without the consciousness of this discrepancy (still quite apart from any particular understanding of the Good) there is no moral problem. The problem of guilt, understood as the contradiction in existence of the *is* and the *ought*, is the moral problem.

But it may be asked, why is the consciousness of *guilt* fundamental? The actual situation of a human being is a complex of *good* as well as of evil. Isn't it only theological prejudice on Kierkegaard's part to insist that the Eternal demands an accounting for every moment and is satisfied with nothing less than perfect purity of heart? Can conscience demand any more of a finite being than the maximum (for him) possible preponderance of good over evil in his actions? Kant's answer to this question is the only answer possible. If I interpret the moral law not as a demand for perfection but only as a demand for the greatest purity of motive possible for a person of my capacity, then I fall inevitably into one of two traps. Either I trim the moral requirement to suit my own indulgent estimate of my abilities, that is, make it "compliant to my convenience." Or I deceive myself with a fantastic vision of my limitless possibilities for perfection, a deception by which I conceal from myself the gravity of my moral predicament (*Kant's Critique of Practical Reason*; cf. also Doescher, "Kant's Postulate").

The inevitability of this dilemma is not the inevitability of logical necessity. It is an existential necessity. But that is precisely the kind of necessity with which the existing human being must grapple in his practical conflicts. Consider the nature of moral evil. The evil that I do is not the product of a cosmic or psychological flaw for which I am not responsible and which I can therefore tolerate without self-accusation. Even if it could be demonstrated in general that there is a recalcitrance to the good woven into the fabric of existence, still in any particular case I could not without deception disclaim responsibility for what I do: to do so would be a pretense to a more perfect self-knowledge and a more perfect understanding of my own motives than I may legitimately claim. I am therefore bound to assume responsibility for what I do even in those cases (and that really means *all* cases) where my autonomous agency is not clearly discernible. That, at least in part, is what it means to say that freedom is a *postulate* of practical reason.

I cannot regard the evil I do as proceeding from a source outside or beyond my will. Neither, however, is it remediable. The evil that I do is indeed my own doing, but because it is past and done, it is not something I can undo. I can try to balance the evil by a compensatory good, but this is not to alter or eradicate the evil. The past that I have built for myself stands, and though I may make improvements in it and additions to it, I cannot tear it down and build a new structure. Moral evil is neither inevitable nor eradicable, but actual. It is the work of my freedom by which I have bound myself. And when I awaken to a consciousness of the moral problem, *that problem has already defined itself so as to admit of no moral solution.* The phenomenon of guilt defines and creates the moral problem. But it also makes a moral solution of the problem impossible. In the face of the demand of conscience for absolute purity of heart, and in the face of the fact of absolute guilt, all exhortations to self-improvement and all further delineations of the moral task become irrelevant, save insofar as they serve to deepen the consciousness of guilt itself. Thus the moral situation, according to Kierkegaard, is a *stalemate*. I cannot evade my responsibility for guilt, nor can I do away with it.

But must we now accept the religious alternative Kierkegaard offers? Is there no other way out of the dilemma? There is another alternative which is not only thinkable but capable of existential enactment. I may simply forget about guilt. I may choose to regard remorse as no more than regret, and I may content myself with getting along and hoping for better times. And better times will come, of course. Time does heal all wounds, and the wound of regret will heal over by itself if I do not perversely insist on reopening it by continual self-accusation.

This is the naturalistic—or as Kierkegaard calls it, the aesthetic—way out of the moral predicament. It can be successful, as all of us know. But it is nevertheless an evasion of the issue. I may find it impossible to live with my past, but the success of forgetting it is contingent upon my willingness to renounce my responsibility and my moral agency. The naturalistic "solution" of the moral problem is a refusal of the problem, by default if not by election. Or, as Kierkegaard says, the Eternal (manifesting itself as the demand of conscience for purity of heart) must not be confused with what is most unlike it, human forgetfulness (PH, 45).

This is why Kierkegaard insists that when a perfect moral disposition is unattained and unattainable, when the Good is not willed with purity of heart, then the moral demand, *not changed in its essence but radically transformed in its actuality*, is a demand for *penitence* (cf. PH, 38). This is what he means by his statement in the *Concluding Unscientific Postscript* (468–93), that the highest moral achievement possible for a man is the everlasting recollection of guilt. "For every human being is an unprofitable servant, and the human being who is inspired by ethical enthusiasm differs from others only in knowing this, and in hating and abhorring every form of deception" (*Concluding Unscientific Postscript*, 122).

If this argument is correct, then the moral situation itself, by its own dialectic, has specified the demand of conscience as a demand for penitence. The continued re-collection and re-cognition of guilt is not essentially different from that integrity of motive which is described as purity of heart. It *is* purity of heart, in the only form in which it is available to a human being. Penitence is the existential-dialectical satisfaction of the essential demand for moral perfection. And this means that the moral situation, existentially understood, is a religious situation.

But is this really so? Remorse and penitence, as thus far described, may simply name an existential tragedy with no religious significance whatever. Still, we have before us a characterization of the situation of man, and it is within this situation, if anywhere, that the Good must be recognized and its power made efficacious. Whatever the Good is, it must either be *good for* (that is, powerful in) the situation of remorse and penitence, or it is *no good for* the individual who desperately needs it. Where and what is the Good in this predicament?

"The Good," says Kierkegaard, "without condition and without qualification, without preface and without compromise, is absolutely the only thing that a man may and should will, and is only one thing" (PH, 54). Consistent with his doctrine that subjectivity is truth, Kierkegaard holds that the Good can only be defined in terms of the mode of its acquisition: it is that which *can be* willed absolutely. In one sense there is nothing that can be willed absolutely: all the goods a man may conceive and set for himself are finite, relative, and fragmentary. Yet Kierkegaard continues: "For as the Good is only a single thing, so all ways lead to the Good, even the false ones: when the penitent one follows the same way back. Oh, Thou the unfathomable trustworthiness of the Good! Wherever a man may be in the world, whichever road he travels, *when he wills one thing*, he is on a road that leads him to Thee" (PH, 54).

To will *something* absolutely is the condition of all genuine human individuality. To be an individual means to concentrate one's whole personality in the dynamic of a single will toward a summary and supreme end. But to do so is also to undertake the absolute risk of staking one's life upon the reality of that end. For whatever a man wills absolutely, he thereby comes to depend upon absolutely. But any finite end, if it is willed absolutely, will reveal its insufficiency to sustain the man who so depends upon it. And in so doing it will *expose* him to the Good through the existential reversal of remorse and penitence. The Good, single and absolute, transcends all finite goods, and manifests itself in their dissolution. That which can be willed absolutely is the Good to which man is exposed only in the failure of his will. This exposition to the Good, which is the Good itself in its existential epiphany, is penitence. Kierkegaard is not interested in the nature of any particular object of the will, but in the absoluteness of the willing. It is the necessarily absolute *how* of the willing, conjoined with the necessarily finite character of its *what*, that both breaks the continuity of moral striving and creates the subjective condition for the revelation of the Good in an extra-moral sense.

What Kierkegaard is saying at this point must be sharply distinguished from the romantic thesis that anything a man does is good if only he does it wholeheartedly and with passion. This is no doubt the most attractive form of moral relativism, but there is no relativism in Kierkegaard's position. It is true, for him, that all ways lead to the Good. But this does not mean that anything a man does is just as good (and by that fact, just as bad) as anything else. Rather, Kierkegaard is saying that if we take the idea of an absolute Good seriously, then no man is *excluded* from the Good, no matter who he is or what he does, no matter even what his moral theories are. Differences of moral theory are significant as expressions of the various and sometimes really distinct ways in which we understand ourselves. But in relation to the absoluteness of the Good, there is no preferred moral theory. There is not even a preferred moral condition. The Good is the same for all men, of every shade of better and worse, and it is in fact efficacious precisely at that point where ethical endeavor is impotent, in the consciousness of guilt, where all men are equally condemned each by his own conscience.

But is there any reason why the absolute Good should not be *continuous with* the relative goods? Kierkegaard answers: "But the secret of deception, to which in one way or another all the expressions can be traced back is this: that certainly it is not men that stand in need of the Good, but that it is the Good that stands in need of men" (PH, 132–33). Every ethical system contains within itself the seeds of that self-destruction which Kierkegaard calls despair. Regarded as an interpretation of the human situation and a guide for conduct, every ethical system is a set of answers to the wrong question. For the Good itself is reality and power. But the Good conceived morally is an ideal which awaits our efforts before it can be actual. All ethical endeavor in this sense is a claim upon the Good, and if a man persists in it, he will discover, in the consciousness of guilt, that it is the Good alone which has a claim upon him. If we ask, therefore, what is the good in the experience of remorse and the act of penitence, Kierkegaard's reply is: remorse and penitence *are* the Good exercising its claim on the human will.

In consideration of this conclusion to which we repeatedly and monotonously come, let us examine another passage from Kierkegaard's text: "For as only one thing is necessary, and as the theme of the talk is the willing of only one thing: hence the consciousness before God of one's eternal responsibility to be an individual is that one thing necessary" (PH, 197–98). It is the self-accusation of conscience that is the revelation of the Good in its reality and its power. But the reality and power of the Good so revealed is *God*. The "Eternal," which is vaguely present to consciousness as the moral demand, is revealed in terrible clarity in the situation of guilt as the Good itself accusing conscience.

Conscience for Kierkegaard is *con-scientia*; it is that which a man *knows together with* God. The accuser of conscience is God, and the self-accusation of conscience (remorse and penitence) is the one place in existence where a man's will is reconciled with the Good. It is in the acknowledgement of guilt that a man is conscious before God of his eternal responsibility to be himself. But the self, so understood, is guilt. And the acknowledgement of the self as guilt before God is the purity of heart by which a man wills one thing, for it is here alone that the will of man and the will of God are at one.

This interpretation of conscience (and that is what Kierkegaard's whole argument really is) is indeed extreme. But he would say that to be a man is to be in extremity, and that any other interpretation of this phenomenon is a counsel of despair. Kant's doctrine of autonomy is a case—perhaps *the* case—in point. In his *Journal*s Kierkegaard wrote:

> Kant held that man was his own law (autonomy), *i.e.* bound himself under the law which he gave himself. In a deeper sense that means to say: lawlessness or experimentation. It is no harder than the thwacks which Sancho Panza applied to his own bottom. I can no more be really stricter in A

than I am, or than I wish myself to be in B. There must be some compulsion, if it is to be a serious matter. If I am not bound by anything higher than myself, and if I am to bind myself, where am I to acquire the severity as A by which, as B, I am to be bound, *so long as A and B are the same*. (*Journals of Søren Kierkegaard*, no. 1041: 364–65; my emphasis)

The truth of this comment is not obvious at first, since Kant does distinguish between my pathologically conditioned personal will B and my rational human will A which alone is the source of moral legislation. But this distinction will not hold; for the rational will is made practical only in the private will, so that I am in reality required to be a law unto myself. Practical reason transcends every individual man, but it does not transcend humanity. And humanity is actual only in men. Under the conditions of existence A and B *are* the same.

The doctrine of autonomy is therefore either fatuous or presumptuous. Either the moral man is, as Nietzsche jibed, the civil servant as thing-in-itself raised up to be judge over the civil servant as phenomenon: Sancho Panza spanking himself. Or he is required by his autonomy to be his own God. But as Kierkegaard demonstrated—what must certainly be obvious—no man is stronger than himself.

The practical consequences of Kant's ethics are in line with this dilemma. I am to treat men as ends in themselves, not as means merely. But how, concretely, does one treat a man as an end in himself? A man *is* an end in himself by virtue of his freedom, which I cannot touch. I can only act on him through his desires; that is, I can make him happy or refuse to make him happy, so far as it lies in my power to do either. Plainly it would be wrong to gratify the desires of men indiscriminately. I can therefore *either* do nothing at all to others, rather than run the risk of violating their freedom: but this would be fatuous. *Or* I can decide which of their desires *ought* to be satisfied and act accordingly. But this means manipulating men for their own good, and it is presumptuous (cf. *Kant's Critique of Practical Reason*, 352–57).

We cannot regard conscience as the self-discipline of the will. On the contrary: it is the recognition of the inefficacy of self-discipline. "A man may be so severe with himself that he understands: all my severity is nothing, I must have another to help me, who can be severity itself, even though he is gentleness itself" (*Journals of Søren Kierkegaard*, no. 1041: 365). What Kierkegaard has tried to show is that the moral situation of man *is* the situation of remorse, and that this situation, existentially apprehended, transforms itself dialectically into the *religious* situation, the situation in which the Good manifests itself as God. The existential analysis of the experience of remorse leads to the being of God as the presupposition and the meaning of that experience. The experience of remorse is dialectically the experience of the Good which imparts itself in the very act of annihilating every effort to achieve it.

How, finally, does the Good impart itself? In Kierkegaard's analysis the self-imparting of the Good works no magical transformation in human nature or in the world. The Good makes all things good, else it would not be the Good in reality and power. But it makes all things good in the sense that the recognition of it enables a man to respect the absolute difference between himself and the Good, and to accept his humanity, particularly its guilt, with the consciousness that in his moral impotence and nonbeing the Good is potent and real. "God in heaven is not as a young girl's folly. He does not reward the impressive with admiration. The reward of the good man is to be allowed to worship in truth" (PH, 67). Remorse and penitence are affirmations as well as negations: they are acts of worship. To "worship" (a technical term in Kierkegaard's works) is to acknowledge one's absolute difference from God as this is revealed in the consciousness of guilt. But the consciousness of guilt, as the content of the act of worship, thereby reveals the existence of God and man's relationship to Him. God and man are at one when the absolute difference between them is respected. Life is good when it is accepted as guilty before God (*Concluding Unscientific Postscript*, 369; cf. also *Gospel of Suffering*, 212).

It would not be altogether wrong to interpret all of Kierkegaard's writing on ethics as a commentary on the saying, "It is a terrible thing to fall into the hands of the living God." The existence of God is a possibility, the terrifying nature of which is not usually evident from philosophical discussions of it. That, according to Kierkegaard, would be due to the fact that such discussions are normally carried on in a way that prevents the real problem of

God's existence from arising. The reality of God is not a postulate or an hypothesis or a puzzle, but an existential possibility which, if it is acknowledged as an actuality, amounts to a complete upheaval of human existence and a complete reversal of human self-understanding. The reality of God, appearing in remorse and penitence, is the sole and sufficient ground of the possibility of the phenomenon of guilt, and is itself the paradoxical meaning of that phenomenon. The consciousness of guilt is the reality of the power of the Good in human existence.

That is why Kierkegaard could write discourses on "the edification contained in the thought that before God we are always in the wrong" and on the theme that "man's need of God is his highest perfection." God is the *absolute fact*, and therefore the one fact of absolute importance, the one thing that is absolutely needful for a man to acknowledge. The only condition for a man's receiving the Good is his awareness that he needs it. And this need is, *dialectically and for a human being*, the Good itself. Thus the prayer set at the beginning and the end of *Purity of Heart* concludes: "Oh, Thou that givest both the beginning and the completion, give Thou victory in the day of need, so that what neither a man's burning wish nor his determined resolution may attain to, may be granted unto him in the sorrowing of repentance: to will only one thing" (PH, 32, 219).[1]

This is the sense in which Kierkegaard takes the consciousness of guilt to be uniquely revelatory of the existence of God and of His relationship to men. Of course his analysis is not a proof of the existence of God. Regarded as such it is circular: the being of God to which it concludes is easily revealed as the hidden premise on which it builds. The argument as argument is a *petitio*. Existential, as opposed to Hegelian, dialectic cannot terminate in a final synthesis. What it can do—and all Kierkegaard

---

1. The human situation, with its dialectic as here described, should not be confused with the dialectic of sin and reconciliation in the situation of the Christian believer. The present discussion is not concerned with a specific religious content but with the general structure of the religious consciousness. According to Kierkegaard, Christianity radically transforms this religious consciousness. Cf. *Concluding Unscientific Postscript*, 493–519.

expects it to do—is to move rigorously toward a final *either/or*: the Good is *either* God *or* it is nothing at all.

This is the substance of Kierkegaard's argument in *Purity of Heart*. It epitomizes his view of the relation of "the ethical" and "the religious." I have tried to state it in such a way as to show what I believe is its validity, and I have tried to anticipate the most obvious objections. Rather than embark on a further critique of the view, I shall in conclusion suggest what I take to be its position in the tradition of philosophical ethics.

If we take the Platonic ethics as a representative high point in ancient ethics, and the Kantian theory as a strong modern position, the views of Kierkegaard can be seen more clearly against the contrast of these two. Both Plato and Kant are moved to ethical reflection by the observed contradiction between men as they are and men as they ought to be. For Plato the discrepancy between Socrates and a man like Alcibiades poses the moral problem. For Kant it is the inwardly sensed conflict between the moral law and the propensity to evil.

Plato, following Socrates, has no difficulty in accounting for the reality of goodness. The Form of the Good is the supreme cause, the source and destiny of all being, goodness, truth, and beauty. But if the world is good and has a good cause, why are not all men like Socrates? It is the existence of evil that is problematic. Plato vacillates between attributing evil to ignorance and referring it to perverse affections. In reality the two are intimately bound up together and inseparable. Virtue is knowledge, but knowledge is also virtue. What is important is that in any case evil is not attributed to the will of man. There is no power of freedom in man capable of choosing evil. There is no doctrine of the will at all in Plato's theory of man, since what is called spirit has no agency of its own but is always in the service either of the mind or of the appetites. The human self is seen as the point of interaction of cosmic forces, incarnate in men as reason and passion, drawing against each other in a cosmological contest of uncertain issue. Plato's final answer to the question, "How is a man like Alcibiades possible?" is: that's the way the *world* is, though in *Reality* the Good holds undisputed sway. Thus the Platonic ethics transcends itself in an aesthetic metaphysics; Plato resolves the moral problem of evil by rising above the level of moral conflict.

By contrast, Kant is easily able to account for evil. Indeed his ethics is built on the possibility if not on the fact of evil. Whereas Plato begins with the assumption that all men by nature desire the Good, Kant begins with the contradictory assumption that all men do not by nature desire the Good though they are by nature obligated to produce it. Kant has inherited and secularized the Christian conception of human freedom, a conception of which Plato had no inkling. The existence of evil is not problematic but normal in Kantian ethics.

What is problematic for Kant is the possibility in a practical respect of the highest Good. For Kant the Good is no longer, as it was for Plato and his Christian successors, a prevenient reality, but an end to achieved, an ideal to be made real by moral striving. But just as Plato cannot account for evil in moral terms, so Kant cannot demonstrate the practical possibility of the Good. All the devices by which he endeavors to prove that the Good is possible serve only to exhibit its impossibility. The consciousness of obligation posits the conflict of the *is* and the *ought* as the given moral condition of man. Kant's doctrine of respect does not offer a unique incentive for practical reason, but rather demonstrates that the moral conflict—and hence evil—persists as long as man lives (*Kant's Critique of Practical Reason*, 191). His doctrine of immortality simply prolongs the hopeless moral situation endlessly. As for his practical faith in God: even if we pass over the purely supernumerary role God plays in Kant's ethics, the fact remains that God is not the power of the Good, but a claim man is entitled to make on his own moral destiny, the demand of practical reason that reality answer to its rational necessity.[2] Kant's postulate of the existence of God is, from a moral point of view, hardly irresistible. Religiously it is absurd. As Kierkegaard said, it would be the very devil to be God in that way.

> 2. It is significant that when Kant criticizes the ontological argument, he interprets it as a demand of theoretical reason that reality be rational. He interprets the argument as he or any modern thinker would have formulated it, as a demand that Being conform to thought. But Anselm's argument is thoroughly dialectical in Plato's sense. It is *fides quaerens intellectum*, the love of wisdom seeking its transcendent

Thus Plato and Kant begin with the Good and with evil respectively. The one, beginning with the Good, cannot explain evil. The other, beginning with evil, cannot get to the Good. Where does Kierkegaard stand in this context? Obviously he combines elements of both views. It should be clear from the foregoing discussion that he shares with Plato the conviction that the Good must be the absolute reality and power: God. But he has a conception of human freedom no less radical than that of Kant. As distinct from Kant, Kierkegaard denies that the Good is an ideal men can actualize or that it is a right which they are privileged to expect the universe to honor. But as distinct from Plato, he denies that men's need of the Good expresses itself as a love of the Good; men's need of the Good is their guilt before God.

The power at work in the Platonic ethics is the Form of the Good, drawing men to itself as best it can out of their estrangement amid error and evil. The power at work in the Kantian ethics is human freedom, advancing by its own law, defining its own Good, and claiming this Good as its birthright. The circularity of Kierkegaard's religious ethics is the consequence of his paradoxical affirmation of both Plato and Kant. With Plato he allows the primacy of the Good over man, though this Good is manifested only in the situation of guilt self-incurred by freedom. With Kant he allows that the Good is efficacious by human freedom, but only at that point where freedom, in the consciousness of its impotence, surrenders itself to the Good. In a word, the Good is God; and the reality of God in human existence is remorse, contrition and repentance. In Kierkegaard's analysis of the Good, the ethical is both suspended and fulfilled in worship.

Would it be wrong to compare Kierkegaard with Socrates as

---

ground, believing reason discovering its origin, goal, and measure in Being. In some ways the difference between ancient and medieval thought on the one hand and modern thought on the other is a fundamental difference of orientation resulting from the acceptance by the one and the refusal by the other of the substance of Anselm's ontology as a basis for philosophic inquiry. The development of modern thought reaches the antipode of the ontological argument in Nietzsche's saying, "God is dead."

his nearest philosophical kin? He did after all characterize his own "religiousness A" (which *Purity of Heart* represents) as the Socratic religiousness. I think we may consider Kierkegaard's *Purity of Heart* as a modern version of the Socratic ignorance and the Socratic piety. In his *Apology* Socrates states his belief that wisdom belongs to the gods alone, that all human wisdom is folly, and that the wise man is the man who acknowledges his own ignorance. In the *Phaedrus*, Socrates is made to profess ultimate ignorance about himself and his destiny, and the *Apology* closes with his confession of ignorance regarding the value of the death which awaits him as opposed to the value of the life to which his Athenian judges will return. There is no reason to suppose that he is being ironical in these utterances. At any rate Socrates' irony about his ignorance is not the irony of a man who seems to say one thing but who really means the opposite. It is the irony of a man who says one thing so as to seem to mean the opposite, but really means exactly what he says.

The fact is that Socrates' ignorance is the same as his piety. His ignorance is the expression for his submission to the direction of the Good. Confronted (in his ignorance) with the alternative of escape or death, Socrates sees this as a choice of either acknowledging that his death itself is a good thing, or admitting that the Good by which he claims to be constrained is impotent in the face of death and therefore an illusion. Is not Socrates' death the demonstration—circular perhaps, but the only existentially possible demonstration—of his conviction that the power of the Good is made effective in and through the weakness and the ignorance of men? It seems to me that the point which Kierkegaard is trying to make in *Purity of Heart* is just this: in the matter of self-understanding we may go as far as, but no farther than, the Socratic ignorance, and in the matter of good and evil we may hope for as much as, but no more than, the Socratic piety.

Kierkegaard of course had a conception of freedom that was Christian in origin if not always in spirit. It was this conception of freedom that put the broken world of modernity in the place of the cosmos of antiquity. Kant and Kierkegaard would have been impossible in antiquity. The absence of their like in the Middle Ages must be traced to the strength of Augustine's synthesis of the Platonic vision of the cosmos with his Christian conviction of sin as man's bondage and man's responsibility. Men like Kierkegaard and Kant could appear only after the Renaissance, which affirmed the Christian doctrine of freedom by refusing the Christian universe and the Christian God.

Kierkegaard is therefore, like Kant, a Christian by heritage living amid the fragments of a broken Christian world. Nevertheless I believe that his ethics is more Socratic than Kantian, inasmuch as it is a religious ethics. Socrates' piety was a piety without freedom. Kant's idea of freedom was so secular as to exclude the possibility of piety. Kierkegaard's religiousness A (Kant's ethics of freedom suspended) is the fulfillment of freedom in its self-surrender to the Good. Kierkegaard is the "Christian Socrates" in that his religious ethics is a recapitulation of the Socratic piety in a world riven by the Christian conception of freedom. Such a religious ethics, with or without its special theological context, is a permanent possibility for human thought and a strenuous demand for human decision. It is the unique contribution of Kierkegaard to modern ethics that he made the possibility unmistakably clear and set out the demand with uncompromising rigor. The philosophical understanding of Kierkegaard's ethics terminates in the comprehension of the possibility he defined; the ethical understanding goes through the contemplation of the possibility to a confrontation with the demand.

3.
THE VIEW FROM PISGAH:
A READING OF *FEAR AND TREMBLING*

Fear and Trembling, by Johannes de Silentio, is an attempt to understand the story of Abraham and Isaac recounted in Genesis 22. Of course it may be assumed that the author is familiar with the whole saga of Abraham: God's faithfulness to Abraham from the time he first left his home in Ur of the Chaldees to sojourn in a strange land until the day of the miraculous birth of Isaac in the senescence of his parents, and Abraham's faithfulness to God throughout all the trials and disappointments of his long pilgrimage. It is only against this background of promise, delay, frustration, and eventual fulfillment that the scene on Mount Moriah exhibits the bitterness and poignance that it held for Abraham himself and still holds for Johannes de Silentio.[1] It also goes without saying that Johannes had read St. Paul's interpretation of the faith of Father Abraham in Romans 4 and the roll of the heroes of faith in Hebrews 11.

---

1. For the story of Abraham, see Genesis 12–25. For an interesting literary treatment of the story, see Erich Auerbach, *Mimesis*, chap. 1. Cf. also my essay, "Kierkegaard's Lyric of Faith: A Look at *Fear and Trembling*."

His interest, however, is not exegetical but existential. After a short preface (of which more later) the book opens with a "Prelude" or *stemning*. The literal meaning of *stemning* is "tuning" or "tone," so that a better translation might be "mood" or "atmosphere." For it establishes the mode and the tonality of the considerations to follow. In the manner of a fairy tale it begins, "Once upon a time . . ." there was a child who heard, revered, and in his simplicity comprehended the story of Abraham and Isaac, how God tempted Abraham, how he kept the faith, and how he received his son again by a miracle. But the increase of years brings about a dissociation of sensibilities. Maturity separates the passion and the reflection that are united in the pious immediacy of the child, and the man finds that the greater his enthusiasm, the less his understanding. In his disenchantment he desires to achieve an imaginative contemporaneity with Abraham in the moment of his ordeal. If only I could be with him on Mount Moriah, he thinks, I might understand how he felt and why he did the things that made him the father of faith! He does not wish for a philosophical comprehension that "goes beyond" faith by fitting it into a system of metaphysics; he simply wants to know the feeling of the reality of faith. He is not a "learned exegete," for he cannot even read Hebrew, though he is willing to assume that those who do experience no difficulty at all understanding Abraham.

The irony of this last suggests irresistibly that the perplexed young man of the Prelude is none other than the author, John of Silence. Johannes de Silentio: if we read "de" as the aristocratic particle it seems to be, then he is John of the realm or kingdom of silence. In another reading the title page of his book says "Fear and Trembling, a dialectical lyric, by John, *about* silence." Either or both will serve: for silence is his domain, and silence the burden of his dialectical lyric. Johannes' character, which is part and parcel of his literary method, is presaged by the motto he has picked for his book: "*Was Tarquinius Superbus in seinem Garten mit den Mohnköpfen sprach, verstand der Sohn, aber nicht der Bote.*"[2]

---

2. *Fear and Trembling* and *The Sickness Unto Death* (Princeton: Princeton University Press, 1968), 21; H, 3. Further page references to this edition will be given in parentheses in the text. I have tacitly corrected Lowrie's translation where it is in error. I have also given page refer-

If there is any message about faith in *Fear and Trembling*, it will be an enigmatic message. Only the sons, those who are already members of the spiritual household of Abraham, will understand it, but not the messengers, those—perhaps philosophers and theologians—who like Abraham's servants witness the mystery from a distance and even convey information about it, but do not comprehend their own witness and their own message. Johannes de Silentio seeks an understanding of faith. But he is saying nothing about it that can be understood by those who do not already understand. True to his name, he is keeping silent.

Perhaps he is silent because there is something that men need to listen for, a still small voice that cannot be heard amid the clamor of the intellectual marketplace. Something of the sort is indicated by his respectful Preface. In these days, he complains (the allusions are topical and local, but the complaint itself is timely enough), faith is being sold, or sold out, at bargain prices. In fact the price is so low it is doubtful if anyone will care to buy. The intelligentsia have doubted everything, transcended faith, and understood all truth. At least they say they have, and it would be bad taste to doubt their veracity. But it is strange that they should appeal to Descartes as their patron. For Descartes was "a quiet and solitary thinker"—a man of silence—"not a bellowing night-watchman" (22; H, 6), who never doubted *de fide*. Strange, too, that every philosophy professor has got beyond faith. For how many and how great are the saints and martyrs who had all they could do just to *keep* the faith until death. Nowadays, Johannes sighs, we all start where the saints

---

ences (in the form: H followed by page number) to the new translation of *Fear and Trembling* by Howard V. Hong and Edna H. Hong (Princeton: Princeton University Press, 1983), but I have preferred to cite Lowrie's version. The German says: "What Tarquinius Superbus spoke in the garden by means of the poppies the son understood, but not the messenger." Tarquin, king of Rome, was bent on the destruction of Gabii. His son, having worked his way into the confidence of its people, sent to his father asking what to do next. Tarquin, distrustful of the messenger, took him into the garden, where he proceeded to cut off the heads of the tallest poppies with his sword. This was reported to the son, who understood thereby that he was to cause the death of the leading citizens of Gabii, and went straight to the task.

and martyrs left off, and faith has gone begging for takers. As for himself:

> The present writer is nothing of a philosopher; he is, *poetice et eleganter*, a supernumerary clerk who . . . writes because for him it is a luxury which becomes the more agreeable and more evident, the fewer there are who buy and read what he writes. He can easily foresee his fate in an age when passion has been obliterated in favor of learning, in an age when an author who wants to have readers must take care to write in such a way that the book can easily be perused during the afternoon nap. . . . He foresees his fate—that he will be entirely ignored. (24; H, 7–8)

There is the dissociation of sensibilities again, in the demeaning of passion by learning. There, too, is an "afternoon nap" that will make its major appearance later in more solemn and dreadful surroundings. And there is Johannes, an idler who writes for himself because he enjoys it and can afford it, retreating once more into his characteristic silence.

The words *"poetice et eleganter"* are reminiscent of the subtitle of *Fear and Trembling*, "Dialectical Lyric." A suitable translation might be "philosophical poem" or "poetic philosophy." The former is recommended by the fact that Johannes' lyric is substantive and his dialectic adjectival, though there is plenty of lyric in his dialectic (the Problemata) and an abundance of dialectic in his lyric (the Prelude and the Panegyric). With the "profoundest deference" (24; H, 8) to the philosophers, before whom he prostrates himself at the close of his Preface, Johannes de Silentio will attempt to write the poetry of faith.

The attempt fails. In the remainder of the Prelude Johannes offers a series of four dramatic scenes, each of which imagines one way Abraham might respond to the divine command: "Take Isaac, thine only son, whom thou lovest . . . , and offer him . . . for a burnt offering . . ." (27; H, 10; cf. Gen. 22: 2). He may, in preparing the sacrifice, prefer to let Isaac think that his father is an idolatrous and bloodthirsty monster, rather than jeopardize the boy's faith in God by insisting upon the truth. The command may destroy Abraham's own faith and deprive him of that joy in God and in Isaac that was the substance of his life. Having obeyed the command, he may still suspect that it was not God's will but his own sinfulness that made him willing to kill his son; he becomes a perpetual penitent, his confidence in God and in himself is weakened, and he has lost Isaac forever by doubting his paternal love. Or perhaps, at the moment Abraham draws the knife, he reveals to Isaac a hand clenched in anguish and a body shuddering with terror; the ram appears and Isaac lives, but he lives in despair ever after, having lost faith in God and in his father.

> Thus and in many like ways that man of whom we are speaking thought concerning this event. Every time he returned home after wandering to Mt. Moriah, he sank down with weariness, he folded his hands and said, "No one is so great as Abraham! Who is capable of understanding him?" (29; H, 14)

Nothing the imagination puts together can contain all the data of the biblical account: that Abraham loved Isaac and yet was willing to sacrifice him, that having given him up he could yet receive Isaac again with rejoicing and without remorse, that through it all Abraham kept faith with the God of the covenant while yet obedient to the God of the command. These are contradictions that exceed the poet's capacity for representation and stop the mouth of lyric fancy. So John of Silence is brought to silence.

Almost. For Johannes is not a pettifogging philosopher who measures enthusiasm and passion by the finite yardstick of the understanding. What he cannot understand he may yet admire. From his aborted essay in religious drama Johannes turns to compose a hymn of praise to Father Abraham and the power of faith which passes the power of poesy. His Panegyric opens with a meditation on heroism and poetry. Life were desperate, he writes, if there were no eternal consciousness in man, if the greatest of human achievements were but the byproduct of an aimless and chaotic play of natural forces. Empty and comfortless were life, if transience were its essence and oblivion its end. But it is not so. As God created both man and woman to assure the continuance of the race, so He created the hero, that there might be no dearth of magnificence, and the poet, that the hero's renown might remain forever in the remembrance of mankind. Abraham is the hero of faith, and John of Silence the poet who will jealously guard the entrusted treasure against the assaults of time.

But how shall the poet measure the magnitude of his hero? Every man is great in proportion to that which he loves: Abraham loved God. Every man is great in proportion to his expectation: Abraham, trusting the promises of God, expects the impossible. Every man is great in proportion to that with which he strives: Abraham strives with God. So

> Abraham was greater than all, great by reason of his power whose strength is impotence, great by reason of his wisdom whose secret is foolishness, great by reason of his hope whose form is madness, great by reason of the love which is hatred of oneself. (31; H, 16–17)

Greater than the greatness of Jeremiah lamenting in exile is the greatness of the father of faith rejoicing in his son and seed. For it is human to weep and to grieve, greatly human to give up one's life and one's hope. But it is greater than human to believe against understanding, to hope against expectation, and to hold onto one's life with joy.

Abraham's struggle to hold fast to the promises of God in the face of His demands is a struggle against time:

> . . . Abraham believed, and believed for this life. Yea, if his faith had been only for a future life, he surely would have cast everything away in order to hasten out of this world to which he did not belong. But Abraham's faith was not of this sort, if there be such a faith; for really this is not faith but the furthest possibility of faith which has a presentiment of its object as the extremest limit of the horizon, yet is separated from it by a yawning abyss within which despair carries on its game. But Abraham believed precisely for this life, that he was to grow old in the land, honored by the people, blessed in his generation, remembered forever in Isaac . . . (34–35; H, 20)

Had Abraham doubted, he would have driven the sacrificial knife into his own heart and forfeited the world for the sake of his "eternal consciousness." The heroism of doubt is easy to understand and a pleasure to admire. But Abraham believed and by believing became "the guiding star which saves the anguished" (35; H, 21). Had he in irresolution discovered the ram before he drew the knife, he would have been remembered forever not as the father of faith but as the author of consternation. But he did not doubt and he did not waver: he believed, and he drew the knife, and still he believed.

The encomiast is forced to conclude that his hero is no ordinary human hero; Abraham's constancy is beyond man's capacity as it is beyond man's understanding. It was God who required of an old man his only son, the son of promise. But it was God also who gave strength to his arm to draw the knife and strength to his soul to hold onto his faith. The God of the covenant does not fail to keep His promises: the God of the trial provides that which He demands. The God of promise and the God of temptation are one God. By God's election Abraham became the father of Isaac and the father of faith, but God Himself is the author and finisher of faith as He is the father of all paternity in heaven and in earth. Johannes' title is from a Pauline text, and his lyric a rhapsody on its theme: "Work out your own salvation with fear and trembling. For it is God which worketh in you both to will and to do of his good pleasure" (Phil. 2: 12–13).

The panegyric cannot continue. John of Silence is reduced to dumb apostrophe: "Venerable Father Abraham! . . . thou hadst no need of a panegyric . . ." (37; H, 22). Abraham does not need the eulogy of a poet to protect him from forgetfulness and the acids of time. In the power of faith he has already conquered time and won the temporal. "Thousands of years have run their course since those days, but thou hadst need of no tardy lover to snatch the memorial of thee from the power of oblivion, for every language calls thee to remembrance . . ." (37; H, 23). The poet has chosen a hero who wants and will suffer no poet. Not even the most reverent lover can praise a power which is impotence, a wisdom which is foolishness, a hope which is madness, and a love which is hatred of self. These are contradictions that disarm even admiration. A man can give up the temporal for the eternal, but only God can restore the temporal. It is the power of God that returns Isaac to Abraham's faith after Abraham's obedience has given him up. And no man can fitly praise God.

Once again Johannes de Silentio sinks in awe before a heroism that his rhetoric cannot duly celebrate nor his fancy adorn. He who would praise the father of faith ends by begging indulgence for the insufficiency of his decorum:

> . . . Forgive him who would speak in praise of thee, if he does not do it fittingly. He spoke humbly as if it were the desire of his own heart, he spoke briefly, as it becomes him to do, but he will never forget that thou hadst need of a hundred years to obtain a son of old age against expectation, that thou didst have to draw the knife before retaining Isaac; he will never forget that in a hundred and thirty years thou didst not get further than to faith. (37; H, 23)

The lyricist is through, his powers broken against the paradox of faith. And so the dialectician, whose business it is to deal with contradictions, takes the field.

Johannes the dialectician wants to examine some problems that are posed by the story of Abraham and Isaac. But there is something he must first spit out of his system before he gets to the problems themselves. Hence his Preliminary Expectoration, which is methodological preparation for the Problemata just as the Prelude provided an atmospheric setting for the Panegyric. At the beginning and end of his expectoration Johannes contrasts the function of the dialectician with the role usually assumed by the preachers when they are moved to uplift their congregations with the story of Abraham and Isaac. The dialectician ideally is an honest and honorable thinker who does not "lack the courage to think a thought whole" (41; H, 30). So honest is he that, should he run across a thought that terrifies him, he will refuse to think it at all rather than edit it. If worst comes to worst—for example, if a dialectical inquiry should disclose that Abraham is simply and solely a murderer—then the dialectician is honorable enough to keep it to himself rather than initiate others into such dreadful torments of the spirit. Not the least of the talents required in a dialectician is the ability to keep his mouth shut.

The parson, however, prates merrily away to all and sundry about the greatness of Abraham, who was willing to offer to God the best he had. Of course he takes care to keep this "best" quite vague, so that no one is troubled by the consideration that in Abraham's case the best happened to be his only son, to whom he owed the duty of solicitous paternal love and whom in fact he proposed to kill. Fortunately most of the congregation sleep through the sermon (there's that nap again), and no one is misled by his reverence's prattle. But should there chance to be an insomniac in the pews who hears the sermon and goes home resolved to emulate the heroism of Abraham on his own family: in that case the parson is on the spot bright and early Monday morning to confront, accuse, convict, and convert the wretched sinner—who only wanted to murder his son in obedience to the pastor's counsel. So thoughtless that he can, without noting the discrepancy, contradict on Monday what he said on Sunday, the parson is the very opposite of the honest dialectician, who thinks a thought whole or not at all. So insensitive that he can with his ranting pro and con breed chaos in the souls of his parishioners, without observing in himself any more than a tendency to excessive perspiration and a swelling vein in the forehead, the parson is the opposite of the honorable dialectician, who turns the chaos inward and keeps his suffering to himself. It's a good thing, Johannes observes in a footnote, that there is more sense in the world than you would expect from the average sermon (40 n.: H. 29 n.)

Or perhaps the parson explains that Abraham's experience is only a test of his faith. Fair enough. But the preacher depicts the trial in foreshortened perspective, with the outcome deceptively assured in advance. Should a sufferer from insomnia happen to hear the sermon, he may feed on the false hope that all his own troubles are but temporary. If only I wait a moment, he thinks, I shall surely see the ram and hear the voice of the angel, just as the parson says. The parson, finding his charge in this state on Monday, might denounce his indolent optimism with the admonition that "all of life is a trial." This is so true that it may be the main point of Johannes' book. But it happens to contradict the impression that the same preacher so carefully contrived to produce on Sunday in his capacity as pulpit poet.

Alas, complains the honest dialectician. Who speaks in honor of faith? Love still has its priests in the poets. But who in these days glorifies faith? Philosophy does not revere the paradox; philosophy goes beyond faith to resolve (or dissolve) all mysteries. Theology sits painted and rouged at the window offering her favors to philosophy. What it is but whoredom when the custodians of the paradox undertake to make the scandal of faith respectable to the scientific worldview, or tailor it to fit the latest fad in German philosophy?

Johannes will have no part of these cheap editions of Abraham. If I were to preach on Abraham, he says (in a passage that describes exactly what he has done, is doing, and will continue to do throughout his book), I would first of all take my time at it. I would drag out that three-day journey to Mount Moriah for at least a month of Sundays. I would distill every drop of manly and paternal feeling out of Abraham's sufferings. My auditors would smell the smoke of the sacrificial wood, feel the edge of the knife, see it glint in the morning sun, hear the weeping of Isaac begging for his life on behalf of the promise still hidden in his loins. In short I would do everything in my power to prevent my hearers from lightly undertaking an imitation of the dread deed of Abraham. I would go out of my way to give them the opportunity to avoid Abraham's problem altogether. For if a dialectician is to speak about Abraham, then he is duty-bound to be painfully clear about the incomprehensible difficulty of Abraham's case, not covering over the contradictions, but letting them stand out in all their starkness and horror. The job of the dialectician is to keep silence in the presence of the paradox, which speaks louder and more forcefully than all the oratory of the preachers.

That the story of Abraham contains paradoxes there can be no question, in view, first of all, of the ambiguity of his motives. He proposes to offer his *son* to *God*. Ethically speaking Abraham wanted to murder Isaac; religiously speaking he was prepared to sacrifice him. It is this contradiction between murder and sacrifice, between the ethical and the religious interpretations of his action, that generates the "dread and distress, the fear and trembling" of Abraham's situation. Within the religious dimension alone there are further agonies. The God who—presumably, for Abraham has no surety that the voice he hears is the voice of God—asks for the sacrifice of Isaac is the same God who miraculously gave Isaac in the first place. Or again: it is possible that God—if it is God and not a demon who speaks—demands the death of Isaac only to discover if Abraham has the moral courage and the paternal devotion to refuse. If Abraham is any kind of dialectician, i.e., if he is at all an honest man, he will not be able to sidestep the thought, and the prodigious dread of the thought, that he may be tempting God when he draws the knife on his son.

These and a multitude of like contradictions make up "the dialectical conflict of faith and its gigantic passion" (43; H, 32). John of Silence has encountered the cul-de-sac of dialectic:

> . . . When I have to think of Abraham, I am as though annihilated. I catch sight every moment of that enormous paradox which is the substance of Abraham's life, every moment I am repelled, and my thought in spite of all its passion cannot get a hairs-breadth further. (44; H, 33)

He cannot "think himself into" (44; H, 33) Abraham because Abraham is the paradox that repels thought. Before the paradox every honest thinker is mute.

But this side of Abraham there is plenty to be understood. Though he cannot comprehend faith, Johannes can at least manage the preliminary expectoration. The movement preparatory for faith he calls "infinite resignation." Infinite resignation means, algebraically, the renunciation of the finite and the temporal for the infinite and the eternal. Faith means, after one has renounced the finite and the temporal, the confidence that one will receive them again. Abraham's willingness to sacrifice Isaac in obedience to God's command was his infinite resignation. His certainty that God would nevertheless not take Isaac was his faith.

The "knight of resignation" believes that God transcends the world incommensurably. If need be he will evacuate his worldly life for the sake of an ideal relationship to God. If I were in Abraham's shoes, says Johannes, I would sacrifice Isaac and continue to believe that God is love. But it would be all over between God and me as far as this world is concerned. My act of renunciation would be noble and poetic, like the magnificence of a tragic hero. But it would also show that I did not love Isaac as Abraham did. And if God were to restore him to me, I would be nonplused, as a young man who has taken monastic vows because he cannot have the girl he loves would be embarrassed to find her in his arms after the cowl is already about his ears.

Abraham on the contrary receives Isaac with joy and thanksgiving. Not because he did not really give him up, for he cut the wood, bound Isaac, and drew the knife. But even while he gave him up, Abraham believed that God would not require Isaac or that, requiring him, He would yet give him back. By resignation Abraham gave up the finite, by faith he got it back again "every inch" (48; H, 37). This movement of faith, Johannes confesses, I cannot understand and certainly not execute. Abraham's faith is a faith "by virtue of the absurd." By faith he receives the world—symbolized by Isaac—after he has let it go. His whole life after faith is a new creation in which he does not the least thing but "by virtue of the absurd."

"Virtue" is "power" (*Kraft*). The power by which a man makes the movement of faith is not a power indigenous or intelligible to himself. It is a power "from beyond" and therefore from the human point of view absurd and paradoxical. A man believes "by the power . . . of the absurd, by the power of the fact that with God all things are possible" (57; H, 46). The only power that can save a man in Abraham's situation, a man who has drained all his own potencies in the act of resignation, is the paradoxical power of God. And this is the impossible possibility that can only be grasped by faith. "He who loves God without faith reflects upon himself; he who loves God believingly reflects upon God" (47; H, 37). On his own Abraham does nothing but give up Isaac; he gets him back by virtue of God.

It would be a terrible error, of the sort to which parsons are prone, to hurry on to faith without making the preliminary expectoration by which one spits out the world. Abraham is great by reason of his strength which is weakness, for it is only in the weakness of man that the power of God is efficacious. God cannot be deceived out of the necessary condition of resignation, and no man can acquire faith by a too previous assurance of the "result." Only he that loses his life saves it; only the man who draws the knife gets Isaac. When a man has compressed the whole meaning of his life in a single object, as Abraham poured himself wholly into Isaac, and when that object is unattainable, as the continued possession of Isaac was made impossible by God's command, then he relinquishes his claim to the object and with it his whole claim on life itself. In so doing he becomes a "knight of infinite resignation," and his resignation is the extreme limit of human possibility (cf. 52 n.; H, 41 n.). For a man's "eternal validity"—the acme of his dignity as a spiritual creature—is his ability to transform his love for the world into a love for God, the power to renounce the world without hope of recompense. At this farthest outpost of his manhood, where the finite and the temporal have become dust and ashes, the knight is at one with God "in the infinite," and his love for the creator so consumes his entire passion that he retains the creation in spirit by giving it up in fact. In the pain of renunciation he is reconciled to existence by the "eternal consciousness" which he gains by cleaving to God alone and letting all else go. To do great things in the world is magnificent; even more magnificent, the summit of human greatness, as the case of every tragic hero shows, is to relinquish the world altogether.

This, Johannes adds, I can do. And I do not hesitate to call him a coward who wants to believe that he cannot make the movement of infinite resignation. He who will not draw the knife is no knight; he who anxiously looks back over his shoulder for the ram when it is time for the resolute step forward to the altar is a "cowardly and effeminate" nature, a cithara player and not a man (cf. 38, 59; H, 27, 48).

Johannes is aware that his view of man and human dignity is not a reasonable view. So he says, "To this end"—that is, the end of infinite resignation—"passion is necessary. Every movement of infinity comes about by passion, and no reflection can bring a movement about" (53 n.; H, 42 n.). Reason never produces a decisive and resolute action of any sort, for reason is "the broker of the finite" (47; H, 36). Its domain is the marketplace of probabilities and comparisons, wherein a man calculates shrewdly how he may meet the demand of the age, how he may satisfy his friends and neighbors, how much he may gain on X by giving up a little on Y, and the like. No man ever vowed his love to a maiden as the result of such rational deliberation. And no man ever truly married a wife because of reflection, though indeed many men have *taken* wives as they take shares in a corporation. Reason says that the rich brewer's widow is quite a respectable match, but the knight—the man of passion—would rather recollect his hopeless love for the princess in the solitude of his monastery cell than stretch his legs in the privileged marriage bed with the wealthy and quite respectable, but unloved, brewer's widow.

The conclusions of passion, Johannes says, are the only reliable and convincing conclusions (109; H, 100). Passion produces action, while reason continues to shuffle the counters of probability in defense of an inhumane and philistine self-interest. Passion, not reason, defines the human, or as Lessing observed, the passions make all men equal (77 n.; H, 67 n.). For all men experience passion, and each man learns its meaning from scratch. Reason is a "differential attribute," a talent which some men have and some do not, a resource that some possess in abundance and others in short supply. Fortunately, the results of rational investigation can be inherited: as the result of our fathers' ingenuity this generation may go to the stars or blow itself up. But every man must learn the joy of love, the bitterness of hatred, the bliss of union, and the pain of separation for himself; and every man learns them in the same way: from experience, or as passion literally says, from suffering (130; H, 121–22).

Passion defines man; and the extreme passion, which is therefore the extremest human possibility, is the passion of infinite resignation. More than this no man can do by and for himself. By resignation he acquires his "eternal consciousness," but not a thing more. If a man is not just to let go the temporal in order to gain the eternal, but beyond that to regain the temporal, then more than human power is needed. For this the power of faith is needed, and faith, as Johannes has already noted, is not of man but—paradoxically—of God. Yet for all its absurdity, faith is a far more blessed thing than resignation, a consummation devoutly to be wished if indeed it may even be hoped for. It is better to get the princess than to recollect her in the cell, better to go home rejoicing with Isaac than to return a tragic hero. "The knight of faith is the only happy one, the heir apparent to the finite, whereas the knight of resignation is a stranger and a foreigner" (61; H, 50). So when Johannes asks, Why did Abraham do what he did? he answers himself: he did it for God's sake, because God required it, and for his own sake, because he would do what God required. Likewise, what Abraham receives from God's hand is simply his own life. In action and in passion Abraham and God are happily one: such is the paradoxical union of finite and infinite that is realized in faith.

So paradoxical is faith that Johannes the dialectician can no more talk sense about it than Johannes the poet can imagine it or praise it. Faith is something which "no thought can master, because faith begins precisely there where thinking leaves off" (64; H, 53). And indeed no one should talk about faith at all if talking means the thoughtless babble of the preachers or the philosophers' pretension to total comprehension. But a dialectician may still talk, if he can by his talking make clear that faith is "a tremendous paradox—which is capable of transforming a murder into a holy act well-pleasing to God, a paradox which gives Isaac back to Abraham . . ." (64; H, 53). If he defines the absurdity of faith with precision, the dialectician does service in the forecourt of the temple to protect the paradox against the ineffectual assaults of enemies who know not what they attack, and against the impotent and meretricious embraces of those philosophers and theologians who foolishly believe that they have understood and surpassed faith. Johannes' Problemata embody his attempt at rigorous dialectical definition of the paradox of Abraham.

Each of Johannes' three problems begins with a paragraph describing something he calls "the ethical," and the second paragraph of each problem begins with a statement that "if this is the way it is, then Hegel is right," etc. Everything that is said about the ethical in this division of the book is qualified by the "if," for it is Johannes' intent to demonstrate that there may be something which escapes an ethical interpretation of human life: faith. The "ethical" in this context does not refer to any particular system of ethics, but simply to the attitude that reads all of human life in ethical terms and measures every human action by a moral yardstick.

Problem I asks, Is there a teleological suspension of the ethical? The answer is, from an ethical point of view, no. If man achieves his highest destiny in the fulfillment of moral obligation, and if this obligation applies without qualification to all men at all times and places, then there is no way a man may justifiably assert his individuality in opposition to the universal norm of ethics. The man who acts so as to set himself outside the universal is simply evil. And since, on this supposition, the moral universal is the highest court of appeal, there is no possible redemption and no conceivable pardon for such an "exception."

But the story of Abraham suggests that in the situation of faith the individual does find a justified standpoint outside the universal:

> For faith is this paradox, that the particular is higher than the universal—yet in such a way, be it observed, that the movement repeats itself, and that consequently the individual, after having been in the universal, now as the particular isolates himself as higher than the universal. (65; H, 55)

Abraham (the particular) was faithful to the universal (his duty to his son) until it broke against the command of God. Through his fidelity to the universal he entered into that "absolute relationship to the absolute" by which he became "the individual who as the particular is superior to the universal."

> Faith is precisely this paradox, that the individual as the particular is higher than the universal, is justified over against it, is not subordinate but superior—yet in such a way, be it observed, that it is the particular individual who, after he has been subordinated as the particular to the universal, now through the universal becomes the individual who as the particular is superior to the universal, for the fact that the individual as the particular stands in an absolute relation to the absolute. (66; H, 55–56)

It should not surprise anyone that Johannes' description of faith is full of contradiction, for faith is a "teleological suspension of the ethical," a suspension of the ethical imperative for the sake of a higher *telos*. In Abraham's case the father's duty to his son is lifted for the sake of his obedience to God. From the ethical point of view that is absolutely paradoxical. Johannes, here as everywhere a man of silence, has nothing to say about this claim of faith. He only wants to clarify the absolute disjunction: *either* there is such a suspension of the ethical, in which case the ethical is not the norm and goal of human striving; *or* "If this be not faith, then Abraham is lost, then faith has never existed in the world . . . because it has always existed" (65; H, 55). If there is no teleological suspension of the ethical, then the position of supremacy claimed by faith is in fact occupied by ethics, and there is no faith because faith—i.e., the highest *telos*—has always existed in the form of ethical action.

Abraham is not, like Agamemnon, Jephtha, and Brutus, a tragic hero who sacrifices a private to a more universal good. The power in tragedy is the ethical power of infinite resignation, but the religious power of faith is the *vis comica*, the spirit of comedy. The tragic hero stays well within the ambience of ethics. What Abraham does is strictly between himself and God, and whatever value it has it has for Abraham—and God—alone. Johannes repeatedly argues that Abraham cannot be mediated; his action cannot be reconciled with the universal it violates. He remains forever alone with God in the dread and distress of his trial. Significantly the only figures Johannes can find to compare with Abraham are the Mother of God who, although she was highly favored among women, was also Our Lady of incomparable Sorrows, her soul pierced by the sword; and those disciples of the Lord who, in spite of the scandal and the offense, sat at meat with Him, believed in Him, followed Him to Golgotha, and became the Apostles of the Crucified. Like Abraham these cannot be mediated; they too are beyond human understanding, their faith a miracle beyond human working.

Problem I suggests Problem II: Is there an absolute duty toward God? Johannes' solution is again simple: if a man's ethical obligations define his whole duty, then these are the only divinity there is. The ethical norm is the supreme power to which man owes his allegiance, and compliance with it the last end toward which he strives. But the claim of faith is that the individual—as an individual and not as an instance of the universal—has an absolute duty toward God—the Absolute Individual and not the ethical universal—which reduces his moral duties to relativities. Thus Abraham's duty to God supersedes his duty to his son.

This is a paradoxical kind of duty. Duty by definition is universal, but the particularity of the bond between God and Abraham defies reduction to universality and mocks the ethical understanding of obligation. Yet if this paradox does not hold, there is no such thing as faith. Worse: the inclination to faith is a temptation that every man is morally bound to avoid. But the alternatives are clear: *either* faith, *or* Abraham is a murderer and there's an end of it.

In this connection Johannes quotes a parallel from the New Testament, Luke 14: 26. The verse, following directly upon the parable of the great supper and the little excuses, introduces its own interpretation:

> 26. If any man come to me, and hate not his father, and mother, and wife, and children, and brethren, and sisters, yea, and his own life also, he cannot be my disciple.
>
> 27. And whosoever doth not bear his cross, and come after me, cannot be my disciple.
>
> 28. For which of you, intending to build a tower, sitteth not down first, and counteth the cost, whether he have sufficient to finish it?
>
> 29. Lest haply, after he hath laid the foundation and is not able to finish it, all that behold it begin to mock him,
>
> 30. Saying, This man began to build and was not able to finish.
>
> 31. Or what king, going to make war against another king, sitteth not down first, and consulteth whether he be able with ten thousand to meet him that cometh against him with twenty thousand?
>
> 32. Or else, while the other is yet a great way off, he sendeth an ambassage, and desireth conditions of peace.
>
> 33. So likewise, whosoever he be of you that forsaketh not all that he hath, he cannot be my disciple.

Johannes argues, against a euphemistic exegesis, that in this context the word "hate" is meant in a strong sense. If "hate" is softened to *"minus diligo, posthabeo, non colo, nihil facio"* (82, H, 72), one arrives at the curious notion that an absolute devotion to God enjoins pallid halfheartedness toward self, kindred, and fellows. That love for God should demand the renunciation of all other affections is credible and a "worthy conception of the

Deity" (84; H, 73). But no man would be so stupid or so conceited as to regard defective filial devotion in his wife as a proof of her connubial passion. Shall the sign of religious commitment be a lukewarm fellow feeling? Johannes' own exegesis is more rigorous:

> The absolute duty may cause one to do what ethics would forbid, but by no means can it cause the knight of faith to cease to love. This is shown by Abraham. The instant he is ready to sacrifice Isaac the ethical expression for what he does is this: he hates Isaac. But if he really hates Isaac, he can be sure that God does not require this, for Cain and Abraham are not identical. Isaac he must love with his whole soul; when God requires Isaac he must love him if possible even more dearly, and only on this condition can he *sacrifice* him; for in fact it is this love for Isaac which, by its paradoxical opposition to his love for God, makes his act a sacrifice. . . . Only at the moment when his act is in absolute contradiction to his feeling is his act a sacrifice, but the reality of his act is the factor by which he belongs to the universal, and in that aspect he is and remains a murderer. (84; H, 74)

The man who recognizes an absolute duty toward God does not cease to love what is other than God. He does not cease, for example, to acknowledge his moral obligations. Otherwise his infinite resignation is a sham. But by his duty to God he is bound to be prepared to do things which, objectively and in reality, have the moral character of evil.

Most men think in terms of two categories of practical reason: the ethical (the universal) and the selfish (the particular). Faith claims, and the proper understanding of Abraham requires, that there is a third category: that of the individual who does not by self-interest sink beneath the universal, but through the universal rises to a particularity superior to the universal. At the subethical level there is Cain, who killed Abel out of self-interest and hatred. At the ethical level there is the tragic hero, who, whatever sacrifices he may have to make, reposes securely in the universal. And at the level of faith: Abraham. Such at least is the claim of faith. Whether the claim is true no one can say. But unless it is true, Abraham is condemned, and "faith" is a terrible temptation to be resisted with all possible vigor.

Of course, Johannes adds, there is a mark whereby one can distinguish the genuine knight of faith from the counterfeit. To wit, the true knight is always incommunicado. He keeps to himself, whereas the false knights are great sectarians, always clubbing together for mutual encouragement and plotting holy wars against the infidel. Johannes sports with the Rotarian temper of the pseudo-knights of faith, but a sober reader may wonder who is really the butt of this joke. The sole criterion by which to tell a knight of faith is his silence and his secrecy. Is this not the most futile of all criteria, that a knight of faith can be recognized only by the fact that he cannot be recognized? So it is, and this becomes the subject of Johannes' Problem III.

The problem is, Was Abraham justified in keeping silent about his purpose before Sarah, Eleazar, and Isaac? The moral imperative demands revelation. Every man shall be prepared to declare to his fellows the purpose and intent of his actions. Only thieves, murderers, and adulterers need the cover of night to obscure their deeds. The honest man acts openly in the light of day. Readiness for community is part of the universal good commanded by ethics.

But Abraham keeps silent. He has to keep silent, for there is no way he can explain to anyone else what he intends to do with Isaac on Mount Moriah. His only recorded utterances are instinct with the most terrible irony. To his servants at the foot of the mount he says: "I and the lad will go yonder and worship, and come again to you" (Gen. 22: 5). The remark is true, but it says nothing about his real intentions. More terrible still is the dialogue with Isaac at the place of sacrifice:

> And Isaac spake unto Abraham his father, and said, My father: and he said, Here am I, my son. And he said, Behold the fire and the wood: but where is the lamb for a burnt offering? And Abraham said, My son, God will provide himself a lamb for a burnt offering. . . . (Gen. 22: 7–8)

Jehovah-jireh: the Lord will provide (cf. Gen. 22: 7–8, 14). That, of course, is the whole import of the story of Abraham and Isaac. The irony of Abraham is a holy irony, but it is no less ironical for all that. *Jehovah-jireh* tells Isaac precisely nothing; for all practical and moral purposes Abraham is silent.

An overingenious reader may wonder if the silence of Abraham has anything to do with the silence of Johannes de Silentio. Is the lyric-dialectical persona only a satyr mask hiding the countenance of a knight of faith? Since he cannot be recognized as such, he might be another Abraham. But these are surely vain speculations, for we have Johannes' own word for it that he is only an ironist.

Be that as it may. Faith paradoxically asserts that there is a silence and a concealment superior to ethical community and revelation. Either this paradox, or else faith is a demonic temptation. That there are many kinds of silence is the theme of Johannes' protracted digression on aesthetics. There is an innocent silence that seeks to spare the feelings of others; for example, *de mortuis nil nisi bonum*. There is the frivolous secrecy beloved by comic playwrights: the mistaken identity, for example, without which very few comedies could be written. And there is demonic silence: the enforced secrecy of a man committed to evil. Kierkegaard's Seducer is bound to silence by his nefarious purpose; his way of life includes a commitment to that silence without which he cannot carry through his program of betrayal.

The ethical verdict on all such forms of silence is easily arrived at. Of the innocent silence ethics says that it is the product of a misconceived and misdirected sympathy; better to have the matter out than to presume to shield another from the truth. The secrecy employed by the comedian is a nugatory fiction unworthy of ethical consideration. The silence of the demon is unqualified evil. He must be compelled to speak, even as Christ caused the dumb man to speak by casting out the devil that possessed him. For if the demoniac is made to reveal himself in public utterance his demonia will be annulled by the community of the good.

If the ethical is coterminous with the human, Abraham's silence is the involuntary silence of the demon. And yet faith sees his reserve as the sign of his complicity not with the devil but with God. Either there is a silence that is justified over against ethical revelation, or Abraham is lost and the incommunicado of faith is but the horrible and vacuous isolation of the demoniac. Johannes once again gets no further than to faith. Not even that far, for he always ends short of faith with his monotonous either/or: either there is a teleological suspension of the ethical, an absolute duty toward God, and a justified silence, or—. Either faith, or—the rest *is* silence.

It might be supposed, from his constant reference to "the ethical," that the terms of Johannes' disjunction are faith and ethics. Either faith or ethics provides the guide for human life and the norm for human achievement. *Fear and Trembling* has often been read as a comment on the discrepancy between ethics and religion. But there is that mighty "if" that qualifies everything John of Silence says about "the ethical." His conviction—which he holds with exceptional vigor and tenacity—that infinite resignation is the supreme act of a man shows that his book has nothing to do with those questions about the propriety of waiving ethical rules which his commentators have so often foisted upon him. Equally irrelevant are all attempts to parallel the case of Abraham with made-up instances of unmotivated evil or real examples of supererogatory sanctity. John of Silence is not concerned at all with sanctions, human or divine, and the paradox he poses is not religion versus ethics. A man on trial, an Abraham, could never parcel out his dilemma in these tidy compartments. The real alternative is: either faith or despair. His analysis of Abraham ironically dissembles Johannes' belief that a faith which passes understanding and exceeds human agency is the only alternative to a resignation that heroically expires in an ecstasy of impotence

In plainer terms: Christianity is the only power that can extricate a man from the predicament of suffering and guilt into which he precipitates himself by his own efforts to secure his relationship to God. It is not without reason that John of Silence has introduced New Testament allusions into his discussion at several critical points. His reference to the Blessed Virgin and the disciples of the Lord, as well as his analysis of Luke 14: 26 and his citations of the dumb demoniac, not only illumine the situation of Abraham; they also suggest the use Johannes wants to make of his patriarch-hero. These, plus the text from which the title of his book is lifted (*"Work out your own salvation* with fear and trembling, for *it is God which worketh* in you . . ."), show clearly enough that whatever Johannes says about Abraham is to be understood obliquely of the Christian believer.

There are two other passages in the New Testament that are decisive in this connection. Although he does not wish to be classed as a "learned exegete," Johannes has betrayed no slight expertise *in sacra pagina*, and it may be supposed that he knows the verses in question. First from the Epistle to the Hebrews:

> By faith Abraham, when he was tried, offered up Isaac: and he that had received the promises offered up his only begotten son, of whom it was said, that in Isaac shall thy seed be called: accounting that God was able to raise him up, even from the dead; from whence also he received him in a figure. (Heb. 11: 17–19)

The second is from St. Paul's explanation of Abraham, "our father, as pertaining to the flesh," in his letter to the Jewish Christians at Rome:

> He staggered not at the promise of God through unbelief; but was strong in faith, giving glory to God; and being fully persuaded that, what he had promised, he was able also to perform. And therefore it was imputed to him for righteousness. Now it was not written for his sake alone, that it was imputed to him; but for us also, to whom it shall be imputed, if we believe on him that raised up Jesus our Lord from the dead; who was delivered for our offences, and was raised again for our justification. (Rom. 4: 20–25)

The words that stand out in the passage from Hebrews are the words "in a figure." It is reasonable to suppose that *Fear and Trembling*, in its own lyric and dialectical way, is an essay in the figural reading of the Old Testament. Abraham is the "father of faith" because he is a type or figure of faith, foreshadowing the faith of the New Covenant. The typology is reduplicated in *Fear and Trembling* itself: whatever John of Silence says about Abraham is also to be understood as "in a figure." To be sure the figure is presented by understatement and dissemblance. But the clues are there, and for all its irony this problematic book demands typological resolution.

Along with this general observation it is necessary to look more closely at the kind of figural interpretation found in *Fear and Trembling*. According to the predominant medieval tradition, a scriptural text, besides its literal meaning, may carry three modes of spiritual significance: the allegorical, the moral, and the anagogical. At the literal level, the story of Abraham and Isaac probably has something to do with the elimination of human sacrifice as a cultic element in primitive Semitic religion. Johannes de Silentio may or may not have known about this, but in any case it is clear that he is not interested in that dimension of the biblical record. In the allegorical reading favored by the author of the Epistle to the Hebrews, the sacrifice and restitution of Isaac prefigure the redemption of the world by the passion and resurrection of Our Lord Jesus Christ. But neither is Johannes concerned to read the story at this level. His reading is guided by the words of the Pauline text: "Now it was not written for his sake alone . . . But *for us also* . . . *if we believe* . . ." (Rom. 4: 23–24; my emphasis). It is the moral sense alone that interests John of Silence. Abraham's faith is the pattern after which the Christian must model his own belief. Or as Johannes says, Abraham is the *paradigm* of faith. As *femina* is the paradigm for all first-declension nouns, so Abraham is the paradigm according to which all instances of faith are to be declined in all cases. Not for his sake alone, but for us also if we believe, God is able to perform what He has promised.

A "learned exegete" in the Middle Ages, expounding the faith of Abraham tropologically, would have viewed it from within as a confirmed believer examining the sources and prophecies of his own salvation. His lyric-dialectic character, his profession of unfaith, and his running polemic against the parsons and theologians besotted with philosophy exclude Johannes from the promised land of churchly theology. Like Moses, he can see but he may not enter. But from his standpoint on Mount Pisgah he casts down a few hints as to the Christian-moral significance he glimpses in the saga of Abraham and Isaac. In the course of Problem III, after sifting through a handful of literary parallels, Johannes notes that none of these is strictly analogous to Abraham's case. He continues:

> If there might be any analogy, this must be found in the paradox of sin, but this again lies in another sphere and

cannot explain Abraham and is itself far easier to explain than Abraham. (121; H, 112)

This is a typical twist of irony, better suited to unsettle than to satisfy the understanding. For the condition of the sinner who needs forgiveness and can only have it by virtue of the absurd is, *mutatis mutandis*, exactly the analogy Johannes is trying to draw. Earlier in Problem III he says as much, though again in an offhand way as an ironist might. In the course of reviewing the legend of Agnes and the merman[3] he speculates that the merman (a demonic figure) might be saved for marriage with Agnes, but only by

> recourse to the paradox. For when the individual by his guilt has gone outside the universal he can return to it only by virtue of having come as the individual into an absolute relationship with the absolute. (108; H, 98)

If the reader's attention has dozed off during this lengthy and somewhat pedantic literary exercise, the sentence immediately following should awaken him and put him on guard: "Here I will make an observation by which I say more than was said at any point in the foregoing discussion" (108; H, 98). A footnote explains:

> In the foregoing discussion I have intentionally refrained from any consideration of sin and its reality. The whole discussion points to Abraham, and him I can still approach by immediate categories—in so far, that is to say, as I am able to understand him. As soon as sin makes its appearance ethics comes to grief precisely upon repentance; for repentance is the highest ethical expression, but precisely as such it is the deepest ethical self-contradiction. (108 n.; H, 98 n.)

---

3. The legend of Agnes and the merman is enshrined in the ballad, "Agnete hun stander på højelandsbro," which may be found in *Danske Sange*, 6–7. See also Matthew Arnold's poem, "The Forsaken Merman," which recollects the story from the merman's point of view.

From other pseudonyms and from the *Edifying Discourses*: repentance (or the eternal recollection of guilt) is the "highest expression" of that religion which itself is only a tensing of ethical passion to the uttermost. But the uttermost is the breaking point. Repentance not only sums up all that a man can do to bind himself to God; it also reveals that his God-relationship is consummated negatively in self-denial, and is therefore the "deepest ethical self-contradiction."

> Sin is not the first immediacy, sin is a later immediacy. By sin the individual is already higher (in the direction of the demoniacal paradox) than the universal, because it is a contradiction on the part of the universal to impose itself upon a man who lacks the *conditio sine qua non*. . . . An ethics which disregards sin is a perfectly idle science; but if it asserts sin, it is *eo ipso* well beyond itself. (108; H, 98–99)

Sin is the paradoxical Christian obverse, the transcendent dialectical reversal, of the immanent and pathetic consciousness of guilt. It is not the "first immediacy" of creation, to which Abraham belongs. That immediacy is exhausted in the strenuous exercises of Kierkegaard's Religion A, but Abraham has not yet reached the *terminus ad quem* of total guilt. His trial is, so to speak, a special case. Sin is the prologue to the "later immediacy," the new dispensation of grace by which a man is returned in virtue of the absurd to the unity and simplicity of childhood wistfully recalled in Johannes's Prelude. The man originally flawed by sin is beyond the end of his ethical rope and beyond the reach of the universal imperative. He is already higher—demonically—than the universal and may through faith be reconciled to the universal by his "absolute relationship with the absolute." But

> What is said here does not by any means explain Abraham; for it was not by sin Abraham became the individual, on the contrary, he was a righteous man, he is God's elect. So the analogy to Abraham will not appear until after the individual has been brought to the point of being able to accomplish the universal, and then the paradox repeats itself. (108; H, 99)

More irony. Of course sin does not explain Abraham. (Or does it?) But Abraham, with his lesser problem and his patriarchal promise, does explain, as a figure explains its fulfillment, the predicament of the man for whom the ethical is permanently suspended by sin and to whom is given, by virtue of the absurd, the promise of the grace of forgiveness. And in such a knight of faith—the Christian believer—the paradox of Abraham will repeat itself when he attempts to live the new life that is given to him beyond the extremity of guilt and condemnation.

It would be unseemly for a messenger to expound too confidently—and to other messengers at that!—the meaning of that enigma which can only be understood by the son. In an epilogue that harks back to the "clearance sale" of his preface, Johannes tells of a trick once hit upon by the merchants of Holland to improve the market in spices.

> One time in Holland when the market was rather dull for spices the merchants had several cargoes dumped into the sea to peg up prices. This was a pardonable, perhaps a necessary deception. Is it something like that we need now in the world of spirit? Are we so thoroughly convinced that we have attained the highest point that there is nothing left for us but to make ourselves believe piously that we have not got so far—just for the sake of having something left to occupy our time? Is it such a self-deception the present generation has need of, does it need to be trained to virtuosity in self-deception, or is it not rather sufficiently perfected already in the art of deceiving itself? Or rather is not the thing most needed an honest seriousness which dauntlessly and incorruptibly points to the tasks, an honest seriousness which lovingly watches over the tasks, which does not frighten men into being over hasty in getting the highest tasks accomplished, but keeps the tasks young and beautiful and charming to look upon and yet difficult withal and appealing to noble minds. (129–30; H, 121)

Is *Fear and Trembling* an exercise in pious self-deception or an honest and serious call to the task of believing? Johannes' irony suggests the former, but his lyric and dialectical intensity belies the latter. Perhaps the case is Socratic. For if the suspicion is correct that our age, which has gone far beyond faith, is already sufficiently self-deceived, then to deceive this generation out of its self-deception is the best service an honest seriousness can render to the times. In a figure and for us also, deception and seriousness may be the same thing. In a world where all men stand on their heads an upright man is bound to look queer. One thing is sure in any case:

> Faith is the highest passion in a man. There are perhaps many in every generation who do not even reach it, but no one gets further. Whether there be many in our age who do not discover it, I will not decide, I dare only appeal to myself as a witness who makes no secret that the prospects for him are not the best, without for all that wanting to delude himself and to betray the great thing which is faith by reducing it to an insignificance, to an ailment of childhood which one must wish to get over as soon as possible. But for the man also who does not so much as reach faith life has tasks enough, and if one loves them sincerely, life will by no means be wasted, even though it never is comparable to the life of those who sensed and grasped the highest. (131; H, 122)

The parson spoke more truly than he knew: all of life is a trial. Those who finish with life before life has finished with them are like children who finish playing before their holiday is over: as these are wretched and deficient children, so those are miserable and unprofitable servants. Even the man who does not get as far as faith will find occupation enough for a lifetime. But the high passion of faith is like the speed of light: the only absolute in a world of relativities. And the man who is too eager to exceed it may find himself moving steadily backward.

So John of Silence ends, without the understanding of faith that he sought. His prospects, he confesses, are "not the best" (131; H, 122). He catches a glimpse of the possibility of faith, imminent just over the edge of his imaginative and intellectual horizons, but he cannot testify to its reality. Denied the joy of possession, he must rest content with the promise and the vision.

4.
ONCE MORE WITH FEELING:
KIERKEGAARD'S *REPETITION*

> There is only one real tragedy in a woman's life. The fact that her past is always her lover, and her future invariably her husband.
>
> Oscar Wilde

The title of his book is *Repetition*. But his subject will be . . . woman. *Repetition*? About woman? Yes, in the only way it can be. By being about everything else under the sun. Woman is reality. This is not under the sun.

The book describes itself as "an essay in experimental psychology."[1] In his epistle to the reader the author reveals that the subject of his experiment is a fiction and his adventure a fabrication. The narrative metonymies of the text dissimulate a meta-

---

This essay previously appeared in *Kierkegaard and Literature: Irony, Repetition, and Criticism*, edited by Ronald Schleifer and Robert Markley. Copyright © 1984 by the University of Oklahoma Press.

1. I have quoted from the translation of *Repetition* by Walter Lowrie (New York: Harper and Row, 1964); hereinafter cited in this essay as R), tacitly correcting Lowrie's version where necessary. I have also given page references (in the form: H followed by page number) to the new translation of *Repetition* by Howard V. Hong and Edna H. Hong (Princeton University Press, 1983), but I have preferred to cite Lowrie.

phoric identity of truth and fiction. Unsuccessfully. This too is not in the world.

I

The first part of the text, not entitled, is uninterrupted narration. Its typographical continuity suppresses an intricate scheme of divisions and relations. Brought to the surface, it looks like this:

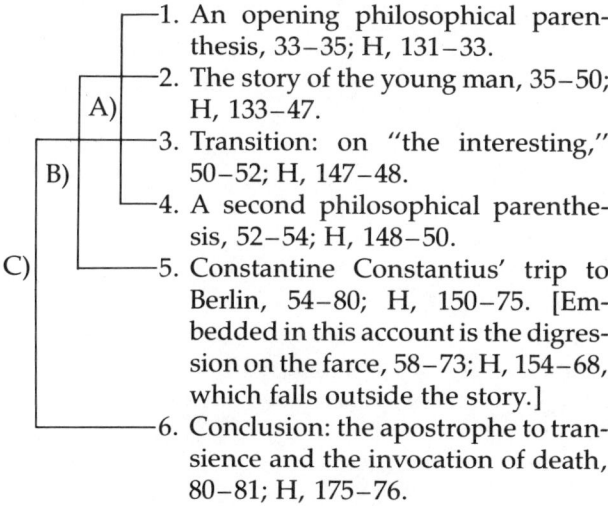

1. An opening philosophical parenthesis, 33–35; H, 131–33.
2. The story of the young man, 35–50; H, 133–47.
3. Transition: on "the interesting," 50–52; H, 147–48.
4. A second philosophical parenthesis, 52–54; H, 148–50.
5. Constantine Constantius' trip to Berlin, 54–80; H, 150–75. [Embedded in this account is the digression on the farce, 58–73; H, 154–68, which falls outside the story.]
6. Conclusion: the apostrophe to transience and the invocation of death, 80–81; H, 175–76.

(A)1. In the philosophical parenthesis that opens the book, Constantine Constantius reflects: recollection glances off the present moment into an idealized past, while hope turns away from the present toward an idealized future. The point would be to recuperate every present moment for the ideal and to install the ideal in every present moment, so that the actual becomes the repetition (re-presentation) of the ideal and the ideal becomes the repetition (the meaning and truth) of the actual. In this way repetition would redeem what is lost in hope and recollection alike.

In another sense, recollection and repetition are the same movement turned in opposite directions. What is recollected is repeated backward; what is repeated is recollected forward. Retreating from the present that is, recollection is unhappy; advancing to meet the present that comes, repetition is happy. It has "the blessed certainty of the instant" (R, 34; H, 132), which is the power of endurance. Repetition is "reality . . . and the seriousness of existence" (R, 35; H, 133). Without it one would be a tablet on which time writes at every instant a new inscription or a mere memorial of the past: the present irrecoverably past or perpetually passing.

Recollection is to repetition as the ancient (i.e., pagan) view of life is to the modern (the Christian). On the ancient view time is without direction and without order, so that one can only "escape backwards" (upward?) into eternity; one tries "to find a pretext for stealing out of life, alleging . . . that he has forgotten something" (R, 33; H, 131). (An umbrella, perhaps?) On the Christian view time is ordered and directed; eternity, to which one moves through time, lies ahead at the end of history. The ancient and the modern views of life offer alternative soteriologies. The former recommends a redemption from time. The latter proposes to redeem time itself: fruits, not flowers. Repetition is incarnation and resurrection.

(A)4. The discussion of repetition with which the book begins prefaces the story of the young man's unhappy love. In the brief passage that introduces his own failed attempt at repetition Constantine says that modern philosophy has not yet developed the category of repetition, but must do so.

> Repetition is the new category which has to be brought to light. . . . The dialectic of repetition is easy; for what is repeated has been, otherwise it could not be repeated, but precisely the fact that it has been gives repetition the character of novelty. (R, 52; H, 148)

The novel is such only in relation to a past and a constant of change; else it were opaquely unique. Radical novelty is radically unintelligible and cannot even be comprehended under the rubric "novel."

> When the Greeks said that all knowledge is recollection they affirmed that all that is has been; when one says that life is a repetition one affirms that existence which has been now becomes. When one does not possess the catego-

ries of recollection or of repetition, the whole of life is resolved into a void and empty noise. (R, 52–53; H, 149)

Temporality is intelligible only in relation to the eternal. Apart from recollection or repetition, which are the possible forms of this relation, existence in time is sound and fury, signifying nothing. "Repetition is the *interest* of metaphysics, and at the same time the interest upon which metaphysics founders." One asks, who am I? in the sense of, where did I come from? in order to know, what shall I do? The temporalizing of essence makes metaphysics interesting. But since metaphysics is properly disinterested, it is also the rock on which metaphysics goes aground. Therefore "repetition is the solution contained in every ethical view." Everything merely temporal is discretely and unrepeatably "this now." Only the continuity provided by the eternal allows for the repetition necessary to moral decision and the development of character. But the eternal alone is also an uniterated "now," and only its distribution along the course of time yields repetition. Without the possibility of repetition, the moral ideal remains a bondage from which there is no release, a problem without a solution. Repetition is, finally, "a *conditio sine qua non* of every dogmatic problem" (R, 53; H, 149). On the other side of faith, "repetition will have the meaning of atonement" (*Søren Kierkegaards Papirer*, IV B 120, 309). From the standpoint of Christian doctrine, repetition means the restoration of fallen human nature to the image of God.

Apart from faith, "a religious movement by virtue of the absurd" (*Søren Kierkegaard's Papirer*, IV B 120, 309), "the finite spirit falls into despair" (*Concept of Dread*, 17 n.).[2] The first part of *Repetition*—at least the first part—is the despair of the finite spirit.

(B)2. A young man falls in love. He represents immediacy. Constantine Constantius tells his story. Constantine is reflection. Or language, which is the actuality of reflection. Falling in

---

2. The whole of the long note on pp. 16–17 of this work is relevant to Kierkegaard's concerns in *Repetition*. Cf. *Johannes Climacus or, De omnibus dubitandum est*, 146–55. *Papirer* IV B 97–124 deal with *Repetition* and with J. L. Heiberg's review of the work. Some of these materials are quoted in Lowrie's introduction to his translation of *Repetition*, 7–28.

love is an immediate passion. But no sooner has he fallen than the young man begins to recollect his love as a thing past. His recollection takes the form of language. As falling in love is to the recollection of love, so the young man is to Constantine Constantius.

However, in the letter to the reader with which he concludes his book, Constantine confesses that he has imagined the young man. And Constantine himself is a pseudonym of Søren Kierkegaard. The plot(s) thicken(s). Constantine's immediacy is his concern to know if repetition is possible. He creates the young man and his story as a "psychological experiment" to try the possibility of repetition. But there is also Søren Kierkegaard's immediacy, which impels him to inscribe this fiction and ascribe it to a figment. Kierkegaard's immediacy is his unhappy relationship to Regine Olsen. The book is, in its multiply indirect way, Kierkegaard's attempt to scout the possibility of repetition with Regine. The faulted repetition of the young man is, across all the intervening distances of reflection, Kierkegaard's own.

Like Kierkegaard himself, the young man cannot marry the girl. And so, saved not by the grace of God but by the magnanimity of woman, he becomes (take that word in the strongest possible sense) . . . a poet. The actuality of Søren Kierkegaard is his texts. He is a discourse. Everything—Kierkegaard, his fictions, and his fictions' fictions—is language.

In the first part of *Repetition* there is no repetition. No recuperation of immediacy on the other side of reflection. In the book as a whole (we shall have to ask if it is a whole) there are none but faulted repetitions. Unless we count Job. But we shall have to ask: in what sense is Job (*Job*?) in this book?

The young man's recollection of his love distances the girl. It also breaches his identity with himself. He is in love with the girl. Call that relation 1: YM—^{R1}—G. He recollects his love for the girl. Call that relation 2: (YM—^{R1}—G)—^{R2}—[YM]. He recalls his love by repeating again and again a stanza of Poul Møller's *The Aged Lover*. Call that—his anticipation of senility—relation 3: (YM—^{R1}—G)—^{R2}—[YM]—^{R3}—(YM old). Reflection preserves the virginity of the girl by effecting the impotence of her lover.

The young man's recollection of his love for the girl, a recollection that follows directly upon his first falling in love, effaces his presence to her by thrusting it into the past. Being in love is transformed by reflection into the preterite: having been in love. The same recollection thrusts the young man into the future and effaces his presence to himself. By reflection he becomes an old man who has lived his life and can only recollect it in the impuissance of absolute seniority. The agent of this double effect is language: poetry.

In the event there is no presence at all. The young man and the girl are absent from each other and from their original relationship. The young man is distanced from himself. Only the girl abides intact in the self-presence of her immediacy—an immediate self-presence, however, which as such must remain a fruitless *an sich*. In the absence of a unity of immediacy and reflection there is no hope of repetition. The young man has lost his immediacy, the girl has not attained to reflection (she does not speak in this book), and their love can never enter upon the repetition of marriage.

The condition of woman's virginity is the impotence of her lover. Woman is reality, a reality not enlightened by the sun of reflection. Existence remains pristine because reflection is powerless to invade it. Being is forever too young; reflection is always already too old. Reality not illumined by consciousness remains in the dark. In the glare of reflection it cannot be seen. In the day as in the night all cows are invisible. There is neither marrying nor giving in marriage.

(This story, which is at first presented as a case history, is at the end re-presented as Constantine's recollection of his own creation. Constantine's visit to Berlin both repeats an earlier visit and parodies the young man's dilemma. Yet Constantine has imagined the young man, and all that he says and does is calculated to "throw light upon him.")

When the girl finally marries someone else (the young man reads about it in the paper), her loss of innocence restores the young man's potency—as a poet, not a husband. His repetition, which only doubles his reflective self-awareness, is not perfected. A Job would have married the girl, *quia absurdum*. But the young man can do nothing. Constantine says:

> He was in love, deeply and sincerely in love; that was evident, and yet at once, on one of the first days of his engage-

ment, he was capable of recollecting his love. Substantially he was through with the whole relationship. Before he begins he has taken such a terrible stride that he has leapt over the whole of life. . . . Recollection has the great advantage that it begins with the loss, hence it is secure, for it has nothing to lose. . . . His mistake was incurable, and his mistake was this, that he stood at the end instead of at the beginning. But such a mistake is certainly a man's undoing.

And yet I maintain the correctness of his mood as an erotic mood, and the man who in his experience of love has not experienced it thus precisely at the beginning, has never loved. Only he must have another mood alongside of this. . . . It must be true that one's life is over at the first instant, but there must be vitality enough to kill this death and transform it into life. (R, 38–40; H, 136)

But there is no vitality at all. The lover can only recollect his love and spout poetry. The girl can never become a woman. She is merely the occasion that awakens his poetic gift. By making him a poet—turning him into language—she signs her own death warrant. She is remanded to perpetual virginity, and he is committed to a guilt he cannot expiate.

Of course he has options. He could go ahead and marry the girl anyway. But that would be a lie, since they are essentially unmarriageable. He could tell her the truth, that she is only a semblance of the ideal, a figure of something more important than herself. But that would mortify her, and his pride will not allow him that. Or he might arrange to make himself despicable in her eyes. Following Constantine's plan, he might cause her to believe that he is living in sin with a loose woman. Believing that, she would surely break off the relationship herself. Thus retaining her own integrity, she would restore his freedom. But he lacks the strength for this option.

He remains, therefore, the melancholy knight of recollection. A Job would have married the girl.

(B)5. Though it is prophesied on the first page of his book, Constantine Constantius' second trip to Berlin parodies the sad story of his young friend. Having once experienced (i.e., recollecting) a half-day of absolute contentment, certain that he will never enjoy the same experience again, Constantine nonetheless becomes interested in the possibility of such a repetition. As an experiment to test this possibility, he undertakes to repeat an earlier sojourn in Berlin, of which he has the most pleasant memories. Hoping to match his recollections of the first visit, he settles in the same apartment, frequents the same cafes, attends the same theatres. But all the particulars have altered, Berlin is not the same, and the experiment fails.

That's the parody. Or part of it. In the young man's case repetition would have to occur at the level of spirit through the agency of freedom. For him, repetition would have meant the recovery by an alienated spirit of its lost immediacy. But Constantine expects immediacy to confirm his recollections. And that expectation spoils the whole thing. Constantine himself is clear about this . . . more or less:

> I discovered that there is no such thing as repetition, and I had convinced myself of this by getting it repeated in every possible way. . . . Time and again I conceived the idea of repetition and grew enthusiastic about it—thereby becoming again a victim of my zeal for principles. For I am thoroughly convinced that, if I had not taken that journey for the express purpose of assuring myself of the possibility of repetition, I should have diverted myself immensely on finding everything the same. What a pity that I cannot keep to the ordinary paths, that I will have principles, that I cannot go clad like other men, that I will walk in stiff boots! . . . How . . . can one get so foolish an idea as that of repetition, and, still more foolishly, erect it into a principle? (R, 76, 79–80; H, 171, 174)

Constantine's parody, like any worthy of the name, exposes the weaknesses, the lines of stress, and the concealed hiatuses in the structure it "copies backwards" (*Philosophical Fragments*, 63).[3] To make a principle of repetition, to try for it, is exactly what makes it impossible. Repetition must occur in the realm of the spirit: it is the recovery of nature by and for freedom. It does not

---

3. "Parody" in this passage renders *bagvendt copierer*, "to copy backwards."

just happen. But it may not be contrived. Shrewdness is of no use. The recovery of immediacy by and for reflection is not another immediacy (though it may be a *new* immediacy), neither is it a further reflection. Immediacy is gone as soon as it is there, and reflection is incurable.

Job might say: it takes a thunderstorm. But Constantine Constantius does not believe in thunderstorms.

And yet. Although Constantine's experience is a travesty, it is still a repetition. A parodic repetition. And it does incorporate several repetitions. Constantine's failure to achieve a repetition is repeated so often in Berlin that he finally becomes weary of repetition (R, 76; H, 171). But these *are* parodies, repetitions in reverse, in which life takes again [*tager igjen*] what it gives without giving a repetition [*Gjentagelse*] (R, 77; H, 172).

Constantine's serious preoccupation is something he calls "the interesting." In principle unrepeatable, the interesting is a token of transience, which is a portent of death. Figures on the ground of nothingness.

(C)3. The interesting "does not lend itself to repetition" (R, 50; H, 147). "A girl who does not crave the interesting believes in repetition. Honor to her who is such by nature [immediacy], honor to her who became such in time [by repetition]." But "a girl who craves the interesting becomes the trap in which she herself is caught" (R, 52; H, 148). The interesting is something from which a wise girl can save a man, something that a foolish girl might elicit from him. The interesting is not defined, but Constantine's metaphor is sexual. And a metaphor, while it may be no argument, is no accident either. It is the metaphor of accident. What is it that women (the wrong kind) desire in a man, from which other women (the right kind) would redeem him? Seduction, from which a man (!) is saved by marriage. By the magnanimity of woman.

It is not accidental that the metaphor of accident dominates this transitional episode in the text. The interesting is the confinium between the actual and the ideal, conceived aesthetically as the occasion of surprise. A threshold. The same threshold, ethically conceived, is opportunity. The opportunity, earnestly desired by the resolute will, to actualize the moral ideal. Marriage, for example. For sure. Interest, as opposed to the interesting. Repetition is reality and the seriousness of life, the interest on which metaphysics founders, and the solvent of ethics. The interesting, a thing of no essential interest, is the interruption of the ideal by the anomalous actual. From which, once you succumb to it, there is no salvation but repetition: the *sine qua non* of dogmatics. For example?

Seduction cannot be repeated. The seducing male requires novelty and variety: a constant supply of original sexual occasions. He is obliged to run wild. For the feminine victim seduction is, *simpliciter*, the loss of innocence, *einmalig* and irreparable. A trap. Virtue is something that men must acquire but women can only lose. There is no repetition in seduction. You can only (be) seduce(d) once. Marriage is the renunciation of seduction. Seduction is either an interminable pursuit or a dead end. For the male transience, for the female death. The two are indistinct.

The feminist phalanx will advance on this argument. But it's only a metaphor. It is interesting (is it an accident?) that Constantine fills this interval of his story with the account of an occasion on which he refused a chance at seduction. He does that more than once.

(C)6. Transience and death. The first part of *Repetition* ends with that. Constantine apostrophizes the post-horn ("that is my instrument"), which is a symbol of transience and the impossibility of repetition. On this instrument you can never play the same note twice. Or what's worse, you can't be sure of it (R, 80; H, 175).

Temporality is the rhetoric of death. Life, neither comic nor tragic, is interesting. But life does not captivate like death. Death has the superior eloquence: *peisithanatos*. By the transience of life it persuades all things to mortality. A conclusion of sorts. Of this, no repetition. That is the despair, and the hope, of the finite spirit.

Hors-texte.

The first half of *Repetition* ends with Constantine Constantius (and we may presume the young man) giving up on repetition. The whole of part 1 is calculated to enforce this defeat. But there is a part of the first part that falls outside its structure: at once outside and inside the trinity of binaries that organizes this region of the text. We have:

(A)1 & (A)4: Recollection vs. Repetition.
(B)2 & (B)5: The stories of the young man and Constantine Constantius.
(C)3 & (C)6: Repetition (in the sense: redemption from "the interesting") v. the triumph of transience and death.

Embedded in (B)5—in the structural center of the text—is the digression on the theater occasioned by Constantine's visit to the Königstäter in Berlin. This is no accident.

Concerning the theater in general, Constantine writes:

> Surely there is no young man with any imagination who has not at one time been captivated by the enchantment of the theater, and desired to be himself carried away into the midst of that fictitious [*kunstige*] reality in order to see and hear himself as an *alter ego* [*Doppeltgaenger*], to disperse himself among the innumerable possibilities which diverge from himself [*i sin al-mulige Forskjellighed fra sig selv*], and yet in such a way that every diversity is in turn a single self. Of course it is only at a very early age such a desire can express itself. Only the imagination is awake to its dream of personality, all the other faculties are still sound asleep. In such a dream of imagination the individual is not a real figure but a shadow, or rather the real figure is invisibly present and therefore is not content with casting one shadow, but the individual has a multiplicity of shadows, all of which resemble him and for the moment have an equal claim to be accounted himself. (R, 58; H, 154)

Through the agency of that fictitious reality, the theater, the youth, all of whose egos are alter, is enabled to disperse himself among numberless possibilities. All of these selves are imaginary, mere shadows; and equivalently, since his other powers are dormant, each of them is himself. Or would be, were it not for that invisible presence.

> Every possibility of the individual is therefore a sounding shadow. The cryptic individual no more believes in the great noisy feelings than he does in the crafty whisper of malice, no more in the blissful exaltation of joy than in the infinite sigh of sorrow; the individual only wants to hear and see with pathos, but, be it observed, to hear and see himself. However it is not really himself he wants to hear. That is not practicable. At that instant the cock crows, and the figures of the twilight flee away, the voices of the night fall silent. If they continue, then we are in an entirely different domain, where all this goes on under the alarming observation of moral responsibility, then we are at the demoniacal. In order not to get an impression of his real self, the cryptic individual requires that the environment be as light and ephemeral as the figures, as the frothy effervescence of the words which sound without echo. Such an environment is the stage, which for this reason precisely is appropriate to the shadow-play of the cryptic individual. (R, 59–60; H, 155–56)

The play provides a show of possibilities for the *cryptic* one: the person who is still hidden within himself, buried in the crypt of his immediacy. Until the cock crows (for the third time?), announcing the dawn of moral responsibility, such a man can only imagine his being, still secreted from himself, as a procession of shadows through a drama of evanescent passions. Because he requires an ephemeral environment, figures of foam, and words without resonance, a man like this desires the serious theater: all the reality he has, the stage is "not merely for pleasure" (R, 67; H, 162).

But the mature person turns to farce:

> Although in the individual life this moment vanishes, yet it is reproduced in a riper age when the soul has seriously collected itself. Yes, although art is perhaps not serious enough for the individual then, he may perhaps have pleasure in turning back occasionally to that first state and rehearsing it [repeating it, not practicing it] in sentiment. [Once more with feeling: *i en Stemning*.] He wishes now to be affected comically, and to be himself in a comically pro-

ductive relation to the theatrical performance. Therefore, though neither tragedy nor comedy can please him, precisely because of their perfection, he turns to the farce. (R, 61; H, 157–58)

Second time as farce. All the characters and situations of farce are types: abstract generalities represented in fortuitously concrete particulars. (Constantine is having a bit of fun at Schiller's expense. Naïve is to sentimental as serious theater is to farce. Naïveté diffuses its reality in the imaginary; or rather, since it has no reality as yet, it *is* the imaginary. Sentimentality recovers the reality it has never lost, farcically, in the instantiation of the imaginary by the accidental.)

After the ideal comes in the very next place the accidental. A wit has said that one might divide mankind into officers, serving-maids, and chimney-sweeps. To my mind this remark is not only witty but profound, and it would require a great speculative talent to devise a better classification. When a classification does not ideally exhaust its object, a haphazard classification is altogether preferable, because it sets imagination in motion. A tolerably true classification is not able to satisfy the understanding, it is nothing for the imagination, and hence it is to be totally rejected, even though for everyday use it enjoys much honor for the reason that people are in part very stupid and in part have very little imagination. When at the theatre one would have a representation of a man, one must either require a concrete form corresponding absolutely to the ideal, or else the fortuitous. . . . In the case of farce, the subordinate actors produce their effect by means of that abstract category "in general" and attain this by a fortuitous concretion. With this one has got no further than to reality. Nor should one seek to go further; but the spectator is reconciled comically by seeing this fortuitous concretion claiming to be the ideal, which it does by treading into the fictitious world [*Kunst-Verden*] of the stage. (R, 66–67; H, 162–63)

The superiority of the farce (for mature persons) consists in this: in the farce the accidental secures reality—or the effect of reality—for the essential. Comically, the ideal generality achieves fortuitous concretion. Like Beckmann's ability to "come walking" (literally *at komme gaaende* [R, 68; H, 163], "to come going"), by which he creates an environment for himself.

Farce therefore is the comical repetition. You don't even have to follow it closely and carefully; you can watch it as casually as it presents itself. In the farce the ideal and the actual are reconciled in laughter. A laughter produced as much by the capricious attention of the observer as by the wholly gratuitous events on the stage.

Of course: this farcical repetition has its serious side. The girl in the box opposite Constantine's, maybe also the lady at the inn, surely the farm girl whose idyllic ambience concludes the digression on the theater. All of them women Constantine scrupulously refuses to seduce. The tender gravity of these scenes is a necessary supplement of (is it also finally superior to?), the raucous laughter of the Königstäter's gallery. The farcical repetition, "blissful" as it is (R, 71; H, 166), is an experience of exuberance, but for that reason unsettling. It needs to be put to rest (R, 71; H, 166) by the reality (or is it the dream?) of innocence (R, 72; H, 167) and by the promise (or is it the illusion?) of true love. "Happy girl! If ever a man should win your love, would that you might make him as happy by doing everything for him as you have made me by doing nothing for me" (R, 73; H, 168).

The digression on the farce tells what the first part of *Repetition* shows. As in the farce, so in the first part of this book, the only viable meaning of repetition—is it unsettling or pacifying?—is the chance conjunction of the abstract ideal and the unmotivated actual. Freedom and nature accidentally made one. An uncertain and unstable recuperation that begs, sentimentally, for the reality it comically dissimulates.

Like life itself the farce is neither tragic nor comic but ambiguously shuttles back and forth in the space between. Interesting. It may even be of interest.

A whore-text? Maybe a pretext. . . .

———

II

The first part of *Repetition* is untitled. Part 2, repeating the title of the book, calls itself "Repetition." A repetition within the work of the work as a whole. (What does that do to its integrity?) And the accomplishment at last of that project which in the first part was abandoned in despair. Now it begins in earnest. Again. (What does that do to the accomplishment?)

The architecture of part 1 was intricate and insidiously concealed. By contrast the divisions of part 2 are simple, symmetrical, and plainly marked:

(A) Constantine Constantius: introductory essay, R, 82–91; H, 179–87.
(B) The young man: letters to Constantine Constantius (August 15–February 17), R, 92–120; H, 188–215. [These letters include the discourse of *Job*.]
(C) Constantine Constantius: second essay, R, 121–24; H, 216–19.
(D) The young man: letter to Constantine Constantius (May 31), R, 125–27; H, 220–22.
(E) Constantine Constantius: letter to "N. N., this book's real reader," dated at Copenhagen, August 1843, R, 129–37; H, 223–31.

(A) Constantine's introductory essay, written some time after his return from Berlin, assesses the young man's condition in the wake of his unfortunate engagement. "There is nothing left for him," Constantine says, "but to make a religious movement" (R, 87; H, 183). The realization of his love being impossible—it "cannot be declined in accordance with the case forms of the regular declensions" (R, 87; H, 183)—it can only come about, if at all, "by virtue of the absurd" (R, 88; H, 185). He is melancholy by nature (R, 83, 87–88, 91; H, 180, 184, 187). And his nature is androgynous (R, 84, 87; H, 181, 183–84).

In the first part of this book Constantine Constantius is the androgyne. He is moved to feminine devotion by the melancholy beauty and the passionate intensity of his young friend.

But he is masculine-manipulative at the same time, in relation to the youth and all the other subjects of his psychological experimentation. Part 2 of *Repetition* (the "repetition") begins with a reversal of roles.

Like a woman the young man requires positive assurance of the legitimacy of his confidant: some token of trustworthiness. But like a man he wants a negative guarantee: he would as soon unburden himself to a madman or a tree (R, 86; H, 183). The sexual ambiguity of the young man puts Constantine in an equally ambiguous position. He is both being and nonbeing, at the whim of his friend (R, 83–84; H, 180). Constantine, whom formerly he regarded as queer, he now describes (Constantine alludes proleptically to the young man's letter of August 15) as mentally deranged. Constantine does not resent this attribution. It almost flatters him. As he says, "Now he knows my most intimate secret" (R, 83, 86, 87; H, 180, 182, 183). Eventually, Constantine conjectures, the young man will kill him with his confidences. The position of an observer is dangerous.

The girl, when her fiancé disappears, is at first unaffected and only gradually slumbers "gently into a dreamy obscurity as to what has occurred and what it might mean" (R, 84; H, 181). Another ambiguity. Both physically and spiritually the young man has vanished to a place unknown, leaving behind him a girl adrift, a confidant in a contradictory situation bordering on madness and death, and . . . uncertainty. A story that begins abruptly, ends indecisively, and bears ambiguous meanings. Or none at all.

The youth himself is in a state of ambivalence. Really, but only, he imagines himself still in love with the girl, an imagining thrown up by his melancholy and his androgynous sympathy. He is, more than all else, captivated by the regret that he may have done the girl a terrible wrong. May have. This too is not certain. Is his guilt real or, like his love, only imagined?

At the outset of part 2 the position of the personae is perfectly indeterminate and the future of the narrative obscure. Three undecided people in an undecidable relationship. Equivocation on all hands has settled into indifference. But: a troubled indifference. It may be the quiet just before the storm.

The young man wants to "come back." His problem has narrowed itself to a point:

Indubitably it is not possession in the strictest sense which concerns him, or the content which develops from this situation; what concerns him is return, conceived in a purely formal sense. Though she were to die the day after, it would not any more disturb him, he would not feel the loss, for his nature would be at rest. The discord into which he has been thrown by contact with her would be resolved [*forsonet*] by the fact that he had actually returned to her. So again the girl is not a reality but a reflection of the movements within him and their exciting cause. The girl has a prodigious meaning, he actually will never be able to forget her, but what gives her meaning is not herself but her relation to him. She is as it were the boundary of his being. But such a relation is not erotic. Religiously speaking, one might say that it was as if God himself employed the girl to capture him; and yet the girl herself is not a reality but is like the artificial flies one sleaves upon hooks. (R, 88–89; H, 185)

What concerns the young man is return in a purely formal sense. The girl is not the obscure object of desire but only a reflection of the movements within himself. And their efficient cause. She has momentous significance, not erotically but as the limit of his being. She is, like the characters and situations in a farce, the fortuitous intrusion of transcendence into the circuit of reflection. But her effect is not comic. Her reality slants the indifference and disturbs the ambiguity of the dialectic. Something stirring in the depths that ever so slightly ruffles the surface.

She is like the bait on a fishhook with which God proposes to capture the young man for himself. The cross of Christ is a fishhook and Christ himself the bait with which God catches the devil.

What baffles the young man is neither more nor less than repetition: return in the purely formal sense (R, 90; H, 186). And repetition is always transcendence: the irruption of the other into the circuit of the same. No other way to the reconciliation of the alienated. Therefore the young man gets no help from Constantine Constantius nor from the philosophers ancient or modern. Immanence—here: reflection—is of no use. His problem is religious, and no man can solve it. So he turns to Job.

Job too was bait. The stake, ostensibly, in a wager between God and Satan. But in fact: the bait with which God caught his unruly son.

Constantine will not deny the reality of repetition. How could he? But he cannot manage a religious movement. And his desire—that he might induce the girl to persuade the young man that she is married in order to disengage him from his melancholy conviction that he loves her—is offset (ambivalence again) by his misgiving—that the bait might be tempted to play God, that the girl might decide to capture the youth for herself by appealing to his melancholy (R, 90–91; H, 187). In that case, Constantine fears, the matter will come to a bad end—for the girl. The young man's revenge on existence, for making him guilty when he was innocent, would become the revenge of existence on the girl, for wanting to exploit his guilt (R, 89, 91; H, 185, 187).

Suppose that Job—or Christ—had decided to catch the Devil himself.

Constantine's assessment of the situation ends, as part 2 begins, uneasily poised between the absurd possibility of repetition and the dreadful possibility of irrecoverable loss.

(B) *August 15.* We have already had, in Constantine Constantius' opening essay, a review of this letter. The original first appears as the revisitation of a revision. It repeats, from the young man's point of view, what has already been repeated from Constantine's perspective. The indeterminateness and ambiguity of the situation, reported dispassionately in Constantine's essay, are here pathetically suffered. Constantine's madness, which concerns himself only analytically, is here confronted with fervent horror. The repetition of the repetition is the origin of the beginning.

The young man (he has never been named) has lost his own name and acquired a false name. He desires no name. Not his own, which (still unnamed) belongs to the girl (whose name he never utters), and not a glorious name if it is not his own (R, 99; H, 194). Throughout this correspondence he signs himself "your devoted nameless friend," "your nameless friend," "devotedly yours," and sometimes "   " (R, 100, 103, 108, 111, 116, 118, 120, 127; H, 196, 199, 203, 206, 211, 213, 215, 222).

In his self-imposed exile (he's in Stockholm but gives no address), the young man exhausts himself in aimless and fruitless activities. "The man who believes in existence," he says, is as well insured as the man who, to hide his feelings when he prays, holds before his face a hat without a crown (R, 100; H, 196). But life evokes no feelings and existence is void of meaning: it smells of nothing (R, 104; H, 200). The nihilism is bleak and total: Constantine, the girl, and the young man, are all brought to nothing, like clouds that tumble down into the womb of earth and there make their grave (R, 100; H, 195).

That, depressingly enough, is the state of affairs at the beginning of the second part of the story. The decisive event reported in the August 15 letter is the young man's loss of his name. The loss of his name—a name that he has never had—expands to become the loss of name-in-general: the loss of the function of the name. Identities evaporate on every hand: impending madness, inexponible grief, the distraction of unaccountable guilt. Impotently ambivalent, language collapses in the confusion of tongues. Words, words, words.

The Job Letters

Beginning with the letter of *September 19*, a new language and a new text are woven into the language of this text: a text and a language called *Job*. A different discourse altogether. Job contends with God and makes his complaint before Him. A loud complaint that echoes in heaven and evokes, in response, the voice of the thunderstorm. The language of Job breaks through the bounds of immanence and forces a word from beyond. As Job is to his comforters, so the young man to is the "miserable shrewdness" (R, 102; H, 198) of Constantine Constantius. As Job is to God, so the young man is to . . . ? The movement of transgression begins. Transcendence hangs in the air like the calm before a storm.

In the letter of *October 11* the speech of Job is contrasted with human language, a wretched invention that says one thing and means another, the miserable jargon of a clique, a collection of poems, proverbs, and pithy sayings gleaned from the classics and from Balle's Lesson Book. Human language has no words for the young man; it cannot without contradicting itself tell the truth about his condition. At this moment, however, the young man is already beginning to speak of himself in the language of *Job* (R, 104; H, 200). Even as he complains of the inadequacy of human speech, he inscribes his predicament in this new and (from a human point of view) paradoxical system of signs. The canonical text, breaking into the discourse of man, restructures and rewrites it. But to describe himself in the language of Job is not to make himself intelligible to men. The young man and his problem remain (from a human point of view) nameless.

The transcendent, which here takes the form of the sacred scripture, bursts irrationally into the normal and (from the human point of view) normative conversation of the world. Where did Job come from? He appears abruptly and without explanation at the beginning of the letter of September 19: "Job! Job! O! Job!" (R, 101; H, 197). His eruption into the correspondence at this point has the effect of deforming all its words and deranging all its significations, from henceforth.

"Existence," the young man writes, "is surely a debate—" (R, 104; H, 200). Between God and man? Man is rationality is language. The other than man is the irrational, the language man cannot speak. God?

In the letter of *November 15* the young man says that he sleeps (not with the girl but) with the words of Job under his pillow. He makes transcripts of them in characters of all sorts on sheets of all sizes. But he will not (though in these letters he repeatedly does) quote them. That would be to appropriate them. Even as he makes them his own, the young man knows they do not apply. Except as therapy: The words of Job, transcribed, are a divine poultice, laid like the healing hand of God upon his sick heart.

Job is stationed at the confines of poetry (R, 110; H, 204). In the same breath: he stands at the limits of faith (R, 115; H, 210).

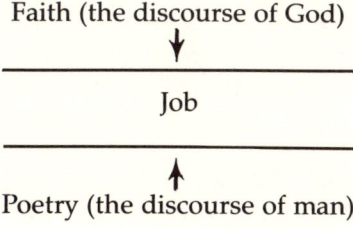

As the language of God, Job cannot be quoted. His speech is inappropriate and may not be appropriated. But if Job is "a poetical figure, if there never was any man who talked like this, then I make his words mine and assume the responsibility" (R, 110; H, 205). The real Job may not be represented in the discourse of man. Job as *figura dictionis* goes without remainder into the letters of the young man, himself at most a poet and at last a poetic figure.

Between faith and poetry there is only silence. A silence broken by Job's anguished cries. "This I understand, these words I make my own. The same instant I sense the contradiction, and then I smile at myself as one smiles at a little child who has put on his father's clothes" (R, 111; H, 206). Were anyone but Job to say what he says, the effect would be humorous. And still the mere reading of these words produces dread.

Job and the girl are beginning to converge. She too is a boundary. The boundary of the young man's being, as if dropped there by God to captivate him. Nothing in herself, she is, like fishing lures, artifice to the angler and reality to the fish. At the limit that divides being from nonbeing (R, 89; H, 185). The boundary situation is the scene of this text and the place at which repetition is (not conceivable, but) by virtue of the absurd possible.

The interesting is also at the borderline. The confinium between life and death. Repetition is the interest of metaphysics, but where the possibility of repetition beckons the threat of seduction looms. There is more than one way to be surprised.

The next three letters are preoccupied with categories of the boundary. *December 14.* Job is in the right. But his rectitude transgresses the limits of human jurisprudence. Every interpretation of his case misunderstands it. He and God understand one another, but this understanding cannot be rendered in human language. The passion of freedom within him "is not stifled or tranquilized by a false expression" (R, 112; H, 207). Beyond the jurisdiction of man, he takes leave of his friends, certain that God can explain everything, if only one can get Him to speak.

Job is subjected to a trial of probation. But this is a thing unspeakable, a phenomenon that escapes every science. Job is made the exception, in whom ethical and religious categories (the human and the divine) collide. Both sacrifice and phoenix, he burns and blooms in the fire of purification. "The border conflicts incident to faith are fought out in him." He is "the whole weighty plea presented on man's behalf in the great suit between God and man." Therefore "probation" is not expressed in the discourse of immanence. "Neither aesthetic, nor ethical, nor dogmatic, it is entirely transcendent" (R, 115; H, 210). To be on trial as Job is on trial is to stand in contradiction to the divine: Job is the plea of man spoken against the judgment of God. Of a single man. Job's trial is *his* thing. It exceeds explanation "at second hand." Not the sublation of time into eternity, which would "erase . . . reality as a whole" (R, 116; H, 210). Job's probation is the confrontation and reconciliation of time and eternity in time. A repetition. Dealt into this game by the wager in heaven, advised by an expert to "curse God and die," the chosen one plays out his hand. He cannot win. Barring a change in the weather.

January 13. Job gets his repetition. At the precise moment when it is perfectly clear that all is lost, the storm breaks:

> Job is blessed and has received everything *double*. This is what is called a *repetition*. How much good a thunderstorm does after all! How blessed it must be after all to be reproved of God! . . . Who could have conceived this conclusion? And yet no other conclusion is conceivable—and neither is this. When everything has come to a standstill, when thought is brought to a halt, when speech becomes mute, when explanation turns homeward in despair—then there must be a thunderstorm. Who can understand this? And yet who can discover anything else?
>
> Did Job lose his case? Yes, eternally; for he can appeal to no higher court than that which judged him. Did Job win his case? Yes, eternally, because he lost his case *before God*.
>
> So then there is a repetition. When does it make its appearance? That is not easy to say in any human language. When did it appear for Job? When all *conceivable* human certainty and likelihood had found it impossible. (R, 117; H, 212)

And so (*February 17*) the young man awaits *his* thunderstorm: the repetition that will restore his potency and make him a husband.

Job is acquitted . . . by the *Donnerwort* that condemns him. Had he won his case against God, he would have demonstrated conclusively that life cannot be endured. The swift logic of a woman. It is a parlous thing (the education of Eve) to win your case against God. Happily Job loses and so, absurdly, wins.

When human language has exhausted its powers and broken against the boundary of transcendence, then God may speak. When the discourse of man has talked itself out, then the voice from the whirlwind may ask its devastating and redeeming questions.

———

(C) Constantine is not impressed. He thinks the young man badly confused. Against all logic he expects a thunderstorm to make him a husband. But, though he thinks himself fortunate that he did not "follow your admirable clever plan" (R, 118; H, 213), he would still be well advised to get rid of the girl. That is the way of a man with a maid, or the way of reflection confronted with an awkward and inconvenient reality. The youth suffers from an "untimely melancholy magnanimity" (R, 121; H, 216) that only a poet's brain could nurture. Let him take a religious view of his predicament and misread nervous apoplexy as divine intervention. He would have done better to exhaust his human shrewdness. Or Constantine's, since the young man himself seems to have none.

As usual Constantine is right in his way. Human shrewdness must be carried at least to the breaking point, and the young man may too previously have cast himself as an erotic Job. How does one know when he has reached the limit?

The young man is a disappointment to his mentor. (His poet.) He has not respected the ideal possibilities inherent in his situation. No help may be expected from the girl. Women (so Constantine) are incapable of the ideal, though they routinely use it as a ruse with which to dupe poets. The unhappy lover has not employed the idea as a regulative principle in the conduct of this affair. Even he admits that his flight to Stockholm, a particularity infinitely remote from the ideal, was a bungling and mediocre move. In these circumstances there is little chance of a thunderstorm.

Into the young man's overheated and long-winded pathos, his frantic invocation of Job, and his fascination with thunderstorms, Constantine's Olympian detachment, his algebraic summary of the ideal options, and his curt dismissal of the whole performance as a mass of confusion and misprision come like a blast of cold analytic air. The place needed airing. Repetition is possible, by virtue of the absurd, only after the exhaustion of human possibility. But to use up the humanly possible means not only to carry oneself in passion to the point at which, all passion spent and all the discourse of passion voided, one is exposed to the whirlwind. It also requires the dialectical reduction of this passionate evacuation to ludicrous misconception and bungling malfeasance. The romantic agony is incomplete without the ironic deflation.

Both Constantine and the young man are textual fictions produced by Constantine Constantius. (It is not so clear about Job.)

(D) Reality (not Søren Kierkegaard) surprises both of them. Without consulting her lover or his confidant or (presumably) the ideal possibilities, the girl finds a husband:

> She is married—to whom I do not know, for when I read it in the paper it was as though I had a stroke of apoplexy, and I lost the notice and have not had patience to make a closer inspection. I am again myself, here I have the repetition, I understand everything, and existence seems to me more beautiful than ever. It came as a thunderstorm, too, though I owe it to her magnanimity that it happened. (R, 125; H, 220)

When his beloved marries someone else, the young man loses no time in fulfilling Constantine's predictions. He calls it a thunderstorm, though he admits it felt a bit like apoplexy (cf. R, 121; H, 216). And he attributes his release to feminine magnanimity (cf. R, 46, 48, 123; H, 143, 145, 217).

But he gets his repetition. "I am again myself. . . . The discord in my nature is resolved, I am again unified. . . . Did I not get myself again, precisely in such a way that I must doubly feel its significance? . . . The magic spell which bewitched me so that I could not return to myself has now been broken. . . . I am born to myself" (R, 125, 126; H, 220, 221).

"I belong to the idea" (R, 126; H, 221). The self to which he is restored is not his immediacy. That he could only have recovered in marriage by virtue of the absurd. A religious movement. He is instead restored, by virtue of the magnanimity of woman, to the idea. He is (re)born as a poet—to "the flight of thought . . . the service of the idea" (R, 127; H, 222)—when the girl (woman is reality) takes herself out of the way. Ilithia unfolds her hands (!), and a man is born again. But he returns not to his primal state, that first fine rapture of first love, but to his subsequent recollection of love. A recollection that has made him happy at last by making him miserable at first. He is released not to the sobriety of the actual, but to the inebriation of the ideal.

His repetition, therefore, is ever so slightly faulted, his return ever so slightly abbreviated, and his rebirth ever so slightly aborted. It is difficult not to sense an undertone of cynicism, ever so slight, in his panegyric to the magnanimity of woman.

Like the letter of November 15, which wonders whether Job is a real man or a poetical figure, this one has no closure. Like all of them, it bears no signature.

(E) Constantine Constantius' concluding letter is addressed to "Mr. N. N., this book's real reader" (R, 129; H, 223). The real reader of this book is masculine. He is also "a fictitious figure [*en poetisk Person*]" (R, 131; H, 225). N. N., who is "not a plurality but only one" (R, 131; H, 225), is something of an ideal reader, who reads the book, as opposed to the host of unreal readers (carefully listed and identified by Constantine) who read in(to) the book only their own anxieties, prejudices, desires, professional psychoses, and privileged doctrines.

Constantine writes like Clement of Alexandria, so that the heretics will not be able to understand him. But the real reader will perceive, through the "inverted development" (R, 132; H, 226) of the thought, what the book is about: the dialectical struggle whereby the exception breaks with the universal and is justified not by getting around it but by going through it. Like Jacob/Israel wrestling with the angel. Like Job contending with God. Like the one sinner who repents, over against the ninety and nine just persons who need no repentance. Or like the poet emerging victorious from his conflict with existence.

The poet, as a justified exception to the universal, is a stage on the way to that superior exception, the religious man. The universal, that which is required of every man (the word *Almene* also means, "common, general, public"), is a coherence of freedom and nature confected by duty. Marriage, for example. And in principle: the marriage of Kant's practical freedom and Hegel's ethical substance. Constantine's young man is justified when existence itself (reality is woman) absolves him from his guilt: that he has defaulted his obligation to being by recollecting it rather than wedding it. In the nick of time the girl withdraws her accusing presence and releases the poet into his exceptional absence. The debt is canceled, and the account is cleared.

His liberation *ab extra* is quasi-religious. But only "as if." He is never more than latently religious. For the young man repetition is not "reality and . . . the seriousness of life" (R, 35; H, 133). It is just "his own consciousness raised to the second power" (R, 135; H, 229). To make him a religious exception, the shock would have to come from higher up. From God, who can do what no ordinary woman, no matter how self-effacing her magnanimity, can even aspire to. Man is reflection, and woman is reality. But only that reality which is (defined as) alienated by language. Both male and female lie this side the boundary of immanence. They are conceivable, and only conceivable, together, as the othered and the othering. Within this domain the Hegelian logic plays its nasty little game in never-ending closure. God is reality in an altogether different sense: the transcendent. The wholly Other, which language can neither distance nor appropriate, because He is always already infinitely far off and infinitesimally proximate.

The young man's problem is solved and his repetition achieved within the circuit of the same. As the shifting sexual identities in this story indicate, the difference between male and female structures an immanent dialectic, of which man and woman are the terms always posited and ever again sublated. The ideal and the actual are two mirrors reflecting each other to infinity.

Job, however, is addressed by the Other. His transgression is precipitated and his protest silenced by the divine prerogative, which neuters the dialectic of man and woman as it moots the argument between Job and his comforters. The unspeakable transcendent takes Job through the universal and beyond it: the universal (marriage) from which the poet is conveniently exempted by the amiable dispensation of existence becomes in the religious instance the universal (justice) from which Job is terribly redeemed by the connivance of God and Satan.

There remains the difference of infinity between religion and a poetry which has the presentiment of religion. This text, which is poetry of a sort, can incorporate the religious only by excluding it. The sacred gloss, appropriated by the young man to describe his own perplexity, is written in the margins of *Repetition*. Intruding ambiguously into Constantine's fiction, *Job* proposes an unaskable question.

Constantine's fiction. Who is Constantine Constantius? A ventriloquist's dummy. A psychologically necessary presupposition. A serviceable spirit who serves by repeatedly becoming someone else. His name is a mockery . . . of the name. Who is the real author of this book? Who concludes by offering his real reader (who?) the barest hint of a possibility of reconciliation (a repetition?) after all the bewildering transformations through which the book has led him (R, 137; H, 230–31). Whose name goes in the blank marked "N. N."? The blank marked "C. C."? There is a blank marked "Søren Kierkegaard." There is also . . . a mark.

But this is serious business. In part 2 of *Repetition*, called "Repetition," the repetition vainly sought in part 1 is finally achieved. After a fashion. The story of the young man repeats, in its own way, the story of Job, which repeats, in its own way, the story of the young man. At the end of it all the "real reader" is offered a chance at his own repetition. (*Forsoning*. In theological terms, atonement.) He is invited to "be reconciled" to the text that has brought him to this pass.

A young man in Stockholm (no address given) is failing to contact a girl in Copenhagen who has recently changed her name. He's lost his own. Job on his ash heap is shouting at the wind. His words are blown back in his throat. Someone has just finished reading an illegible script. A repetition of sorts. This is getting us nowhere. Where were we?

Some birds can only be taken from the rear. Here's a little salt for the tail:

> The idea of the book is the idea of a totality, finite or infinite, of the signifier; this totality of the signifier cannot be a totality, unless a totality constituted by the signified preexists it, supervises its inscriptions and its signs, and is in-

dependent of it in its ideality. The idea of the book, which always refers to a natural totality, is profoundly alien to the sense of writing. It is the encyclopedic protection of theology and of logocentrism against the disruption of writing. . . . If I distinguish the text from the book, I shall say that the destruction of the book . . . denudes the surface of the text. That necessary violence responds to a violence that was no less necessary. (Derrida, *Of Grammatology*, 18)

Bound securely between its covers, *Repetition* appears to be a book. A finite totality of signifiers, organized by a superintendent meaning that assigns to beginning, middle, and end their rightful places in a system closed upon/within itself. We expect it to contain, or be contained by, all it expresses.

Yet it begins with a digression remarking the contrast between the Eleatics' absurd denial of motion and Diogenes' equally absurd denial of that denial. It ends with an open letter to the reader, Mr. N. N., that asks him to be reconciled to the errant ways of the narrative. To continue (for how long?) the dialectic of repetition which the book begins to enact. Or perhaps to achieve for himself (how?) the repetition that Constantine's experimental psychology has shown to be impossible. An invitation to an indefinitely postponed atonement. The middle of the book is a blank: a silence and a silent passage of time between the death with which part 1 concludes and the "repetition" with which part 2 begins.

The putative totality of the signifiers called *Repetition* is exceeded by the digression on the farce. It is breached and invaded by the canonical discourse of *Job*. It is the work of a protean author, a shape-shifter ironically named "constant," and it is addressed to a real/ideal reader who is only a blank without a name. If *Repetition* is a book, it is a book of which there is no definitive edition. A book that does violence to itself as book.

There is reason to think that this "book" is (in the technical sense and *avant la lettre*) a text: writing in which the violence done to writing by the book is countered by the violence inherent in the nature of writing itself. A necessary violence. The book attempts a conquest of being through the consolidation of meaning. But if the guardian of the integrity of being is the impotence of language, then it is expedient that *Repetition* (which says as much) perform the solicitation of this conquest and the dissemination of this meaning. A repetition. Of sorts.

In the body of the narrative there are two proper names, both of which stand (in) for absences. Somewhere in Stockholm the young man takes refuge from the scene of his engagement. Poul Martin Møller, deceased five years when *Repetition* was published, provides a (pre)text for recollection. Remotions in time and space. The letter to the reader is situated and dated, but in the course of the letter Constantine's identity is dissolved at last and for good. "Copenhagen, August 1843" (R, 131; H, 225) marks the place and the moment at which *Repetition* was finished by its "real" author, whose absence from his text is absolute.

It is only where the text transgresses the story—Constantine's *aparté* on the farce—that it is suddenly punctuated by names that function as indices of presence: the Royal Theater in Copenhagen ("not merely for pleasure" [R, 67; H, 162]), the Königstäter in Berlin, the actors Beckmann and Grobecker. Reality enters the text only at that place where the text is beyond itself: being is always the excess of the text. And perhaps at that place where the text is interrupted *ab extra*. The *Job* letters. Perhaps. For who knows whether Job is a human being or a trope? Job? or *Job*? That is only, but always, a maybe. We might check up on the Königstäter and its troupe. There is no way to verify Job. The being that is the excess of the text might be pursued. The being that invades the text—for that we would require a thunderstorm. Whose voice would we hear? And how would we know?

In the hierarchy of life-styles proposed by Johannes Climacus, humor is the proximate confinium of faith. In the Aristotelian sense, its place.

One of the excesses of this text (his name appeared on the Stationer's Register) was a subject of Christian VIII named Søren Kierkegaard. A writer on religious subjects. Through the pseudonym Johannes Climacus he professes an interest in Christianity, proclaimed throughout history as the Incarnation, in history, of the Word of God, and demanding a decision, also in history, for or against the miraculous Presence. So historical is the reality of Christianity that history itself, since the Incarnation, has had no reality but Christianity. Yet Climacus, for all his concern with the concrete historical actuality of Christianity, is exclusively preoccupied with the abstract dialectic of rationality and radical alterity: not the historical reality, but the absurd historicity of Christianity is the sole *topos* of his meditations. He even goes so far as to suggest that we could dispense with the New Testament and the whole of Christian history if only the contemporaries of Jesus had left "this little advertisement, this *nota bene* on a page of universal history": "'We have believed that in such and such a year God appeared among us in the humble figure of a servant, that he lived and taught in our community, and finally died'" (*Philosophical Fragments*, 130). Those few words, alleging the bare fact of incarnation, would have been enough to provide the opportunity for faith and the occasion of offense.

This is a contradiction only if we forget that the historical Incarnation—the Christ who is also Jesus—is, like the characters and situations in farce, a fortuitous concretion. On the one hand, history is beside the point. What matters is the "dialectical movements." But on the other hand, to be a Christian is to be contemporary with the historical Christ and to appropriate the history of Christianity. The Christian is not one who has correctly worked out the logic of incarnation. He is one who lives a perfectly determinate kind of life: *imitatio Christi*. Although the concretion is fortuitous (how could it be otherwise when the category to be incarnated is the Absolutely Other?), yet it *is the* concretion of the Absolutely Other and therefore the Absolutely Other itself. This particular actor, who just happens to work at the Königstäter, *is* the *miles gloriosus*. Likewise the gratuitousness of the incarnation of the Word in the man Jesus, like the second birth of every new Christian, is no accident. Although it is an absolute surprise.

Is it an accident that in *Repetition* the young man and the girl are never made concrete, not even fortuitously? He is described, but description is abstraction (*Søren Kierkegaards Papirer*, VIII[1] A 6222), and he remains for all of it a category: the young man. The girl is not even described. She is never more but never less than the alienated term of an allusion *ins Ferne*.

Reality is, in relation to every movement of reason, the unmotivated. An other that the dialectic can never generate and so never consume. The irrational. Woman is reality. Like the Christ absurdly incarnate in Jesus, that impossible possibility whose reality we call the God-man, woman can save us all. From the interesting. From ourselves. We are all men. The women too. All of us bear, inside out or outside in, the signifier of our lack.[4] This is not under the sun.

This is absurd. Of course. Nevertheless, in *The Point of View for My Work as an Author*, Kierkegaard says that his life has been a love affair with God, who is metonymically identified with Regine, the rejected bride, and Michael Pederson, the dead father. God, his true lover, is also the mother he never had, replacing and effacing the biological mother, whom his father had possessed without right to his lifelong despair. This too is absurd. But the sexual identities in his life as in his texts will not respect the limits of gender. In the possibility opened by the death of the father, God gives himself as mother and bride to the prodigal who returns from harlotry to his true home. A repetition of sorts ("he came to himself" [Luke 15: 17]),[5] in which Kierkegaard returns to that origin from which he never departed. How far is the grace of God from the magnanimity of woman?

In the book, as the forced containment of the irregularity of writing, phallogocentrism asserts its possession of the signifier and essays the appropriation of being. (Ane Lund, so rudely forced.) But if the book is an attempted rape of reality, then the original violence of writing responds to the violence of the book with a gesture of castration that liberates the transcendent. In *Repetition* the signs neuter themselves. The verses of Poul Møller, by which the young man quotes himself into senility. His copybook, containing citations from the classics and the catechism, and his transcripts of the biblical text; his removal from Copenhagen to Stockholm; and his letters themselves, addressed to "my silent confidant" and left unsigned: signifiers of something missing. Occupying the place of an absence and exposing its impotence, *Repetition* renounces dominion and imperium. The mastery of being by the book is unmasked as sterile self-manipulation, the hymen remains intact.

---

4. Cf. Samuel R. Delany, *Tales of Nevèrÿon*, 87–101. See also Jacques Lacan, *Écrits*, 281–91.

5. Cf. *Point of View*, 19–20, 64–65, 76–84 (where the relationship with Regine is characterized as a *"factum"*).

From Philostratus the Elder Kierkegaard took a motto for *Repetition*: "On wild trees the flowers are fragrant, on cultivated trees the fruits" (R, 31; H, 127). The conjunctions—wild/flowers, cultivated/fruits—are paradoxical. These words, Kierkegaard remarks, could stand as an epigram over the relationship between paganism and Christianity (*Søren Kierkegaards Papirer*, IV A 27).[6] Paganism, in all its declensions a religion that centers in fertility and procreation, only flowers. Christianity, which has decentered sexuality to the point of glorifying perpetual chastity . . . bears fruit. Untamed nature expends itself in show. Artifice gives birth. (A virgin birth?)[7] In both cases it's a question of fragrance, and therefore of perception at a distance.

It's paradoxical, and beyond paradox surprising, to be told that Christian fruits smell like pagan flowers. But Christianity repeats paganism, as the fruit repeats the flower. And a repetition is always something of a surprise. To be taken again [*gjentages*] is to be overtaken (surprised): taken over, without warning, perhaps unawares. Seized or captured by that which is always there before you because it runs faster [*overraske, überrasche*]. Faster even than irony, of which surprise is in a sense the opposite. Irony knows everything, and more than everything. It has used up reality and explored possibility and found them wanting. Irony is beyond surprising. Insofar as every text takes itself out of the race by turning on itself in a cipher of emasculation, every text is ultimately troped as irony. Therefore repetition is never inscribed in the text. Especially a text entitled, with double irony, *Repetition*.

And yet: irony is a necessary condition of repetition. Only the unsurprisable is absolutely surprised. The ash heap comes before the thunderstorm. "No authentic human life is possible without irony," and every authentic human life is a function of repetition, "a history wherein consciousness successively lives itself out, though in such a way that happiness consists not in forgetting all this but becomes present in it" (*Concept of Irony*,

---

6. Cf. Gal. 5: 16–23. For the previous paragraph, cf. Gal. 3: 28.
7. Cf. *Concept of Irony*, 47, and by contrast, 262. The virgin birth issues in an incarnation on 259.

338, 341).⁸ Repetition cannot be written. *Repetition* is a way of writing this.

The crucifixion was an event in history, as the creed testifies. He was crucified under Pontius Pilate: a time and a place and an undistinguished agent of the imperial Roman government. (Now forever marked with a distinction he might have wished to decline, from which his wife tried to save him.) After 1,900 years the human race managed, in Nietzsche, to comprehend the crucifixion. This is in the world. But the resurrection took place in accordance with the Scriptures. An event beyond history, of which history knows nothing but an empty tomb. The signifier of absence. Tolkien has said that Christianity is the fairy tale that came true. The man-God, the historical Jesus who died and the eternal Christ who was reborn in him, is the metonymy that becomes metaphor. This is not in the world, although the resurrection (of which the crucifixion is the impossible possibility) is the repetition that contains the world. Creates it anew and for the first time by restoring it to that beginning from which it never departed.

But the crucifixion comes first. Being cannot be forced by the signifier. Like truth, she keeps her legs crossed. The violence of language turns on itself. The catechretic seizure of being by the sign yields only the indefinite deferral of presence and the dispersal of the sign itself in sterile dissemination. Alluring fruit and miserable pittance, which do not satisfy (R, 34; H, 132). Fragrant flowers of evil.

Maybe. These may be dragonseed. It is necessary to pass by the dragon. The impotence of language preserves inviolate the alterity of being. And thereby—perhaps—opens the way of repetition. But the hook must be baited. Irony is the penance of language, by which it acknowledges its original fault: the incapacity to let be. And a kind of reparation. A refusal to foreclose the possibility that reality may, in the extremity of language, bestow itself. The manna that satisfies with benediction (R, 34; H, 132). Beyond irony there is the possibility—*just* the possibility, which

---

8. The Tolkien essay referred to in the next paragraph is "On Fairy-Stories," in C. S. Lewis, ed., *Essays Presented to Charles Williams* (Grand Rapids: William B. Erdmans Publishing Co., 1974).

can be neither activated nor shut off but only allowed to remain in its absolute *dehors*—that being may, gratuitously, give itself. Being is inconceivably conceivable as gift. A graceful and gracious self-giving, of which the restoration of Job is a singularly thunderous instance. Of which the magnanimity of woman (the self-withholding of being) is an ironic inversion.

Or is it? In the first draft of *Repetition* the young man kills himself in febrile imitation of Werther. When Kierkegaard learned that Regine had married Fritz (from whom she had been temporarily distracted by Søren), he rewrote the ending. The magnanimity of woman saved, among other things, this text. Among other things, Søren Kierkegaard? Perhaps: a fortuitous concretion of the young man, Søren in *Repetition* repeats his love affair—and his faulted self-recovery—with feeling. Not quite autobiography, since the life follows and repeats the fiction. The end of the story and the beginning of the history were written by Regine. Regine is the grace of *Repetition*. What saved Regine?

Pogo says, very sensibly, that bait never wins (Kelly, 19). But the girl achieved a repetition. She found another man and began a new life. Who was he and what did she do for him? "She is married—to whom I do not know . . . I read it in the paper . . . I lost the notice and have not had the patience to make a closer inspection" (R, 125; H, 220). His signifier is effaced in the very mention. But he got the girl. The woman who is not in the book marries the man who is not in the book. The unsurpassable is surpassed. The "movement" by which the girl finds a man and enters upon her marriage is made by virtue of the absurd; it is unmotivated by her "ideal" relationship to the young man. This bait died and was resurrected: she had the vitality to kill her death and transform it into life (R, 40; H, 137). What was for her lover a matter of life or death became for her a matter of life and death. The past her lover, the future her husband. Is that a tragedy? Perhaps it's a farce. More than interesting, it is the interest of this text.

Being, which can never be taken at the origin but only repeated, is grace. The beloved and fruitful wife of whom one never tires.

In Hebrew she is the maternal grandmother of our Savior.

5.
A Ram in the Afternoon:
KIERKEGAARD'S DISCOURSE OF THE OTHER

> . . . because it is produced in the locus of the Other, it is first of all for the subject that his speech is a message. By virtue of this fact even his demand originates in the locus of the Other, and is signed and dated as such. This is not only because it is subjected to the code of the Other, but also because it is marked by this locus (and even the time) of the Other.
>
> Jacques Lacan, *Écrits*

    The *Philosophical Fragments* is obsessed with alterity. In particular with the question, how can language give expression to that which is wholly other than language? Although the ostensible subject of the book is Christianity, it is Christianity as *wholly other* that structures its discourse. Since the other than language cannot be uttered, the text of the *Fragments* turns back upon itself and becomes an exploration of the limits of language. But since the limit of language is itself the alterity language cannot express, the *Fragments* neither says nor shows but rather performs the "absolute paradox": that the limit of language, its irreducible other, is also its radical source. It is in this sense that the book is an "indirect communication." And it is only in this absolutely indirect way that the book is, importantly, "about" Christianity.

    I shall try to substantiate this claim by reading crucial passages of the text.

I

The first chapter of the *Fragments* opens with the question, "To what extent can the truth be learned?" (11A; hereinafter cited in this essay as PF).[1] The question is "asked by the unknowing, who does not even know what has given him occasion to question in this way" (PF, 9A). The pseudonymous author, Johannes Climacus, contrasts two answers to this question: the "Socratic" answer and an anonymous view he represents as his own "thought-project."

The Socratic view heads up in the doctrine of recollection, according to which "the truth is not introduced into him [the ignorant man], but was within him" (PF, 11A). On this assumption the temporal moment in which a man "learns" the truth and the teacher from whom he "learns" it are alike no more than occasional. "Each man is his own center, and the whole world centers only in him, because his self-knowledge is a knowledge of God" (PF, 14A). All that concerns me as learner is "my possession of the Truth, which I had from the beginning without knowing it" (PF, 15).

> The underlying principle [*finale Tanke*] of all questioning is that the one who is questioned must himself have the truth and must acquire it by himself. The temporal point of departure is nothing; for as soon as I discover that I have known the truth from eternity without knowing it, that moment is hidden in the eternal, incorporated in it in such a way that I, so to speak, could not find it even if I looked for it, because there is neither here nor there but only an *ubique et nusquam*. (PF, 15–16A)

The Socratic presumption (whether it is the view of Socrates himself is of no concern in the present context, for reasons that will soon become clear) is that there exists an eternal and omnipresent structure of truth centering equally in all men and there-

---

1. In this passage and in many others I have adapted the English translation, usually in the direction of greater literalness. In such cases the letter A is added to the page number(s) of the primary reference.

fore just as much but no more present in one than in another: an *ubique et nusquam* to which time, space, and occasion are strictly irrelevant.

Truth is always and everywhere attainable by everyone. One attains it simply by reverting to its always already presence to himself. That is the meaning of the doctrine of recollection and the presupposition of all inquiry. For which reason it is irrelevant (as Socrates himself would have been the first to acknowledge) whether or not this is the view of Socrates. It is the view (acknowledged or not) of man thinking.

The Socratic answer to the question with which the chapter begins is therefore: truth may only be "learned" if and to the degree that it is always already known by the learner. "Learning" is just the realization of this presence, which is the condition of all questioning. Because its presence in the learner is assumed, the truth is never introduced into him from without.

This presence of truth is a kind of absolute. Therefore, since a man's self-knowledge necessarily incorporates a knowledge of the eternal truth, knowledge of self is knowledge of "God." The title page of the *Fragments* poses this question, thematic for the work as a whole:

> Can there be an historical point of departure for an eternal consciousness? How can such a point of departure be of more than historical interest? Can one build an eternal blessedness on historical knowledge? (PF, iiiA)

From the Socratic point of view this is a pseudo-question. Not that the answer is No. But rather: the question cannot be asked, since it presupposes what is contrary to the presupposition of all questioning—that one might in a historical moment and by a historical occasion come to know something he did not know before, that in a moment of time and by the agency of a teacher a hitherto simply absent truth might become simply present. Or, if the question (asked by one whose ignorance conceals from him even the source of his questioning) is not to be altogether meaningless, then it merely expresses the inattentiveness to truth (the Socratic forgetfulness) in which inquiry (that is, recollection) begins. The absolute (a knowledge of God, eternal consciousness, eternal blessedness) is always already possessed and known: it is impossible to be absolutely surprised.

What is said *in* the *Fragments* concerning the presuppositions of all inquiry must also be said *about* the *Fragments*, which is an inquiry into the limits and conditions of inquiry and therefore perfectly self-reflexive. More of this later.

Impossibly, Climacus goes on to propose his own "thought-project" as an alternative to the Socratic (the only human) option. Beginning with the moment of learning. "Now if things are to be otherwise" (with respect to the question of the title page), "the Moment in time must have a decisive significance" (PF, 16). In this moment the eternal (truth, consciousness, blessedness), *hitherto nonexistent*, must have *come into being*. Were it always already present, the moment would not be decisive. Let us see, Climacus says, what follows from this assumption.

The assumption is that the answer to the question on the title page is Yes. But as we have seen, the question is unaskable. The assumption that it might be both asked and affirmatively answered entails absurd consequences, which Climacus proceeds to unfold.

Prior to learning the truth, the inquirer must not possess it even in principle, as an ever-present recourse. It does not *exist* for him. So alienated from the truth that he cannot be occasioned to recollect it, the learner must be *defined* [*bestemmet*] as *un*truth. He is (not "is in a state of" but *is*) untruth (PF, 16–17).

The teacher may, Socratically, serve as occasion to remind the learner that he is untruth. If he is to be more than occasion, he must give the learner both the truth and the ability to understand it.

> The condition for understanding the truth is like the capacity to inquire for it: the condition contains the conditioned, and the question contains the answer. . . . All instruction depends in the last analysis upon the presence of the condition; if this is lacking, the teacher can do nothing. (PF, 17–18A)

To save the hypothesis, the teacher must impart both truth and condition. Since this is beyond human capacity, the teacher must be divine.

In the moment of learning, which Climacus calls the "fullness of time," the eternal truth (impossibly) comes into being. The learner experiences the transition from untruth to truth as a transition from nonbeing to being: a second birth by which he becomes a new man.

"But," Climacus asks disingenuously, "is that which is here expounded thinkable?" (PF, 24A). Only, he answers, by one who has experienced the second birth. It would be "preposterous" and "laughable" to suppose anyone else (any ordinary human being, here defined as untruth) capable of imagining this passage of eternal truth from the simple absence of nonbeing to the full presence of existence in time. In a deeper than Socratic sense the question of Chapter 1—To what extent can the truth be learned?—and the question of the title page—Can there be a historical point of departure for an eternal consciousness?—are asked in ignorance by one who cannot even know what prompted his asking. For Climacus' thought-project proposes what is strictly unthinkable by any human being. It contradicts the presupposition of all questioning—that he who asks already knows the answer—and of all inquiry—that he who seeks the truth already knows it.

The doctrine of recollection expresses both ontological and epistemological necessities. It is necessary to situate the present against the background of the past. The new is only the making explicit of what was implicit in the old, the actualization of a permanent or preexistent potentiality. Likewise for the conditions of intelligibility: the novel must always be understood in terms of the fixed and familiar. But Climacus' hypothesis defines a *radical* novelty, a coming-into-being unfounded and unprepared for, which of course would be unintelligible to anyone who had not experienced the novelty in question. And to him intelligible only in a radically new way, not by reference to an eternal *prius* but (impossibly) as the incommunicable meaning of a unique event in his own being.

Compounding unintelligibilities, the coda to chapter 1 (a dialogue between the fiction, Climacus, and his imagined interlocutor) argues that Climacus' thought-project is self-verifying. It is ridiculous and foolish, which is just what one would expect if it were true. And it is old and well known: every Sunday school child knows that Climacus' project is no more than orthodox Christian doctrine. Climacus is, his interlocutor says, "like the man who collected a fee for exhibiting a ram in the afternoon, which in the forenoon could be seen gratis, grazing in the open field" (PF, 26). But at the same time the hypothesis was not invented by its purported author, it was not invented by the interlocutor, and it could not have been invented by any human being. Say what you will about human folly, no man could think up something *absolutely* unintelligible.

The fact that the hypothesis exists, that it is unintelligible, that everyone knows it and also knows that he did not invent it, proves its truth. For that is exactly what the hypothesis predicts. At the very least it is clear that something utterly uncanny is afoot in the world. Something that disturbs and dislodges the norms of truth and meaning. Something no less disquieting because familiar to every man, woman, and child—a sickening uncertainty, a wild insecurity, that undermines assurance with the threat of radical unintelligibility, and which yet, through misunderstanding, carelessness, the force of habit—or bad faith—has come to be taken for granted.

Given a ram in the morning free, what is the point of a ram in the afternoon at great price?

It is instructive to transcribe Climacus' argument in (loosely) semiotic terms. Can there be a historical point of departure for an eternal consciousness? may be taken to mean, Can the historical signify the eternal? The question about learning is a search for vestiges of truth in the ignorant consciousness. Generally: terms like "history," "ignorance," "the learner" stand for signifiers, while terms like "the eternal" and "truth" stand for the transcendent signified. The argument investigates the relation of signification.[2] But since Climacus' text is itself a system of linguistic signifiers, the further question arises, How can language be "about" the eternal and "about" the relation of eternal truth to temporal fact? How can the transcendent signified be implicated in/by the play of signifiers?

---

2. Cf. *Concluding Unscientific Postscript*, 86–97, on the relation of accidental historical truths to eternal truths of reason, with special reference to Lessing. Kierkegaard's fascination with proofs of God's existence, in which the same problem arises, is shown by chapter 3 of the *Philosophical Fragments*. Cf. my discussion below, sec. 2.

To put the matter in this way is to undertake that self-reflection which the *Fragments* demands and itself enacts.

On the Socratic view, the signified is given in and with the signifier. To know oneself is to know God. On this view one is already, in history, out of history, so that to talk about anything at all is a way of gathering oneself out of time (the realm of signs) back into eternity (the always already presence of the signified). Language is pure self-transcendence. Instant recall. The signifiers, revoked as soon as they are uttered, collapse immediately into the signified.

On the Christian view (if that is what it is), time and eternity are simply diverse. There is no passage from time (the signifier) to eternity (the signified), only (on the one hand) the play of signifiers and (on the other) the silent alterity of the signified. Truth is not manifest in history save by a rupture of all the categories. Every Christian concept shatters the logic of signification. The terms of Climacus' thought-project, affirming the unsayable, merely open faults in language.

Hence the irony of the concluding dialogue, in which the absurdity of the Christian hypothesis is made a test of its truth. Ironic because Climacus catches discourse in a double bind. He permits either schizogenic signification or none at all. In order for signification to occur, the signifier must be distinct from the signified. On the Socratic view, therefore, there is no signification, only the prevenient reabsorption of all signifiers into the signified. But if signifier and signified are categorically distinct, as in Christianity (if that is what it is), then signification is contradiction. Every linguistic operation (including the *Fragments*) is doomed, either to nullity or to absurdity.

It is not surprising that Climacus (himself a being of language) splits in two at the end of the chapter. For one of him, the interlocutor, the thought-project is old hat. For the other it is so novel as to be unthinkable. "Better well hanged than ill wed" (PF, 2A). But the choice is not a happy one.

II

Chapter 3 of the *Philosophical Fragments*, on the absolute paradox, may be read as an attempt to conceive the Augustinian doctrine of the relation of faith and reason in terms of a Hegelian conception of reason. It argues that reason is fulfilled in faith; that is perfectly Augustinian. But it adds that the fulfillment of reason is the undoing of reason—the crucifixion of the understanding. That is to take "reason" in an idealistic sense.

The passion of reason (according to Climacus) is to think what is not thought. Yet it is the fate of reason to think nothing but thoughts. Realist by desire, idealist by destiny, reason is paradoxically situated in its passion. It seeks its own destruction in collision with its other. Being is either a category of thought or an alterity canceling thought. That reason desires its annihilation is paradoxical. That its annihilation is also its beatification is absolutely paradoxical.

The known is coextensive with the human. That was Socrates' view—all knowledge is implicit in self-knowledge—and it must be taken as normative. The other with which reason seeks collision must therefore be the unknown. "But what is this unknown . . . ? It is the unknown. . . . So let us call this unknown *God*. That is only a name we give it" (PF, 49A).

The text continues: "It could scarcely occur to reason to want to prove that this unknown (God) exists." This introduces a long digression on—proofs of God's existence. But the digression is to the point, and the point is to seal the unknown as such, to certify the absolute discontinuity of the unknown divine with the human and the known. The argument is as simple as the dialectic that sponsors it. The reality of the unknown (God's existence) cannot be demonstrated, for if it could it would not be other than reason.

The unknown is unknown, and there's an end of it. It could hardly occur to reason to make the unknown a *topos* of cognition. Reason could not even imagine the problem, since one of its terms is *de jure* extrarational. Yet the history of philosophy is virtually coterminous with the history of proofs of God's existence. What *did* put this notion into philosophers' heads?

In the ensuing discussion Climacus manipulates a distinction between essence (ideal being) and existence (factual being) that is equivalent to the distinction between the rational (continuous with the human) and the not-rational (discontinuous with the human). Existence, he insists, is never demonstrated but always assumed in demonstration. It is not part of the structure of ratiocination but a *prius* or an *accessorium*—a datum or a supplement (PF, 50). The reality of thinking presumes the thinker's participation in that which is not thought (PF, 46). Before he thinks, he *is*, and to this being-before-thought he persistently returns on the other side of thought. But it is never comprehended in his thinking (cf. *Concluding Unscientific Postscript*, 267–82, 293, 296, 314).

Proofs of God's existence, cosmological or ontological, take "God" as a concept (PF, 51) rather than a name (PF, 49) and proceed to unpack the contents of this concept—among which, of course, is (ideal) being (PF, 50–52, 51n.). But they do not reach through to (factual) being, which is the nub of the matter. The idea of proving that *this* (other than reason) exists could scarcely suggest itself to rationality.

> He, therefore, who wants to prove the existence of God . . . proves in lieu thereof something else, something which at times perhaps does not even need a proof, and in any case needs none better. For the fool says in his heart, there is no God; but he who says in his heart or to men, wait just a little and I will prove it, O what a rare man of wisdom he is! (PF, 54A)

He who would know the unknown only proves himself a fool. And yet this folly of reason is not conspicuously different from its paradoxical passion: to encounter that which, in the encounter, will destroy it.

"A project of this kind would scarcely have been undertaken by the ancients" (PF, 54). Presumably because they were perfectly rational. The thought that something discontinuous with reason might exist had not yet entered the world. Whence then the paradoxical passion of reason and its (decadent?) expression in the foolishness of theistic proof? Cryptically inscribed in Climacus' text is the suspicion that *Christianity* put this notion into reason's head. "What an excellent subject for a comedy of the higher lunacy!" (PF, 54 n.).

There is, Climacus says, one way a man may get to God's existence via demonstration. By stopping:

> As long as I hold on to the proof (i.e., continue to be the prover), existence does not appear . . . ; but when I let go

> of the proof, existence is there. But the fact that I let go . . .
> is indeed my contribution; . . . it is a *leap*. (PF, 53A)

One arrives "rationally" at the other-than-reason by abandoning ratiocination. By a leap. A movement across radical discontinuity. Not by summoning all one's powers and venturing into the unknown. Where or what is the unknown? And what good are all one's powers? One "leaps" by letting go, giving up the attempt at proof, no longer demonstrating anything. There, in that abeyance of reason, reality beyond reason reveals itself.

The unknown makes its appearance when reason "sets itself aside" (PF, 73). Can reason dismiss itself in this way? No. It cannot abstain from seeking that which, found, will rebuff it.

> Thus the paradoxical passion of reason collides continually with the unknown, which indeed exists, but is also unknown, and in so far does not exist. Reason gets no farther, yet it cannot in its paradoxicality refrain from coming to this point and concerning itself with it. . . . (PF, 55A)

It will not do for reason to deny the existence of the unknown, for the denial itself would affirm a relationship between reason and (that which reason conceives as) the nonexistent. To say that the unknown simply cannot be known, and that if it could it could not be expressed, correctly interprets the unknown as a limit. But the cognizance of the limit does not satisfy reason's passion for encounter, it only incites it.

> What then is the unknown? It is the limit to which reason continually comes, and insofar . . . it is the different, the absolutely different.

Because it is the absolutely different, there is no mark [*Kjendetegn*] by which the unknown may be recognized: it is not signified by any sign. To call it the absolutely different may seem close to revealing what it is: it is the negative of everything rational. Not so. It is simply diverse from reason, and "reason cannot even think the absolutely different."

The unknown is no more than a limit. Unless it is left as such, the simple notion of difference turns into a profusion of monsters and ludicrous fantasies: the pantheons of polytheism and the wilder speculations of religious philosophers.

> But this difference cannot be held fast. . . . If the difference cannot be held fast, because it has no distinguishing mark [*Kjendetegn*], then difference and likeness are identical, as is the case with all such dialectical opposites. The difference, which fastens itself to reason, has confounded it so that it does not know itself and quite consistently confuses itself with the difference. (PF, 56A)

Paradoxically, the attempt to conceive—or even to postulate—the absolutely other than reason leads to the absolutely paradoxical indistinction of reason and its other. But this, the paradoxical satisfaction/frustration desired by reason, is indistinguishable from idolatry. "Deepest down in the heart of piety lurks the mad caprice which knows that it has itself produced the God" (PF, 56).

> Thus God has become the most terrible deceiver, because reason has deceived itself. Reason has brought God as near as possible, and yet he is just as far away as ever. (PF, 57A)

The paradoxical passion of reason—to be consumed in collision with the other—leads to the paradoxical impasse that reason cannot distinguish its salubrious immolation in the other from the idolatrous generation of the other in the vanity of its own imagining.

The absolutely different is indistinguishable from the absolutely same. There is no mark by which it may be known and therefore none by which it may be discriminated. The other-than-reason is that which in principle is contained in no rational category and which nonetheless is categorized as nonrational by this statement. With respect to any set of signs, "reality" is that which is included by exclusion and excluded by inclusion. The meaning of a text is the unwriteable inscription, and all discourse (*pace* proposition 7) is about that which cannot be spoken.

By Climacus' argument the Hegelian dialectic is made to generate the ultimate un-Hegelian conclusion. Not the unity of the rational and the real, subject and substance. And not simply their difference. Rather, their *indistinguishable* difference. The paradoxical issue of this paradoxical labor of reason is the interminable dialectical oscillation of the same and the other, the irresolute alternation of reflection aiming at being and recoiling into itself. The inconclusiveness is the conclusion.

At the end of chapter 3, Climacus' alter ego appears to protest that this discourse about the absolute other is so ludicrously absurd that "I must exclude from my consciousness everything that I have in it in order to hit upon it" (PF, 57). Granted. And from this it follows that

> if he is to know anything in truth about the unknown (God), man must first know that it is different from him, absolutely different from him. Of itself reason cannot get to know this . . . ; if it is to learn this, it must learn it from God, and if it does learn this, it cannot understand it, and therefore cannot know it. For how should reason understand the absolutely different? (PF, 57A)

Reason itself, which cannot even imagine the absolutely different, cannot be the source of its own passion nor of the undecidable dialectic of likeness and difference to which it is thereby brought. Christianity is offered as the origin and the interpretation of this predicament of reason. For it is Christianity alone that discovers in man his absolute difference from God (the untruth of sin) and effects the absolute likeness of atonement.

Christianity resolves the residual Socratic perplexity about human nature (cf. PF, 58; and Plato, *Phaedrus*, 230A) and in so doing makes the paradox of reason absolutely paradoxical. As Kierkegaard might have said, potentiates it infinitely (cf. *Sickness unto Death*, pt. 2) by declaring humanity both monstrous (by sin) and divine (by adoption). In order to make himself understood by man, God (the unknown) himself became man.

> Thus the paradox becomes even more terrible, or rather the same paradox has a duplicity that shows it to be the absolute paradox; negatively by producing the absolute unlikeness of sin, positively by proposing to sublate [*ophaeve*] this absolute unlikeness in absolute likeness. (PF, 59A)

Christianity is literally unthinkable, and "reason will have much to urge against it" (PF, 59). And yet

> reason in its paradoxical passion desires its own destruction. But the paradox also wills this destruction of reason, and so they understand one another. (PF, 59A)

Precisely because it is unthinkable (the destruction of reason) Christianity is the satisfaction of that passion of reason (for self-destruction)—of which it is, aboriginally, the origin.

Exceeding in its paradoxicality even the paradoxical indistinction of the same and the different, Christianity (if that is what it is) is the absolutely absolute other than the Hegelian absolute knowledge. The Absolute Paradox (the capitalization is at last necessary) propounds the consubstantial union of reason (the human) and its other (the divine). A union absolutely unintelligible, to be sure, signed and sealed only in the "moment of passion" and the "passion of the moment" (PF, 59). Whatever that may be.

There is no doubt that Climacus' conclusions are paradoxical. Yet one might, in the spirit of his interlocutor, question the dichotomies on which his dialectic is strung. For example, why does he regard existence (factual being) as absolutely different from essence (ideal being), so sundered that there is no rational transition from one to the other? It is not strange or unprecedented to define ideal being as the realm available to thought, or simply as the realm of thought; nor to define factual being by opposition as being independent of thought. In which case reason, by definition restricted to one side of this duality, could not reach across to comprehend its contrary. Existence is in principle incomprehensible.

But there is more than stipulation at stake. Thought, as Climacus points out, is never pure (cf. PF, 46; and *Concluding Unscientific Postscript*, 269–70, 273–79, 292, 296–99). It is always the thinking of a thinker who in his thinking is not just his thought. Thinking presupposes and intends the other than thought. Just as a ghost of significance—a phantom of reference—plays about the margins of even the most self-contained text, so the edges of thought are haunted by the ghost of reality. A ghost that can neither be laid nor made to materialize.

Climacus' text enacts the ambivalent relationship of text-as-such ("reason," "humanity," "self-knowledge," etc.) to its extratextual presuppositions ("God," "the unknown," "the absolutely different," etc.). This beyond-the-text cannot be comprehended or even adumbrated in the text without becoming itself textual: everything in the preceding parentheses—both of them—is a signifier and no more. In that sense there is nothing outside the text. And yet it is this "nonexistent" *hors-texte* that all texts are "about." That is paradoxical enough. The absolute paradox is that the nontext is the source and meaning of the text, the extrastructural foundation, fulfillment, and frustration of every structure.

In Climacus' version of this paradox, "existence" is a name (like "God" it is only a name, no more than a signifier) for (another signifier!) the nonthought from which thinking starts and departs. Thinking starts and departs from existence; it cannot disavow its origin, nor can it turn and devour it. Thought cannot escape from its escape from its point of departure, nor can it arrive at that which is always already its destiny.

Yet the passion of reason is to do just that: to reach back before the beginning or forward beyond the end and to recover by thinking the presupposition which as thinking it makes and loses. The passion and the paradox of thought is a nostalgia for the primordial but always already sundered unity of thought and being. Which in actual thinking becomes an eschatological trajectory toward their always intended but ever unrealized reconciliation.

The passion of thought is as persistent and inescapable as it is desperate. The name for this nostalgia, protended as apocalypse, is the search for truth or the love of wisdom: the signifier "philosophy." It is a desperate passion, because the original unity of thought and existence was never given and is never experienced. There is no such thing as immediate experience and certainly no immediate thinking (cf. *Concluding Unscientific Postscript*, 101–6). All that is given is nostalgia for a primal harmony that is felt as lost but which "in fact" (that is, in reflection) never was. What is experienced is not sameness but difference, not presence but absence.

The desperate passion of reason is desperately self-destructive, for the presence of being would annul thinking by obliterating its difference (both *differentia* and *différance*) and "fulfill" it by engulfing it. The Greek doctrine of recollection is the nostalgia of thought for return to its no-longer-present origin (preexistence), and the modern belief in afterlife (postexistence) is only recollection in reverse. Both of them are expressions of the pathos of death (PF, 11–12, 12n., 26). The passion of reason for reunion with being is simply the present experience of their diremption. *Media vita in morte sumus*, and the attainment of everlasting life, whether a priori or a posteriori, would be the triumph of death. Life is the difference between life and death—and the impatience for its obliteration.

Wallace Stevens wrote, "In the long run the truth does not matter" (*Opus Posthumous*, 180). Truth is at best an external correspondence of signs with realities or a coherence among signs utterly indifferent to reality. Truth would not repair but only perpetuate the breach between thought and existence. In the same vein, "Realism is a corruption of reality" (*Opus Posthumous*, 166).[3] Realism is an act, a form, and a content of thought which derealizes the real by asserting it. "The difference [man] himself produces is identical with likeness, for he cannot get outside of himself" (*Søren Kierkegaards Papirer*, V B 5, 10). "Thus reason has brought God as near as possible, and yet he is as far away as possible; and this is the most ironical thing thinkable, that God has become pure negativity" (V B 5, 8; cf. below, sec. 5).

But "the whole thing is a trick" (V B 5, 5). Not just Climacus' suggestion that what man has put asunder God can join together, but the far more irritating insinuation that perhaps it was not man who put asunder in the first place. Man can neither think the absolutely different nor imagine a likeness that is not idolatrous. The absolute paradox is a "metaphysical crotchet" (PF, 46). A crotchet so outlandish that a man would have to lose his mind in order to hit upon it. Yet as the name [*Grille*] says, it's all in the head. How did it get there?

Like every chapter of the *Fragments*, chapter 3 ends in a dialogue between Climacus and his other. The repeated emergence of these little dissensions reveals two things. First, that Climacus is divided within, or against, himself by the matter under discus-

---

3. Cf. also "The ultimate value is reality" (166) and "The real is only the base. But it is the base" (160).

sion. And second, that the inner contention which surfaces in them has been present all along, agitating the depths of the argument. The argument is not an argument at all, but an agon between Climacus and his alienated self instigated by the "wholly other" that occasioned (spoke?) their discourse in the first place.

In his preface to the *Fragments* Climacus identifies himself as the frivolous exponent of the absolute paradox, but betrays another, more conscientious and socially responsible self. The former is an idler who writes for his own amusement and hopes that his work will make no contribution to the common welfare or the progress of knowledge. The latter, reflecting that perhaps the life of society and the public mind are already badly confused by their all-too-many and all-too-eager teachers and benefactors, surmises that the example of his self-indulgence—like Archimedes' concentration on his circles or Diogenes trundling his tub (PF, 3–4)—may be just what the age demands. At least a "kind and benevolent reader" may find something of use in his "piece" (PF, 5, 3). But even this modest expectation sustains nothing but ambiguity:

> It is not given to everyone to have his private tasks of meditation and reflection so happily coincident with the public interest that it becomes difficult to judge how far he serves merely himself and how far the public good. (PF, 3)

The failure to reconcile his public and private egos (the radical of this failure be what it may) prevents Climacus from formulating a doctrine or espousing an opinion:

> But what is my opinion? . . . Let no one ask me that. For next to knowing whether I have an opinion, nothing could be of less importance to another than knowing what my opinion is. (PF, 5–6A)

To have an opinion would be too much and too little. Too much, because it presupposes the unity and solidarity of the social self—domestic happiness and civic respectability—which the disjunct Climacus cannot count on. And also too little, for Climacus' opinion would be the opinion of a trifler, and if anyone were to be so polite as to assume that I have an opinion, and if he were to carry his gallantry to the extreme of adopting this opinion because he believed it to be mine, I should have to be sorry for his politeness, in that it was bestowed upon so unworthy an object, and for his opinion, if he has no other opinion than mine. (PF, 6)

The duplicity of its author, recollected at the (in)conclusion of each chapter, transforms his work from exposition to enactment. Climacus himself (whoever that is) describes it as a dance, in the service of thought, to the glory of God, and for his own enjoyment. A dance, however, in which his partner is (indomitable thought) the thought of death. A game. But a game played in all seriousness, in which (for reasons that are beginning to become clear) his life is at stake (PF, 6–7).

The appendix to chapter 3 discusses "offense" [*Forargelse, skandalon*]—the rejection by human reason of the absolute paradox—which it describes as an "acoustic illusion" (PF, 61). Reason's encounter with the paradox may issue either in understanding and reconciliation ("that happy passion" [PF, 67] as yet unnamed) or in scandal and alienation. The latter Climacus calls offense. The nature of offense, in particular its linguistic proclivities, shows that the passion of reason, however paradoxical, does not itself discover the absolute paradox. The passion of reason, like erotic passion, wants to find its other in order to be overwhelmed and fulfilled by it. But as erotic passion is fundamentally self-love and desires to surrender *itself* to *its own* other, so reason demands that *it* shall meet *its* other and achieve fulfillment by means of *self*-immolation. Realism, though its accomplishment would mean the end of (idealistic) reason, is to be the work of reason, its *self*-sacrifice. Hegel might have understood that.

The paradox, however, posits the impossibility of a rationally motivated encounter of reason with its other. The other is absolutely unlike reason and could not be met by reason in any course of ratiocination. Thereupon the paradox proposes the abolition of this absolute difference in absolute likeness: a reconciliation of reason and the paradox initiated, empowered, and enacted by the paradox. This (absolutely un-Hegelian) outcome reason cannot conceive—concerning which it must be said "with all possible ambiguity" that it "did not arise in the heart of any man" (PF, 138; cf. 1 Cor. 2: 7–9).

It follows that all offense (like "that happy passion") is passive. Never so passive that reason is wholly annihilated, but never so active that reason can extricate itself from scandal. Reason desires to surrender itself to the other; it cannot desire the dissolution of its autonomy by the other. Offense, like the paradox itself, is paradoxical.

The verbal expressions of offense, while they seem to come from reason, are only echoes of the paradox in the offended consciousness (PF, 63). Hence the acoustic illusion: the language of offense is nothing but a ventriloquism in which the paradox speaks through the mouth of reason. As his interlocutor notes, Climacus' own characterizations of offense are quotations from Tertullian, Hamann, Lactantius, Shakespeare, and Luther—partisans of the paradox one and all (PF, 66–67). As radically other than reason (even its paradoxical passion), the paradox generates its own rejection by reason. "Reason says that the Paradox is absurd, but this is mere mimicry, since the Paradox is the Paradox, *quia absurdum*" (PF, 65). In this way offense is an "indirect proof of the validity [*Rigtighed*] of the paradox," of its origin in the absolutely other than reason. Offense is "the mistaken reckoning [*den feile Regning*]" and the "invalid consequence [*Usandhedens Conseqvents*]" by which the paradox repels reason. Offense only "parodies [*bagvendt copierer*]" the paradox—copies it and gets it all backwards (PF, 63). Like a mimic, it testifies to the absolute priority of its original and its own absolute unoriginality.

The paradox of chapter 3 is identical with the "moment" of chapter 1. It marks the unmediated transition from the nonbeing of untruth to the being of truth. Because it is unmediated and unmediatable, the incursion of the wholly other into the structure of rationality introduces into that otherwise orderly world an unmanageable shiftiness. The appearance of the paradox inaugurates an interminable play of discontinuity and difference. The mere possibility of the absolutely other and the mere suggestion of the (impossible) absolute sameness of the absolutely other—the dialectic of sin and atonement proposed by Christianity—means that reason can no longer trust itself, not even its distrust. Once a hole is made—a breach in the continuity of rational structures—reason is perforated everywhere and always by the irrational. "Is perforated," because reason did not discover the irrational itself.

> The expression of offense is that the moment is folly, the paradox is folly; which is the claim of the paradox that reason is absurd, resounding as an echo from offense. . . . [S]ince the paradox has made reason absurd, reason's regard signifies nothing [*er intet Kjendetegn*]. (PF, 64–65A)

A possibility once is a necessity forever. That is what Christianity (if that is what it is) has introduced into the world: the possibility, once insinuated never eluctable, of an irrationality unmasterable by reason, an unreason which even the cunning of Hegelian rationality cannot surround and make its own. The dethronement, in principle, of all security. All it takes to destroy the confidence of reason for good and all is the rumor (which is now somehow inexplicably abroad in the world) that literally "all things are possible."[4] That little hint is sufficient to expose human thought and discourse intolerably to the infinite uncertainty of all things.[5] In Kierkegaard's language these phrases are names of God. God has become pure negativity. What could be more ironical?

III

Signed and dated. Signed with the sign of the cross and dated from the Incarnation. The mark of a unique and decisive historical occurrence. The temporal point of departure for an eternal consciousness and the historical foundation of eternal beatitude. In chapters 4 and 5 of the *Philosophical Fragments* Johannes Climacus meditates the historicity of the eternal.

That is the gist of the absolute paradox, "the historical made eternal, and the Eternal made historical" (PF, 76). The historical

---

4. *Sickness unto Death*, 173–74: "God *is* that all things are possible, and that all things are possible *is* God."

5. Cf. *Concluding Unscientific Postscript*, 80: "The Deity . . . is present as soon as the uncertainty of all things is thought infinitely."

coming-to-be of the eternal or the fulfilling of time by eternity could only issue (rationally) in the cancellation of time by eternity or the dispersion of the eternal along the moments of temporality. Climacus' concern is not with the concrete historical event of the Incarnation—historical content is irrelevant to his purposes—but with historicity in the abstract. The absurdity of the Incarnation is its structural (in principle) impossibility (PF, 73–74).

To "that happy passion" in which reason and the paradox meet with understanding Climacus gives the name "faith," though as he notes, it is not the name that matters. Faith is the opposite of offense and the God-given condition for understanding the God-given truth. It is also the occasion for a couple of precisions. Faith is not a kind of knowledge. All knowledge is either of the eternal or of the historical, never of their paradoxical conjunction (PF, 76). The relation of the sign (history) to the transcendent signified (eternity) is either a continuity in which the sign is absorbed into the signified (Socrates) or a discontinuity whose overcoming is absolutely impossible (Christianity). On the former view, cognition of the sign has no independent epistemic value: it is only incipient cognizance of the signified. On the latter view, cognition of the sign can never lead to cognition of the signified and vice versa, since they are by definition mutually exclusive.

Neither is faith an act of will. It is impossible to will without knowing what one is willing. Lacking this condition, which on the Christian view is the faith imparted by God, there can be no will. On the Christian hypothesis, the capacity both to know and to will is given with faith (PF, 77). God is neither immediately knowable [*lader sig jo ikke umiddelbart kjende*] nor conceivable [*lader sig ikke forestille*] (PF, 78). He is received and known only in the faith that he himself bestows. And faith is as paradoxical as the paradox itself (PF, 81).

Climacus' conclusion (he is discussing "the case of the contemporary disciple") is that there is no immediate contemporaneity with the paradox. "Contemporaneity" in this context means immediate presence, either the everywhere always presence of the eternal (with which all men at all times are contemporary) or the presence to each other of beings coincident in time (whose contemporaneity would be a function of the intersection of their spatiotemporal coordinates). A being that is at once historical and eternal, itself the breach with every form of immediacy, can have no immediate contemporary (PF, 83 ff.).

The contemporary of the paradox is neither the eyewitness nor the timeless subject of cognition, but the believer. And in the nonimmediacy of the "autopsy of faith," which iterates in the subject the paradoxicality of the Incarnation, every noncontemporary (in the immediate sense) may become a contemporary (in the paradoxical sense) of the paradox (PF, 84, 87). The moment of his transition from untruth to truth is identical with the moment of the coming-to-be of the eternal in time: his knowledge of God-in-time is, by virtue of the gift of faith, at once a vision of himself reborn to eternal consciousness.

If the distinction eternal truth-historical occasion be assimilated to the distinction transcendent signified-immanent sign—as it must, since the "Socratic" philosophy simply enunciates the norms of rationality as such—then problems arise concerning cognition of the sign, of the signified, and of their relationship. Knowledge of the temporal sign would be sensuous awareness or historical witness. Knowledge of the eternal signified would be purely intellectual. Knowledge of their relationship (signification) might be either direct or indirect. If it is direct, then the signified is immanent in the sign, and the sign as mere occasion vanishes as soon as the signified is known. If it is indirect, then there is no transition at all from sign to signified; cognition is arrested at the level of the sign, and passage to the signified is indefinitely deferred. Or else—the Christian alternative—the union of sign and signified (the absolute paradox) is apprehended in the absolutely paradoxical passion of faith.

Pace Hegel, there can be no mediation of time and eternity. Mediate cognition of the signified by means of (immediate) cognition of the sign would require the presence of the signified, if not to the sign, then at least to $sign^1$, $sign^2$, or $sign^n$. At some point either the Socratic view is reinstated—the immanence of the signified in the sign—or else the Christian dichotomy stands fast and the absolute paradox is the only escape from the schizophrenia of cognition. Either presence or absence: either the eternal signified is present in the historical sign, or the signified is simply absent and cannot be recuperated save at the unimaginable and unthinkable limit of the "autopsy of faith." A faith whose "objective" condition (the moment of incarnation) and whose "subjective" condition (the moment of conversion) are themselves unthinkably and unimaginably conjoined.

The relation of sign and signified is both a likeness and a difference. The likeness, which at some point must be identity, cannot be preserved without, at that point, denying the difference and fusing sign and signified. The difference cannot be maintained without denying the likeness and converting the difference of sign and signified into their mutual exclusion. A logic of analogy—of likeness-*in*-difference—would fall prey to the dialectic of likeness *versus* difference—every analogy consists of an element of likeness juxtaposed to an element of difference—which would relocate the problem (*ad infinitum*) without solving it. To say that analogy uniquely and unanalyzably merges likeness and difference is to beg off the problem with a plea of ineffable mystery that is conceptually no advance on, though conceivably more ingratiating than, the absolute paradox itself. This side of mystery, either the knowledge of the signified is given with the knowledge of the sign or indefinitely postponed by it.

The absolute paradox is that the temporal sign and the eternal signified are and are apprehended as at once absolutely other and absolutely same.

But of course the very idea of a sign-signified relation—the concept of signification itself—incorporates the paradox. The sign must participate the being of the signified; else it cannot mediate *cognition* of the signified. But at the same time the sign must be distinct from the signified; else it cannot *mediate* cognition of the signified. Although it contains analytically the notion of the signified (to be a sign is to signify the signified), the concept of the sign insists upon the sign's identity with itself and its difference from the signified. Identity and difference alike are affirmed and compromised by the conception of their relation.

The paradox of the sign is the paradox Augustine found in Platonism: the forms are both known and not known in their appearances. A discomforting paradox, which led to the separation, in the subsequent history of Platonism, of Neoplatonic gnosis (a knowledge of the forms that has sloughed off appearances) and New Academy skepticism (an acquaintance with appearances unstructured by form). It was this paradox to which the Christian-revisionist Platonism of Augustine counterposed as resolution the absolute paradox of the Incarnation.

It was the Christian Augustine who discovered the paradox of the sign in Platonism. Is it possible that the paradox of signification is a Christian innovation? Climacus' fascination with the relation of alterity and identity would suggest as much.

In the (unusually long) dialogue that concludes chapter 5 and the book, Climacus finally concedes his identity with his interlocutor, in response to whose opening (and untypically conciliatory) speech he says: "Well said, I would reply, did not modesty forbid; for you speak as if it were myself" (PF, 133). As the discourse of *his* other (alter ego) the interlocutor is Climacus' unconscious, at first repressed and rejected, now—albeit somewhat grudgingly and with a certain coyness—acknowledged. He is as Climacus' own depth—the cultural language in which Climacus' self is originally encoded—the one for whom this discourse is designed and to whom it is addressed. At the end of the work Climacus and himself are reconciled.

Alternatively, it is possible that Johannes Climacus is the unconscious voice of his more "normal" interlocutor. The latter remarks:

> I have now read your exposition through to the end, and really not without a certain degree of interest, noting with pleasure that there was no catch word [*Stikord*], no invisible script [*usynlig Skrift*]. But how you twist and turn, so that . . . you always manage to mix in a little word [*et lidet Ord*] that is not your own, which awakens disturbing recollections. (PF, 132A)

Otherness is a repeater. And it is just possible that this entire discourse—the *Philosophical Fragments*—is the voice of another than both Climacus and his interlocutor: the suppressed language of Western Christendom, still to be heard beneath its song and clang. A song of mockery, unlicensed but inevitable. A "shrill laughter, like the mocking nature-tones on the island of Ceylon." The revenge of the law of contradiction on an age that preferred wonders and wonder-workers no matter what the cost (cf. PF, 135–36).

Or perhaps—this unspeakably and with "all possible ambiguity"—the *Fragments* is the discourse, unconscious because unutterable, of the Absolute Other, now at last and impossibly reconciled with human speech. The ultimate iteration—and so the closure—of alterity. As the terminal dialogues repeatedly point out, this "did not arise in the heart of any man." Climacus himself—and his other—say so. Is it conceivable that the voice of Johannes Climacus (J. C.) is the voice of God? The historical costume, ill-fitting and unbecoming, is irresistibly proffered.

In which (any) case, while we may not say that the project here unfolded is true, we may at least be certain that it makes an advance upon Socrates. Certain, that is, with all possible ambiguity. For, in conclusion and with respect to the beginning, "'When the question cannot be asked the answer need not trouble us, and the difficulty becomes slight indeed.'—'This does not quite follow; for suppose the difficulty lay in perceiving that one cannot ask such a question'" (PF, 111). That perception may be difficult indeed. Whereof one cannot speak one must keep silent. But how else than by speaking may one perceive that whereof one cannot speak?

IV

Between chapters 4 and 5 of his discussion Climacus inserts an "Interlude," comparable to the entr'acte played during an intermission in the theater. Its purpose is to create the illusion that time has passed, say the 1,843 years that separate the eyewitness of the paradox from the latest generation of noncontemporary disciples. Although there is little more than temporal difference between contemporary and noncontemporary, Climacus' Interlude occupies a tense moment: the moment between acts during which it is possible, among other things, to walk out.

However paradoxical (what else?) its conclusion, the argument of chapters 4 and 5 is the essence of simplicity, based as it is (dichotomies again!) on the strictly exclusive disjunction of time and eternity. The Interlude is meant to clarify this disjunction and pursue its implications so as to substantiate the argument it sponsors. The question it poses is, "Is the past more necessary than the future? Or, does the possible by becoming actual thereby become more neccessary than it was?" (PF, 89A).

To open this question Climacus distinguishes between qualitative change [*alloiosis*] and coming-to-be [*kinesis, Tilblivelse*]. In the former, essence [*Vaesen*] changes while being [*Vaeren*] remains the same. In the latter, essence remains the same while being changes. If essence did not remain the same in coming-to-be, then A could never come to be but would in the process of becoming change into B. Coming-to-be is (just) a change from nonexistence [*ikke at vaere til*] to existence [*at vaere til, Tilvaerelse*], essence abiding. It is, in other terms, a transition from possibility [*Mulighed*] to actuality [*Virkelighed*], where possibility is the being which is still nonbeing and actuality the being which is indeed being.

It is important to note the *pseudo*-Aristotelian character of Climacus' description of *kinesis*. Not quite the movement from potency to act, coming-to-be is the change from possibility to actuality.

By contrast with possibility and actuality, necessity [*det Nødvendige*] cannot change. It cannot undergo anything. Necessity "always relates itself to itself and relates itself to itself in the same way" (PF, 91). Necessity simply *is*.

Possibility is annihilated by actualization. Not only the excluded possibility (−A, for example, when A is actualized), but also the actualized possibility (A), which is negated *as* possibility when it is made actual. Possibility and actuality are mutually exclusive. Each is the nonbeing of the other. Wherefore necessity could not be a synthesis of possibility and actuality, the Hegelian unity of *an sich* and *für sich*, since any such synthesis would be contradictory:

> Possibility and actuality do not differ in essence but in being; how could there from this difference be formed a synthesis constituting necessity, which is not a determination [*Bestemmelse*] of being but a determination of essence, since it is the essence of the necessary to be. (PF, 91–92)

The discrimination is crucial. Possibility and actuality are categories of being—the only categories of being, and contradictories. But necessity is a "determination of essence." It is that the essence of which is to be and thus escapes the disjunction of possible and actual. There is therefore no transition from the realm of being (possibility-actuality) to the realm of essence (necessity), or vice versa. Necessity "stands entirely by itself" (PF, 92A).

Since necessity is excluded from the realm of coming-to-be, the latter (necessarily?) takes places with freedom [*Frihed*]. Becoming has no (logical) ground [*Grund*], though it does have a cause [*Aarsag*]. And all causes terminate in a freely effecting [*fritvirkende*] cause. It is only in the domain of freedom that anything really *happens*. The realm of freedom is the realm of history.

The eternal, which is also the necessary, has no history in any sense. It sustains no relationship to possibility, actuality, change, or freedom. Nature is pure synchrony (spatiality, *Nebeneinander*), save for the fact that it has, as a whole, come into being. History is pure diachrony (temporality), save for the fact that it presupposes space as its locus. Nature has no "dialectic with respect to time" (PF, 94). Strictly speaking, nothing happens in nature. It is always, if cyclically, the same, for which reason there are *laws* of nature. But historical events, for which there are no laws, are the operations of freely working causes terminating in the working of an absolutely free cause.

Climacus' desire to identify the domain of history and distinguish it from the realm of nature prescribes his substitution of the categories possibility-actuality for the Aristotelian potency-act. Aristotle's concern is with nature, which from Climacus' perspective is as a totality not necessary (since it has come to be) but in all its parts is a system of simultaneous nonevents. In potency the act is already contained and will emerge. Every potency, moreover, is rooted in (strictly, *is*) a prior act. But possibility is just the nonbeing of its corresponding actuality. The freedom of history—the unmotivated discontinuity of historical action—is opposed to the quasi-necessity—the explicability and continuity—of natural change.

However, although Climacus' appeal to Aristotle is oblique, the classical allusions strewn throughout the Interlude serve a purpose. By aligning his own discourse with that of the "honest" Greeks, Climacus hopes to ally himself with their integrity and oppose himself to the "mendaciousness" of the Hegelians (*Søren Kierkegaards Papirer*, V A 98). This in spite of the fact that he deploys some of Hegel's categories and says things that no Greek could imagine.

The past (to continue with Climacus' text) is necessary only in the sense that what's done cannot be undone. Its "thus" [*saaledes*] is immutable. But because it did happen, the past was not and is not necessary. Its "how" [*hvorledes*] might have been otherwise. The future is no more necessary than the past, but no less so merely for the fact that it has not yet happened. If the past were necessary, the future would also be necessary. If necessity were to be found anywhere in the realm of happening, past and future could not be distinguished. For a strict determinism time is unreal, and the distinction between past and future nugatory. To claim (as Hegelian philosophers of history did) to discern the necessity of the past is no more and no less rational than to claim to predict the future with certainty. If necessity were once to get a foothold in the process of becoming, then past, future, freedom, change, and history would all be illusions.

But there is no necessity in becoming. The past, having come to be, is uncertain. As actualized, however, it annuls all possibilities including its own. In that sense the past is certain. With its duality of certainty (its "thus") and uncertainty (its "how") the past is confronted in wonder and apprehended in belief [*Tro*]. Belief is an attitude in which (objective) uncertainty is negated by (subjective) assurance. Its epistemological structure corresponds to the ontological structure of the past, which is an actuality that negates a possibility.

What is true of the past is true of all becoming, including the becoming of the present. Even here the conjunction of certainty (annihilated possibility) and uncertainty (the antecedent possibility annihilated in its actualization) engenders wonder. Doubt succumbs to the uncertainty. Belief, comprehending the uncertainty and sublating doubt, affirms the certainty.

Belief is not an act of cognition. All cognition, sensuous or intellectual, is infallible. It apprehends essences, sensible or intelligible, which are constant (necessary). Belief affirms becoming, which is free and fallible. Like its opposite, doubt, belief is a passion, a resolution of the will, not an inference from ground to consequent. In this respect it answers to the free causation that is the instrumentality of becoming.

The contemporary of a historical event has his sensuous or intellectual knowledge of its "what." A noncontemporary has the testimony of contemporaries. Belief follows no more and no less from testimony than from direct cognition. As far as belief is concerned (this is the gist of the argument in chapters 4 and 5), whether one is or is not contemporary with a historical event is a matter of indifference.

Climacus now applies these precisions to the assertion that God has come into existence. As a historical assertion this formula proposes an object of belief [*Tro*] in the ordinary sense. As an assertion that affirms a contradiction—that the eternal (the necessary) has come to be in time (the domain of freedom and change)—it defines the object of faith [*Tro*] in the eminent sense. The Incarnation, as the historical event which in principle could not happen, is apprehended by that faith which is neither an act of knowledge nor an act of will but a divine gift accepted with divine subvention.

The existence of God—properly his eternal and necessary being—cannot be proven, as chapter 3 has shown. Neither is it a matter of faith. The object of faith is the content of the moment: not that God *is*, but that he *has been* in the past and continually *comes to be* in the experience of the twice born.

For Socrates history as a whole is only an occasion for reversion to the eternal. It is from all eternity continuous with the eternal and from all eternity subsumed into the eternal. The being of time, a diminution of the being of eternity, has no reality outside or against its eternal source. On Climacus' Christian hypothesis (if that is what it is), history is abruptly discontinuous with the eternal and set against it, so that the marriage of time and eternity in the moment is absolutely paradoxical. For Hegel history is continuous with the eternal but more than an occasion of eternal truth: history itself is the reality and truth of the eternal. The conjunction of history and eternity is superlatively the work of reason.

That is the "mendaciousness" of Hegel, that he wants the best of both incompossible worlds. He will have his Socratic cake and also, like a good Christian, eat it. The *Philosophical Fragments* is meant to affront that Hegelian option. In the Interlude Climacus has guaranteed the incommunication of time (freedom) and eternity (necessity) and assured that the allegation of their communication in "the fullness of time" is a contradiction which no cognitive inference or determination of the will can resolve.

But surely words like "guaranteed" and "assured" are devious in this context. What makes the guarantee valid and the assurance trustworthy? Only the assumption that the Teacher has already come and gone (PF, 89). Given Christianity, Climacus' definitions and exclusions tell it like it is. Otherwise they are arbitrary and nonsensical stipulations. Only if Christianity is *already there*—by virtue of the absurd, for no man could posit it—does Climacus' very un-Greek diversion of Greek categories and his very un-Hegelian inversion of Hegelian categories make sense. Given that unthinkable presupposition, his analysis is impeccably rational.

Climacus, like Socrates and like necessity, is always "repeating the same things, 'about the same things'" in order to create the "illusion" that time—1,843 years!—has passed. The conjunction of freedom and necessity in the language of the Interlude is no less refractory to reason than the absolute paradox itself. Addressing his reader, Climacus says:

> . . . I do not by any means doubt that you have completely understood and assented to the newest philosophy, which like the modern age seems to suffer from a curious distraction, confusing the superscription with the execution; for what age and what philosophy was ever so great as our own—in superscriptions. (PF, 90A)[6]

If superscription is to execution as possibility is to actuality, then perhaps the Interlude should be subtitled "a possibility." Standing as it does between past and present, the Greeks and Hegel, the Interlude stands also—possibly—between two worlds, one dead, the other powerless to be born. It is—possibly—a piece of becoming in its own right, the coming-to-be of the impossible possibility of the historical coming-to-be of the eternal.

A lengthy footnote coaches this reading of the Interlude:

> The Absolute Method, Hegel's discovery, is a difficulty even in Logic, aye a glittering tautology, coming to the assistance

---

6. Cf. *Stages on Life's Way*, 258–68, "A Possibility," in which the paralyzing terrors of possibility are explored. Cf. also *Concept of Dread, passim*, on the effects of possibility.

of academic superstition with many signs and wonders. In the historical sciences it is a fixed idea. The fact that the method here at once begins to become concrete, since history is the concretion of the Idea, has given Hegel an opportunity to exhibit extraordinary learning, and a rare power of organization, inducing a quite sufficient commotion in the historical material. But it has also promoted a distraction of mind in the reader, so that . . . he may have forgotten to inquire whether it now really did become evident at the end, at the close of this journey of enchantment, as was repeatedly promised in the beginning, and what was of course the principal issue, for the want of which not all the glories of the world could compensate, what alone could be a sufficient reward for the unnatural tension in which one had been held—that the method was valid. Why at once become concrete, why at once begin to experiment *in concreto*? Was it not possible to answer this question in the dispassionate brevity of abstraction, which has no means of distraction or enchantment, this question of what it means that the Idea becomes concrete, what is the nature of coming into existence, what is one's relationship to that which has come into existence, and so forth? Just as it surely might have been cleared up in the Logic what "transition" is and means, before going over to write three volumes describing its workings in the categories. . . . (PF, 96 n.–97 n.)

Does Climacus offer his little Interlude as an abstract and undistracting concretion of the categories, a transition in which the meaning of "transition" is made . . . clear? Ostensibly the Interlude connects the past (the actualized and so abrogated possibility) and the present (the possibility now awaiting actualization by a free cause). So conceived, the Interlude, entirely in the spirit of the newest philosophy, is a mediation. As it connects past and present, so also it mediates essence and existence, necessity and freedom, eternity and time, and so forth. A veritable paragon of the absolute method, perhaps even its paradigm.

Yet it cannot be an accident that the author never explains the relationship of the necessary and the possible, the changeless and the changing. Nor does he clarify the double relationship of essence to the necessary and to the possible. Essence is both that which is necessarily self-identical (relates itself to itself always in the same way) and that which comes to be (is actualized) in every spasm of becoming. These conjunctions are taken for granted but never accounted for, perhaps even prohibited, in Climacus' singularly well-written, brief, and undistractingly abstract theoretical resumé.

The Interlude's "mediation" is ironic. Which is not quite the same as no mediation at all, but rather: a mediation denied. In preliminary drafts of the Interlude Kierkegaard says that it is the passion of philosophy to minimize the concrete in order that the "thought" may not be confused or allowed to fall into oblivion. And in order that the reader may not be fooled with diversions and entertainments [*Ordspil og Vittigheder*: "word games and witticisms"], but enlightened with understanding (*Søren Kierkegaards Papirer*, V B 14; cf. also V B 41). It is therefore crucial to philosophy to be absolutely clear about the distinction between abstract and concrete, ideal and actual. That would account for the irony of this "mediation," as well as the algebraically abstract language of the *Fragments* as a whole. The point is to guarantee that the essential (abstract) shock of the absolute paradox will not be confused by the rich but distracting (concrete) history of Christianity.

If Climacus' project is to go beyond Socrates without, like Hegel, rushing beyond faith as well, then it must be irrational. Becoming and history themselves must be irrational in a way that no Greek would dream of and no German tolerate: a play of the categories between the no-longer-possible serene rationality of the Greek and the never-to-be-actual synthesis of absolute knowledge. *Must* be? Given Christianity, without which neither these disjunctions nor their reconciliation were (!) conceivable. As Climacus says in another work, reality is an *inter-esse* between the actual and the ideal (*Concluding Unscientific Postscript*, 279): a being-between the no longer and the not yet, between the possible which when actualized is no longer possible and the actual which is never possible. The impossible possibility of transforming that *inter-esse*, suspended in abstraction, into the concretion of becoming: that is the awful and consoling thought with which Christianity disturbs and allures the passion of philosophy.

One of Walker Percy's characters has suggested, by not saying so, that Christianity is a technique of reentry from the orbit of transcendence (Percy, 269, 277, 291). Irony, once you hit upon it, puts the self into orbit. Only Christianity can bring it down. That is what Climacus, speaking ironically, says. His Interlude is the ironic moment—the moment of absolute freedom—from which Christianity absurdly promises to save us.

The Greeks defined for Western consciousness the conditions of intelligibility and truth: the "Socratic" view. Christianity has perforated consciousness with the possibility of radical uncertainty, radical insecurity, and radical irrationality. But the inhabitants of that consciousness have, through carelessness, misunderstanding, bad faith, and the force of habit, come to regard this absurdity as a matter of course. His subject matter being what it is—the absolute paradox—Kierkegaard's strategy is to promote not understanding but ineluctable confrontation. His device—the ram in the afternoon—is recommended by the desperate hope that men will pay an exorbitant price to acquire that which they were not sufficiently ironic to recognize as a gift.

V

In 1841 Kierkegaard published his master's thesis, *The Concept of Irony with Constant Reference to Socrates*. From his many characterizations (see 224, 230–34, 238–40, 253, 255, 271–75, 278–79) it is possible to conflate a definition: irony is the principle of infinite abstract negative subjectivity. The discovery of this principle is credited to the sophists, who acted on it without knowing what they were doing, but eminently to Socrates, who formulated it *as* a principle and practiced it systematically (*Concept of Irony*, pt. 1, chap. 3).

"Infinite abstract negative subjectivity" stands for the liberty of the subject to refuse any determination proposed to him or projected onto him. Absolute freedom: the capacity to say No without limit and without qualification. Which negative capability in a deep sense *is* the subject.

Irony in the literary sense, the figure of speech so-called, is the verbal expression of this negative freedom. Of necessity, an oblique and problematic *modus loquendi*. Infinite abstract negative subjectivity could hardly be rendered in the finite concrete positive objectivities of ordinary speech. The principle of irony bespeaks itself in words that negate what they say, indeterminately, as they say it.

The textbook examples of irony, like the usual practice of irony, are most imperfect (see *Concept of Irony*, 264–65). For instance, "Brutus is an honorable man." Antony's statement negates what it says, but not indeterminately. The Roman mob knows that he means exactly the opposite of what he says, that is, "Brutus is a scoundrel." Similarly, the standard textbook definition—"saying one thing and meaning the contrary"—makes irony a special case of allegory: a finite not an infinite negation.

A better example would be the Greek imagined by Kierkegaard, who, invited to dinner, replies: "You can count on me, I shall certainly come; but I must make an exception for the contingency that a tile happens to blow down from a roof and kills me; for in that case I cannot come" (*Concluding Unscientific Postscript*, 81). The very randomness of the excepted contingency makes it clear that the speaker, though he probably will come to dinner, regards himself as in no position to make any commitments whatsoever.

An even better example would be the pious qualification we often (thoughtlessly) append to our assurances: "God willing." A codicil that tacitly acknowledges the infinite uncertainty of all things; that is, indeterminately and in the abstract ("in principle") disallows all certainty (cf. *Concluding Unscientific Postscript*, 80).

Irony—in principle, in fact, and in discourse—is the anomaly of the absolute. Etymologically, the "untied" or the "unbound." Irony is the negative and abstract absolute of subjective freedom, the emancipation of the subject (by which the subject is constituted as such) from every finite ("objective") determination.

The concept of irony instructs the interpretation of Kierkegaard's theory and practice of indirect communication. Indirect communication is a "means of expression" wholly self-consuming. It negates not only the said but also the saying. In a word: communication from the standpoint of irony. All of Kierkegaard's texts are written from that standpoint. It is impossible to understand them unless one keeps this constantly in mind. Whether it is possible to understand them *with* this in mind is another question.

A Kierkegaardian text, like any other, is a system of signifiers.

It is one thing to find an interpretation of this system. In the case of the *Philosophical Fragments*, the interpretation that is irresistibly insinuated is Christianity. It is another thing altogether to ask about the sense of the words. The former is easy, since Kierkegaard has provided all the clues, everything but the "historical costume" (PF, 137). That, he adds, "every divinity student" should be able to furnish (*Concluding Unscientific Postscript*, 14). Finding the meaning is much harder but absolutely indispensable. For unless you know the meaning, the interpretation is worthless. It is not much help to know that Kierkegaard is talking about Christianity if you don't know what he is saying about it. And what he is saying about whatever he is talking about is something you get only by deciphering his language. It is illicit to take the formal properties of the interpretation—some system of Christian doctrine—and read them back into Kierkegaard's words. There is no guarantee that what Kierkegaard is saying about Christianity is what anyone else has ever said about it. Indeed, there is massive reason to think otherwise.

Direct (un-ironic) communication is the use of verbal signs to refer to something, thought or things, with which sender and receiver are both already acquainted. Or perhaps to direct attention to something with which the sender is familiar and with which the receiver may become familiar if suitably alerted. In any case, this ordinary usage is intentionally referential, and it presupposes on the part of both communicator and recipient a common knowledge or capacity for knowledge of a referent signified by language, transcendent of language, and in principle public. Meaning, in direct communication, is taken for granted. The order of the signifiers is either determined by the signified or given in advance by the linguistic code, which is itself an object of common knowledge and thus a kind of referent. In direct communication, sense and interpretation tend to coincide.

An indirect (ironic) communication is a system of signifiers that obviates reference. When we read, we ordinarily construct hierarchies of signification. At least we project a referent, a transcendent signified, of which the text is signifier. Ordinary uses of language encourage this hierarchizing tendency by offering themselves as icons, indices, or what-have-you of facts or ideas. The order of the sign-surface reflects to us our conventional notions about the order of things and its relation to the order of words. But if the sign-surface is disordered with respect to ordinary usage and conventional notions of meaning, then we are led to reflect upon the signs and the sign-function itself.

The language of the *Fragments* proscribes any hierarchizing of sign and referent. "Christianity" is proposed, by the text itself, as the interpretation of this language. But it does not in any ordinary sense "stand for" Christianity; it does not conventionally describe it, picture it, or point to it. It pretends to elicit Christianity deductively from hypotheses, but the pretense is exposed. It pretends to imagine Christianity fairy-tale fashion, but the imagination fails. And so on. As an indirect communication the *Fragments* is a system of signs that systematically severs its bonds with any referent that it might be supposed to designate. The meaning of the text is therefore to be sought exclusively in the interrelations of the signifiers themselves, their reflection upon each other, and not in their allusion to any transcendent thought or thing.

But there is another turn of the screw. A further irony. Indirect communication not only impedes reference, it also confuses connotation. The relations of the signifiers with each other are deranged, so that meaning is indefinitely postponed. Kierkegaard's texts conventionally violate the conventions of the linguistic codes he works in, philosophical and literary. The movement from signifier to signifier does not yield a satisfactory ordering of the whole. The signifiers invite attention to themselves and to the process of signification. But they do not converge upon a core of sense. The *Fragments* begins several times to propound the unthinkable, interrupts itself to underscore the banality and/or unintelligibility of what it proposes, asserts the superior veridicality of the banal and the unintelligible, and begins again. Only to end (inconclusively) with a dubious "moral"—whatever else this may be, it is certainly different—and the claim, doubly ironic, to have made an advance beyond the master of irony himself (PF, 139). The inconstancy of the sign-system, perpetually discounting its implications and cancelling its commitments, prevents the emergence of a stable pattern of meaning.

Indirect communication occurs in the expansion of the interface between sign and referent and in the indefinite deferment of sense procured by the restless play of the signifiers. This is the source of the mystification systematically practiced in Kierkegaard's texts. It is the source, also, of their literary—or as he preferred to say, "aesthetic"—character. For that is what identifies literary language as such: the use of verbal signs to call attention to themselves and to the act of signifying—that is, to block reference and to postpone meaning. Signs as motifs. Poetry and all that.

The pursuit of these exquisite involutions and hermetic introversions prompts an obvious question: why call this a technique of *communication*? Literary language may justify its crypticality and its narcissism by reference to the intrinsic value of the verbal object. But a communication, presumably, communicates something. What is communicated by Kierkegaard's works? In the light of Kierkegaard's own thematic preoccupation with the indecisiveness of reflection it is tempting to suppose that what is communicated is just this indecision itself: the impossibility of halting by reflection the process of reflection and the impossibility of a return by way of reflection to the reality from which reflection is a departure.

The aesthete of *Either/Or* remarks that what the philosophers say about reality is like a sign in a shop window that reads "Pressing Done Here." If you take your clothes in to be pressed, you find that they do not press clothes—they only sell signs (1: 31). It is tempting to conjecture that what is here said about the philosophers is also true of Kierkegaard. For his own texts are like series of signs, each of which reads "This Way to the Sign." It is tempting, that is, to advance the hypothesis that Kierkegaard's texts are "really" about language, and that the purpose of indirect communication is simply to exhibit the capacity of language (= reflection) for uninterrupted self-reference and interminable deferment (*Johannes Climacus*, 146–54). It would certainly be ironic to think that the truth communicated by indirect communication is a truth that can only be communicated by not being communicated at all.

That is tempting and not altogether wrong. But perhaps not good enough. Or better, a bit too ironic (and therefore not ironic at all), like the possibility, entertained and rejected by Climacus, that God might have topped his own understatement in the Incarnation by entering the world and passing through it completely unnoticed (PF, 69; cf. *Søren Kierkegaards Papirer*, V B 5, 8).

That, he suggests, would not be irony but wrath. An ironic communication, albeit incalculably indirect, is still communication—the silence *in* speech, not the silencing *of* speech.

Because it confounds sense and obstructs reference, Climacus' language may be said to undercut itself as language. But that is too facile. How can language, *being* language, undercut itself *as* language? Can language ever do more than repeat itself, even if not especially when it tries to deny itself? Is literary language a special case, an exception, or is it not rather a distillation of the "essence" of language: to question meaning by multiplying meanings and to fold the referentiality of discourse back on itself. Human language, as Climacus observes, is rooted in self-love (PF, 34–35). Its extravagant fascination with itself in literature is not a perversion of language but a singularly pellucid manifestation of its true nature.

Indirect communication—negative capability, the literary or aesthetic principle—is also, Climacus knew, Socrates' maieutic, a *magisterium* perfected in ignorance and ironic detachment. But Christianity is something else again: not man's communication to man but God's communication to man. The expression of God's (strictly unimaginable) love for man and the execution of his (strictly unthinkable) resolve to consummate this love in the union of Incarnation (PF, chap. 2 passim; PS 20–34).

Exceeding the normative indirection of Socrates ("this project indisputably goes further than the Socratic" [PF, 139A]), the *Philosophical Fragments* wills to be the expression of this expression and the execution of this execution. Which it can only accomplish in the mood of audacious suggestion, by asking the unaskable question (cf. above, sec. 1): is it possible that Something Else has invaded language, foisting upon it both an interpretation and a meaning, dissolving its autonomy, enslaving it to a sense and committing it to a referent—all of which, as language, it must and will be free of? Is it possible that there is Something that can make language speak what cannot be spoken? Possible. But scarcely thinkable. And surely unspeakable.

> So then perhaps it is no poem, or at any rate not one for which any human being is responsible. . . . But then my soul is filled with new wonder, even more, with the spirit of worship; for it would surely have been strange had this

poem been a human production. . . . as you yourself voluntarily exclaim, we stand here before the *Miracle*. . . . the poem is so different from every human poem as not to be a poem at all, but the *Miracle*. (PF, 44–45)

But what is the difference between a poem and—the Miracle? That is a question hardly to be answered. Can it even be asked?

Maybe that is what Kierkegaard meant when, in presenting himself poetically to posterity, he ascribed his work to "Providence," and described that work itself as a "teleological suspension in relation to the communication of truth."[7] That God is uniquely revealed as God in man's nothingness and need is a common theme in Kierkegaard's writings.[8] Man's weakness is God's opportunity. So also perhaps the impotence of language to lay hold on being, its necessary and voluntary self-contentment,[9] is the aperture through which the Other intrudes itself into the affairs and the discourse of men. The language of Kierkegaard's texts is not, like the language of Socratic dialogue, self-effacing. It is effaced in advance by the unspeakable which is incredibly given it to utter. More ironical even than the irony of Socrates, the *Philosophical Fragments* is Kierkegaard's discourse of the Other.

VI

In 1852 Kierkegaard made the following entry in his journal:

Melancholy

Somewhere in the Psalms it says of the rich man that he collects a treasure with great care and "knows not who shall inherit from him": and so too I shall leave behind me, intellectually speaking, a not so little capital; alas, and I know at the same time who will inherit from me, that figure which is so enormously distasteful to me, who up till

---

7. *Point of View*, 91 and chap. 3 *passim*. On this whole matter, cf. Edward W. Said, *Beginnings: Intention and Method*, 73–78, 85–88.

8. Cf., e.g., the discourse, "Man's Need of God Constitutes His Highest Perfection."

9. Cf. PF, 18–21, 20n. on the willed but inevitable nature of sin.

now has always, and will continue to inherit all good things: the Docent, the professor. . . .*

*And even if "the professor" were to come across this it would not stop him, it would not have the effect of making his conscience prick him, no, this too would be taught. And this remark again, if the professor were to come across it, would not stop him, no, this too would be taught. For the professor is longer than the tapeworm (which a woman lately got rid of and which measured, according to her husband, who gave thanks in the paper, 200 feet) longer even than that is the professor; and no man in whom there is "the professor" can be freed by another man from that tapeworm, only God can do that, if the man is willing.[10]

Anyone who writes about Kierkegaard (if he is not *all* professor) must confront the tapeworm in fear and trembling. Kierkegaard himself did not escape altogether. Who scribbled that little note in his journal and then doubled back and wrote a footnote to it? Devolutions of the tapeworm.

The image is to be taken with all gravity. Reflection, which is another name for language, is interminable, segment after segment propagating itself and prolonging itself. Without relief. Unless the head is rooted out. The principle must be extirpated. But, as Kierkegaard says, only God can do that.

Who?

---

10. I quote from *The Journals of Søren Kierkegaard*, nos. 1268 and 1269. I have altered Dru's translation. The original may be found in *Søren Kierkegaards Papirer*, X^4 A 628, 629.

6.
THE LOSS OF THE WORLD IN KIERKEGAARD'S ETHICS

Any inquiry into the metaphysical foundations of Kierkegaard's ethics runs into the unique hermeneutical problem posed by his method of indirect communication. On his own admonition, Kierkegaard's books, even those that are richest in theoretical content, are not to be read as doctrinal compendia or philosophical essays. In his ethical writings Kierkegaard offers no system of norms, values, or precepts. Except incidentally, and then usually in a polemic interest, there is no analysis of moral phenomena as such. Certainly there is no explicit concern for the metaphysical basis of ethics. There is only a strategy, calculated, as he put it, "to make aware."[1] His utterances on ethics are the tactics of that strategy. They are elements in a rhetoric of edification, whose meaning is not enclosed within them as their content but projected beyond them as their effect on the reader.

---

1. See, among many references, *Point of View*, 138, 155; and *The Journals of Søren Kierkegaard*, no. 1001.

The effect intended by Kierkegaard's rhetoric is a certain self-relationship ("subjectivity" or "inwardness"), which cannot be formulated and given out as doctrine or information but which the reader is required to achieve on his own. The books provide only the occasion, the impetus, and the demand. For example, the proposition "Truth is subjectivity" (*Concluding Unscientific Postscript*, 179ff.; hereinafter cited in this essay as CUP) is not a philosophical indicative but a rhetorical imperative. Translated into the language of personal address, it says: "You reader! Whatever you believe, whatever you claim to know, remember in fear and trembling that you hold this faith and stake this claim solely on the strength of your own freedom to do so, with no guarantee more ultimate than your own decision, at your own risk, and on your own responsibility!" This charge to the reader, which is the real and indirect import of "Truth is subjectivity," is as far as it could be from the epistemological relativism which the proposition immediately suggests. What the reader is to get from "Truth is subjectivity" is not the comforting assurance that "it doesn't matter what you believe," but rather the existential terror—that glimpse of the abyss which is itself a confrontation with the Absolute—that ensues when "the uncertainty of all things is thought infinitely" (CUP, 80).

It is possible and salutary to read Kierkegaard as he meant to be read, to let the rhetoric have its effect without bothering one's head over metaphysical doubts. And yet Kierkegaard could not really hope that his half-learned readers would refuse to lay their dialectical hands on his work.[2] Precisely because of their rhetorical indirection, his writings do not preclude but demand philosophical interpretation and criticism. Every sustained act of rhetoric, insofar as it projects a determinate state of affairs as its meaning and satisfaction, also structures by implication the universe which makes possible both that state of affairs and the practice of the rhetoric demanding it. The purpose of this essay is to evaluate the suggestion of *acosmism* that is found in the ethical writings of Kierkegaard, especially the *Concluding Unscientific Postscript*. For this purpose it is not sufficient to understand the end intended by Kierkegaard's program. It is also necessary, over

---

2. CUP, "A First and Last Declaration," unpaged (= p. 554).

Kierkegaard's objections, to investigate the metaphysical groundwork by which both program and end are sustained.

The problem of acosmism is posed by two Kierkegaardian propositions central to the argument of the *Postscript*. (1) The ethical reality of the subject is the only reality. (2) All realities other than his own the subject encounters only in the mode of possibility, by thinking them.

From the *Postscript* we know that the "ethical reality of the subject" means neither the subject's inner intentions nor his external actions nor the two together, but rather the *tension* of inwardness *from* will *to* performance. To exist as a human being means *to be between* (*inter-esse*) thinking and being (CUP, 279). The reality of the individual is his *interest* in existing, his passionate *concern*, as he stands in the crisis of decision, *to move from* possibility (thinking) *to* action (being). It is only his own reality in this sense to which the individual has direct access *as* reality. Other realities he can relate to only cognitively or aesthetically, by translating them into possibilities.

The combination of propositions (1) and (2) seems to imply an acosmism—a worldlessness of the individual—that borders on solipsism.

Yet these propositions, like "Truth is subjectivity," must not be taken casually at face value. For we know that the face of any Kierkegaardian utterance is likely to be a pseudonymous persona whose words have a rhetorical significance different from the meaning they directly assert. That this is the case here is indicated by the one passage in his works in which Kierkegaard shows himself sensitive to the suggestion of acosmism and counters it in advance:

> To grant thinking the supremacy over all else is gnosticism; to make the ethical reality of the subject the only reality might seem to be acosmism. That it will seem so to a busy thinker who is out to explain everything, a nimble wit who speedily traverses the entire world, proves only that he has a very limited conception of what the ethical means to the subject. If ethics were to take the whole world away from such a busy thinker and let him keep only his own self, presumably he would think: "Such a trifle is not worth keeping, let it go with the rest!" And so—that is acosmism.

But why will such a busy thinker speak and think so disrespectfully of himself? If the sense were that he should give up the whole world and be content with another man's ethical reality, then he would be right to regard it as a poor trade. But his own ethical reality should, ethically, mean more to the individual himself than heaven and earth and all that therein is, more than the 6,000 years of world-history, more than astrology, veterinary science, and everything that the age demands—which aesthetically and intellectually is a monstrous vulgarity. If this is not the case, then so much the worse for the individual himself, for then he has nothing at all, no reality at all. For to all else he has only a possibility-relationship at the very maximum. (CUP, 305)[3]

The suggestion then is not so much wrong as it is irrelevant and improper. The question of the *reality* of the world, whatever interest it may have for the disinterested science of metaphysics, is *irrelevant* to the ethical concern of the individual. Because it is irrelevant it is also *improper* to raise the question of acosmism. Such questioning is a dangerous distraction—a "parenthesis"— that tempts the individual to forfeit the only reality to which he has entry and for which he is responsible, for the sake of an impressive but illusory pursuit of mere possibilities.

No one who knows the devastation Kierkegaard's own nimble wit can work would lightly put himself in the place of that busy thinker who is here castigated. Yet the sense of Kierkegaard's polemic is not wholly clear without further analysis. The precise respect in which the reality of the world is ethically irrelevant needs to be defined.

It is evident from his works at large that Kierkegaard does not intend to *deny* the reality of the world. When he does touch in passing on metaphysical problems, his most obvious affiliation is with the Greeks, whose "honest" realism he contrasts with the "mendacious" idealism of Hegel. It is not always clear whether

---

3. I have slightly altered the existing English translation. This passage is found at p. 331 of volume 7 of the second Danish edition of Kierkegaard's *Samlede Værker*, hereinafter cited in this essay as SV.

his orientation is Platonic or Aristotelian or that of an orthodox creation-doctrine combining elements of both. But it is clear that he means to defend the reality of an objective world-order against skeptical and sophistical intrusions (cf. *Philosophical Fragments*, 47–48, 46–60 passim; and CUP, 293–95). *Metaphysically*, and *with respect to the extra-subjective realm*, Kierkegaard tends to make the larger assumptions of classical realism. Not that he tries to establish the truth of these assumptions by argument; for the most part they stand in the background of his writing, as "beliefs-which-it-is-not-necessary-to-call-into-question."

But the fact that such metaphysical questions never become matters of importance to Kierkegaard is itself significant. In spite of his devotion to the Greeks and his implicit realism, Kierkegaard can write:

> Instead of conceding the contention of Idealism, but in such a way, be it noted, that one dismisses as a temptation the whole question of actuality (of an elusive *an-sich*) in relation to thought, which like all other temptations cannot be overcome by giving way to it; instead of putting an end to Kant's misleading reflection, which brought actuality into relation with thought; instead of referring actuality to the ethical, Hegel went further. He became fantastic and vanquished the *skepsis* of Idealism with the help of pure thought, which is an hypothesis and, even if it does not so declare itself, fantastic. And this triumph of pure thought (that in it thought and being are one) is something both to laugh at and to weep over, for in pure thought the question of the difference between thought and being cannot actually be raised at all. —That thought has reality was assumed by Greek philosophy without further ado. By reflecting on the matter one would have to come to the same result; but why confuse a thought-reality with actuality? A thought-reality is a possibility, and thought must simply dismiss every further question concerning its actuality. . . . A skepticism which attacks thought itself cannot be stopped by thinking it through, for this would have to be done by thought, which is on the side of revolution. It must be broken off. To answer Kant within the fantastic shadow-play of pure thought is precisely not to answer

him. The only *an-sich* that cannot be thought is existing, with which thought has nothing to do at all. (CUP, 292; SV, 7: 316–17)[4]

Kierkegaard believed that Kant's critical idealism had instituted a skepticism which attacked the validity of thought. His belief is not difficult to understand if we recall several features of Kant's philosophy. Existence in the categorial sense, as a pure concept of the understanding, is constitutive of phenomenal (= thought)-reality only, and not of actuality *an-sich*. Kant asserts that the *existence* of the *Ding-an-sich* can be known, though by what Kantian mechanism it is apprehended is not clear. In any case, the *nature* and *meaning* of existence in this non-categorial sense—that anything is at all—are not open to philosophical inquiry. We cannot, Kant says, ask to know the conditions of the actuality of experience, only the conditions of its possibility.

There are then two senses of existence in Kant's critical philosophy: categorial existence, a constituent of any possible experience; and actual, non-categorial existence *an-sich*, which we must acknowledge as a fact, but with which, as Kierkegaard says, thought has no further dealings.

Kant's view of the existence of the human self derives from his view of existence in general. I can know the phenomenal existence of the phenomenal self; the transcendental unity of apperception, though not properly and substantially a self, is a—or rather *the*—condition of the possibility of all experience, including the experience of the phenomenal self. But the actuality of

---

4. I have altered the existing English translation of this passage in the direction of a more literal rendering. The word I have translated "actuality" is *Virkelighed*. This word is rendered "reality" in the existing translation, and appears as such everywhere else in this essay in phrases like "the ethical reality of the individual." I have kept "reality" for the most part because it is the word familiar to readers of Kierkegaard-in-English. But in this passage Kierkegaard distinguishes *Virkelighed* from *Realitet* (as in "thought-reality"): *Virkelighed* is actuality as distinct from possibility, while *Realitet* is a generic term encompassing both possibility and actuality. The existing translation is obliged to render *Realitet* in this passage by "validity," which is wrong and misleading. But in any case: "actuality" in this quotation is to be understood as synonymous with "reality" elsewhere in this essay.

the self in any further sense is beyond investigation. For theoretical reason, it is a mare's nest of pseudosyllogisms. For practical reason, it is an item, not of knowledge, but of faith. The self, so apprehended, is the one *Ding-an-sich* to which we have access, though not theoretical access. Actuality is for Kant, though in a rather different sense than for Kierkegaard, "referred to the ethical."

Something like this seems to have been Kierkegaard's understanding of Kant. And for Kierkegaard these considerations were decisive. All thinking necessarily makes the assumptions of Greek realism. But all that Greek realism actually assumes is that the object of thought is "real" *as an object of thought*: it is an *essential possibility*. No more than this can or need be assumed for the purposes of theoretical understanding. Existential reality—the actual existence of these essences, thought-realities, or possibilities—cannot be grasped by thinking. The question of actual existence cannot even be formulated as a theoretical and cognitive question. It must therefore be dismissed as a misunderstanding and a temptation.

Hegel's endeavor to think through Kant's *skepsis* is no more likely to succeed than is a squirrel's attempt to get out of his cage by going around one more time. Hegel's objection to Kant—if he knows of a reality that eludes thought, he must already be out beyond the boundaries he has assigned to thought—holds only because Kant asserts that our acknowledgment of the *Ding-an-sich* is a cognitive acknowledgment. This would be "Kant's misleading reflection, which brought actuality into relation with thought" (CUP, 292). Against such a view Hegel is right; but right only in that his idealism is thoroughgoing and consistent, not (as he believes) right in the sense that he avoids or resolves the difficulty. Hence his mendaciousness as opposed to the Greeks, who did not make the reality of the world a *theoretical* problem. The difficulty cannot be resolved, and the contention of Idealism—which is in effect that *this* question of actuality cannot even arise—must be conceded. Hegel did not solve the problem of the thing-in-itself; he simply erased it. And *qua* metaphysician, in a cognitive respect, he was quite correct. He erred by presuming that he had dealt with the problem of the relation of thought and being, when in fact he had only formulated—fantastically—its unformulability.

Therefore, the skepticism which Kant introduced into philosophy cannot be resolved. It can only be broken with. The metaphysical problem of actuality and its relation to cognition must be dismissed as a pseudo-problem, a temptation to absentmindedness and distraction. Actuality must be referred to the ethical—to the subject's existence, his *inter-esse*, which he apprehends not by thinking it, but by existing it in passion and decision.

This is the meaning of Kierkegaard's statements, that the ethical reality of the subject is the only reality, and that to all realities other than his own he has only a possibility-relation. These propositions do not *define* a metaphysical *position*; they *disavow* a metaphysical *problem*. In this light it is clear why Kierkegaard believes that the imputation of acosmism is irrelevant to his concern and ethically improper.

However, although he believes that metaphysical questions have no bearing on ethical matters, Kierkegaard is still a realist—not only in the sense that he believes every object of thought to be real as an object of thought, but also in the more exact sense that there *are* other actualities than my own. Things in nature exist in their own way, and every other human being has his own existence in just the same way that I have mine. Kierkegaard writes books in order to communicate. The very act of communicating, no matter how indirect, implies the being of the recipient and of a world which incorporates both communicants.

Therefore, when he says that the ethical reality of the subject is the only reality, Kierkegaard means to stress that the only reality which the individual can grasp (*faa fat paa*) *as reality*—by *being* it—is his own. Other realities, men and things, he can only get hold of (*faa fat paa*) as *possibilities*, by abstracting from their actual existing.

"Possibility" in this context means *the manner of my relation to realities other than my own*. To assert that I apprehend other realities as possibilities is not to *deny*, but to *affirm*, a relationship, albeit an indirect relationship, holding among real entities. Realities other than my own *are, in themselves; to me* they *are addressed as* possibilities (cf. Lønning, 15, 39ff.).

From an intellectual or aesthetic point of view, other realities are grasped as possibilities to be reflectively or imaginatively entertained. They are taken objectively, as the contents of a transparent intentionality, considered "for their own sake," and not for any relevance they might have to the existential situation of the thinking and imagining individual. From the disinterested poetic and intellectual point of view, Kierkegaard says, possibility is higher than reality (CUP, 282).

From an ethical point of view, other realities are again grasped as possibilities; now, however, not as material for contemplation, but as a *demand for action*, a *claim on my freedom*. Other realities confront me ethically as opportunities—they are alternatives for action—and as requirements—they insist that, either consciously or by default, I do something about them, seize them and actualize them or let them pass. Ethically I am not disinterested, but interested. I apprehend other realities as possibilities, not "for their own sake," but exclusively because they irrupt into my situation so as to make a difference in the way I exist my actuality. Kierkegaard writes, "Ethically regarded, reality [sc.: the individual's ethical reality] is higher than possibility" (CUP, 284). Intellectually and aesthetically, I abstract from my own reality in order to enjoy other realities in the mode of possibility. Ethically, I grasp other realities as possibilities in order to exist my own reality.

For Kierkegaard, the "stages on life's way"—aesthetic-intellectual, ethical, religious—are fundamentally *ways of being human*. They are similar to Heideggerian "existentials." They do not characterize manthings as attributes might characterize substances. They are modes of existing in and by which a free being like man constitutes his own selfhood.

The key word here is *free*. I am free with respect to other realities. They do not impinge on me directly so as to make me what I am, nor do I so impinge on them. *Because* I am free, other realities become for me possibilities, things-which-*I-am-able*-to-do-something-about. I can either stand off and look at them (aesthetically-intellectually), or take them into my existence as opportunities and demands for decision (ethically). Realities other than mine *are*, and they are *related* to me. But they are related to me *externally*. They do not touch me as *realities* in such a way as to determine me. They bear on me indirectly, across the nothingness of freedom, "the alarming possibility of *being able*" (*Concept of Dread*, 40; hereinafter cited in this essay as COD).

Therefore, Kierkegaard would say that the isolation of the individual in his freedom is not a perverse denial of the world, but a *sine qua non* of ethics. "This is profitable preliminary training for an ethical mode of existence: to learn that the individual stands alone" (CUP, 287). Deny that the ethical reality of the subject is the only reality, deny that he is related to all other realities as possibilities, and you have denied freedom. Deny freedom, and you have made nonsense out of ethics and human existence in general.

It is now clear not only why Kierkegaard regards the metaphysical question of acosmism as ethically irrelevant, but also why he believes it ethically *necessary* to recognize that individuals are isolated, each in his own subjectivity sustaining only a possibility-relation to other realities. But a further question arises: is it ethically *sufficient* to hold that the individual is related to other realities as to possibilities?

Consider a case of temptation, say the radical temptation to neglect my proper ethical concern for the sake of some "objective result" my action might have, such as the esteem of posterity. Such results, Kierkegaard rightly says, I cannot guarantee by my free action alone. Factors other than my will help to decide my historical significance or insignificance. The esteem of posterity is "impossible because it is merely possible, i.e., perhaps possible, i.e., dependent upon something else" (CUP, 121–22), and *therefore* "it is unethical to be concerned about it" (CUP, 122).

Now it may or may not be unethical for me to be concerned about the historical fate of my actions. But if it is, and if I am nevertheless tempted to such concern, then I do not believe that the temptation issues from the *impossibility* of my guaranteeing this significance to my acts. The inference: perhaps possible, therefore merely possible, therefore impossible, therefore a temptation, does not hold. No one is tempted by impossibilities or by *mere* possibilities. Men are tempted because they are involved in situations compounded of *real* relations to other men, objects, and events. If I am tempted to seek historical importance, it is because I am *really* involved in history, in the *reality* of other men and their decisions, and in the *reality* of the natural forces that help to shape history.

To be sure, I am free, and for that reason the world—with other men as members of it—confronts me as possibility. But it confronts me as *real* possibility, as possibility arising not only out of my freedom, but also out of my participation in realities other than my own. My freedom, however much it isolates me in responsibility and in risk, *does not altogether sever me from the reality of the world as such.*

If this is not the case, if there is not, e.g., something like a contingent causal relation involved when I am lured by a possibility, then the alternative is that *I tempt myself.* But this is ethical nonsense. I may of course tempt myself in particular cases; that is, I may fancy to myself alluring possibilities. But *fundamentally* I do not tempt myself. Self-enticement is possible only on the basis of a more radical experience of *being enticed*; otherwise temptation is an unimaginably gratuitous experimentation with possibilities. If I am totally isolated by my freedom, then the experience of temptation is illusory and the notion of temptation meaningless.

Yet something like this follows if we accept Kierkegaard's view that I am related to other realities only as possiblities. Unless I am *also* related to them directly as *realities*, I cannot be tempted.

Or take another case. Kierkegaard holds that other realities confront me ethically as demands for decision. They are possibilities which *require* me, not to perform this or that particular action, but to act in a way relevant to the alternatives they establish. Other realities address themselves to my freedom in such a way as to make a claim on me.

Suppose that on my way home I am approached by a shabby stranger who asks me for money, insisting that he needs it for some vital purpose. I may interpret him and his request in various ways, but in any event I either do or I do not give him the money. I am free, and therefore not determined to do one thing rather than the other; I can do either in an indeterminate variety. of ways; but I am required to do something. Even if I view the situation aesthetically—say as material for my next novel—I still either give or do not give what is asked. The same thing is true even if I look the other way and pretend not to notice the fact that another reality has arisen in my situation and calls for action.

Now I believe that another reality, appearing before me as possibility, cannot require me to act unless this other reality and I are in the first place related as realities.

If this is not the case, then the alternative must be that *I obligate myself*. But this is ethically absurd. It is true, of course, that I can and do in particular cases imagine alternatives and determine myself to act on them. But it is also true that, however free I am, fundamentally I do not create my own possibilities and require myself to act in a way relevant to them. The very fact that alternatives are given, and that they insist, will I or nil I, on relevant action—do x or do not do x—is itself a sign that these alternatives emerge not only out of my freedom, but also out of my real community with other beings. Pure self-obligation, like pure self-enticement, is only experimentation. Freedom (the possibility-relation of Kierkegaard) and the "reality-relation" are both *necessary* conditions of ethical action; only together do they constitute the *sufficient* condition of such action.

When I run into the panhandler, the two of us participate, however slightly, in each other and in a common world. We are, however brief and transitory our encounter, really members one of another and of a larger reality that includes us both.

I believe, however, that Kierkegaard implicitly denies this. He means to say that the individual is really isolated from other beings, receiving from them neither support, insistence, opposition, nor allurement. The world is only a cluster of possibilities for him, and as such does not offer him matter, content, locus, opportunity, or exigence for action—these he must generate out of his own freedom. Kierkegaard was rightly apprehensive about the kind of objectivism that threatened to dissolve human individuality in the non-human world, the race, the state, or some other collectivity. But his fear of coalescence and his will to preserve freedom untrammeled led him to sweep away all order, participation, and community. His insistence that the question of the reality of the world is ethically irrelevant, and that only an indirect possibility-relation holds between the ethical subject and other realities, implies a sort of freedom that is separative only and is not supported by the cosmos. Kierkegaardian freedom—perhaps this is the influence of the Romantics—is the negative half of Augustinian freedom. As St. Augustine learned from his own experience—an experience of painful involvement, quite unlike Kierkegaard's experience of withdrawal—it is this half of freedom which, left to itself, can only consume itself in the pursuit of vanity. It often seems that Kierkegaardian subjectivity—the tension of inwardness within itself—far from being concrete and existential, is but an abstraction vibrating in a vacuum.

In any case, unless we allow that I—in my own ethical and human reality—participate in the reality of other beings, then we are forced to the conclusion that I create my own possibilities, tempt myself, and obligate myself. I become my own God and my own devil. And this, depending on one's perspective, is either foolish or presumptuous.

In fact, it is a conclusion that, for other reasons, would be unacceptable to Kierkegaard himself. He jibed at Kant's conception of moral autonomy because it led to this end (*Journals of Søren Kierkegaard*, no. 1041).[5] Concerned as he was with religious faith, he saw in the failure of autonomy God's opportunity. Where the human spirit recognizes itself to be a land of emptiness and want, there God can enter in and fill up man's need with the bounty of his own gratuitous goodness.

For this reason, it might be objected that my previous criticism bypasses the center of Kierkegaard's ethic. It might be protested that he intended *really* to isolate the individual, to deprive him of the illusory securities of community and world-order, so as to bring him face to face with God. Community and world-order are realities, but they are not the absolute Reality, and the individual must not rely upon them or stake his existence upon them. His isolation is not so much metaphysical as it is personal and religious. And the "weakness" I have discovered in the "metaphysical foundations of Kierkegaard's ethic" is actually a deliberate, systematic, and justified tactic in the strategy of indirect communication.

It this is true, my criticism of Kierkegaard serves only to illumine and enhance his effectiveness. The rhetorician has got around the philosopher after all, and my analysis is not a diagnosis but a symptom.

Let us examine this objection. Kierkegaard's rhetoric is meant to drive the reader away from the world, to a confrontation with God. But it seems to me that there is a contradiction in Kierkegaard's account of the God-man relation. Consider his typical de-

---

5. On this point and the following, see "The Analysis of the Good in Kierkegaard's *Purity of Heart*," chapter 2 in this volume.

scriptions of this relation. God is said to be negatively present in subjectivity (CUP, 52); He is present but hidden in the world (CUP, 218); He is present whenever the uncertainty of all things is thought infinitely (CUP, 80); He is present to freedom, where freedom is conceived as infinite possibility (CUP, 124); "God *is* that all things are possible and that all things are possible *is* God" (*Sickness Unto Death*, 173–74). In a word, God communicates with men indirectly, in the mode of possibility (CUP, 139–40, 217–22). Every direct relation to God is branded paganism (CUP, 218–19), and even the Incarnate Presence of God among men is more concealment than revelation (cf. *Philosophical Fragments*, chap. 4; and *Training in Christianity*, pts. 1, 2).

Thus man is related to God, as to the world, by a possibility-relation. The reality of God is apprehended only in the form of negation, radical uncertainty, dread, offense, or faith. The only "natural theology" in Kierkegaard is an extreme form of *via remotionis*; for example, his discussion in *Philosophical Fragments* of the annihilating encounter of human reason with the Absolute Paradox. Such "revealed theology" as there is is strangely lacking in an understanding of creation, redemption, grace, and sacrament; mystery and miracle—the awesome appearing of the infinite richness of the divine reality—are replaced by absurdity and paradox—the self-concealment of the divine in the form of unthinkable possibilities.

The Kierkegaardian individual, when he confronts God, meets Him by the most remote indirection, as an empty or contradictory X. The ethical reality of the individual, freedom tensed between its own passion and its own decision, is isolated not only from the reality of the world, but also from the reality of God.

I believe, therefore, that the Kierkegaardian rhetoric drives the individual, not to an encounter with the Absolute Reality and Power (*Qui Est, ipsum esse subsistens*), but only further back into his own inwardness. The effect of Kierkegaard's position is *to infinitize the freedom of the individual and thereby to absolutize human subjectivity*.

In the last chapter of *The Concept of Dread*, Kierkegaard explains the way in which dread, the experience of the nothingness of freedom, can become an instrument of salvation when taken up into an act of faith. Kierkegaard writes that

> in possibility everything is equally possible, and he who truly was brought up by possibility has comprehended the dreadful as well as the smiling. When such a person, therefore, goes out from the school of possibility, and knows more thoroughly than a child knows the alphabet that he can demand of life absolutely nothing, and that terror, perdition, annihilation, dwell next door to every man, and has learned the profitable lesson that every dread which alarms may the next instant become a fact, he will then interpret reality differently, he will extol reality, and even when it rests upon him heavily he will remember that after all it is far, far lighter than the possibility was. (COD, 140)

And he adds that

> if one is to learn absolutely, the individual must in turn have the possibility in himself and himself fashion that from which he is to learn, even though the next instant it does not recognize that it was fashioned by him, but absolutely takes the power from him.
>
> But in order that the individual may thus absolutely and infinitely be educated by possibility, he must be honest towards possibility and must have faith. By faith I mean what Hegel in his fashion calls very rightly "the inward certainty which anticipates infinity." When the discoveries of possibility are honestly administered, possibility will then disclose all finitudes but idealize them in the form of infinity in the individual who is overwhelmed by dread, until in turn he conquers them by the anticipation of faith. (COD, 140–41)

It is clear from such utterances that Kierkegaard means what he says elsewhere in the same book, that "it is the supreme glory of freedom that it has only with itself to do" (COD, 97). But human freedom, thus absolutized, becomes indistinguishable from the omnipotence of God. Kierkegaardian freedom *does* generate its own possibilities; it *does* both obligate and tempt itself: how significant that Kierkegaard could "associate no definite thought with the serpent" in the myth of the Fall! For the serpent, he complains, "lets the temptation come from without" (COD, 43). Kierkegaardian freedom anguishes itself, makes itself guilty, and at last, by taking-in-advance (anticipating: *at tage forud*) all possibilities, it redeems itself from the perdition it has brought on itself. If it is not itself God, at least it has a handy purchase on the divine omnipotence.

Kierkegaard, like Hegel, operates exclusively in terms of two relations: identity and difference. Whatever is not wholly same is simply other; whatever is not wholly other is simply same. And so, for Kierkegaard as for Hegel, absolute opposition falls back into sameness. Between God (omnipotence) and man (freedom) there is an infinite gulf fixed. They have nothing in common, but for that very reason there is also nothing to distinguish them.

The absence in both Hegel and Kierkegaard of anything like a logic of analogy—a logic that recognizes multiple modes of sameness-in-difference—and the consequent lack in both of a conception such as the "chain of being" necessitate in both a collapse of the distinction between God and man. This indistinction of the finite from the infinite, a union Hegel labored consciously to achieve, occurs in Kierkegaard in spite of himself because he is enslaved to Hegel's dialectic even when he protests against it in the name of the "infinite qualitative difference."

It is not strange that Kierkegaard always formulates the relation of God and man as paradoxical identities: man's need of God is his highest perfection; the only existential evidence of God's love is suffering; the recoil of reason from God is its oneness with God's purposes; the only purity of heart is the consciousness of absolute impurity; the God-man is the historical event which on principle could not happen—and so on.

Now I do not wish to deny that there is a moment of absoluteness in human freedom: the capacity of man, recognized by Augustine and most other theologians, to utter a radical and final yes or a radical and final no to the claim and the grace of God. Nor would I deny that Kierkegaard is the connoisseur without peer of this religious crisis, with its terrible testimony to the reality of God—and its equally terrible temptation, *eritis sicut dii*. But it seems to me that his understanding of subjectivity often succumbs to the temptation, and confuses the *potentia absoluta divina* with human freedom in a way that is close to demonic.

Moreover—and this is just the other side of the demonia—his understanding of human subjectivity *trivializes existence and thereby destroys the very end his indirect rhetoric was intended to achieve*. Kierkegaard's ethical thought is involved in a basic self-contradiction: it makes impossible the very effect it was meant to establish. The Kierkegaardian individual is existentially—in his ethical reality—acosmic if not atheistic. He is infinitely free. But because it is without limitation—by the relative objectivity of the world or the absolute objectivity of God—his freedom is empty of everything but indeterminate possibilities.

In the Interlude of the *Philosophical Fragments*, Kierkegaard effectively shows that nothing really happens in a world without freedom. For if everything is necessary, then everything on principle already *is*, and the historical unfolding of events is a time lag of no essential or existential significance.

But now, from the passages just quoted from *The Concept of Dread*, with their apotheosis of freedom, the same conclusion follows. To the man educated in possibility by dread, nothing that happens in reality matters. Against a background of infinite possibility, every actuality is a matter of indifference. The man educated by dread has *so prepared himself* for *any* reality that *no* reality can overtake him and surprise him either with terror or with joy. Kierkegaard's man of faith is no less fatuous than his speculative philosopher. Both of them are fantastically outside existence. Both absolute freedom and total determinism render actuality superfluous.

This, I believe, is a contradiction in Kierkegaard's own thought, not a difficulty incident upon understanding him in a way external to his own concern. Kierkegaard begins, as we saw, by making in a large and vague way the assumptions of classical realism. It is only by means of such assumptions that he can initially dismiss all metaphysical objections as impertinent, and go on to enforce his ethical claim. His claim, however, is that the individual's inwardness is the only reality to which he has access as reality, and therefore the only reality that is ethically significant. Although the rhetoric presupposes and must presuppose a world as the condition of its own possibility, it ends by isolating the individual not *within* but *without* a world, just as effectively as if that world were not there—and indeed, for all ethical purposes it is not. The practice of the rhetoric of indirect communication demands a world; the end projected by the rhetoric—the inwardness of the individual—is worldless. But an inwardness so projected is not only in conflict with the strategy that urges it; it is at once demonic and effete. Kierkegaard's ethical thought, even in its religious dimension, rests on an acosmism as pretentious as the idealism of Hegel, an acosmism which, furthermore, drains existence of its terror, its passion, its risk, and its responsibility as surely as did the gnostic "System" against which he directed his polemic.

After all this I cannot be insensitive to the presence behind me, applauding enthusiastically and exclaiming, "Very good, young man! Very bravely protested. Why, this sounds almost like seriousness. —Just one little detail: haven't you missed the point after all? The point was really not man or God or the world or metaphysics. The point was—you. The difficulties *you* have finding a metaphysical consistency in my books. But that only shows that you are so absentminded and fantastically *sub specie aeternitatis* that my indirect communication passed you by altogether—or else that in your own way you did get the point, however unimaginatively, but managed to turn it to your disadvantage. In which case, make the most of it. But your theoretical objections and your metaphysical contradictions don't bother me a bit."

"Now hold on there! Can you get off the hook so easily—just by saying you're not concerned? The whole point of my paper was to prove that you *must* be concerned."

"Well, I suppose if one is a serious-minded person, metaphysically and morally a responsible sort, a faithful husband and a good provider, and an ornament of his profession, one must be concerned for the implications of what he says. But suppose one is a wastrel who takes no responsibility, suppose one is a poet. . . ."

And having spoken the magic word he disappears, as he always eludes any reader who wants to lay serious dialectical hands on him. Kierkegaard insists on having the last word. He *will* remain what he is, the poet of inwardness, forever vanishing behind one of an endless series of masks, never present *in propria persona* when you want to hold him accountable.

And does he not in his own way succeed in producing the

effect he desires? If this analysis fails to dissect and expose Kierkegaard, is it not also true that Kierkegaard, by provoking the analysis, *has* led us through freedom to God and to an awareness of the ethical significance of the reality of the world? Such an awareness is neither given nor directly implied in his writing; quite the opposite, if the argument of this essay is valid. But is not this itself the supreme indirection of Kierkegaard, that he thrusts his readers away from him to seek the truth for themselves? By disappearing from the scene, by assuming no responsibility for what he *does* imply, the poet returns his readers to their own situation and leaves them free for *any* implications.

It is not after all un-Kierkegaardian to find Kierkegaard "wrong." The nature of the "subjectivity" Kierkegaard was trying to communicate necessitated a peculiar kind of rhetoric. If poetry be defined as language centripetally drawn and self-contained, and rhetoric as centrifugal other-addressing speech, then it may be said that Kierkegaard's rhetoric had to exhaust itself in his poetry. Only the reader can address himself: subjectivity demands it.

And, finally, it must be remembered that Kierkegaard on his own admission is the "master of irony." Though he himself vanishes, his works remain to take their effect—ironically—by surviving the analysis that would destroy them.

7.
POINTS OF VIEW FOR HIS WORK AS AN AUTHOR:
A REPORT FROM HISTORY

> One might almost be tempted to think that even what was signed 'S. K.' might not for certain be his final words, but only a point of view.
>
> Peter Christian Kierkegaard

> An author is often merely an x, even when his name is given. . . .
>
> Søren Aabye Kierkegaard

Kierkegaard's "literature" is prefaced by a long, densely overwritten, and appropriately indirect essay on *The Concept of Irony*: his master's thesis, published over his own name and publicly defended. As a postscript to the authorship there is a brief, simple, direct communication, a "report to history" entitled *The Point of View for My Work as an Author*. Also over his own name. Written in 1848, at the time of the publication of the second edition of *Either/Or*, the first work in the corpus proper, it was not made public until 1859, four years after the author's death, by his brother Peter.

Both works stand outside the canon of Kierkegaard's writings. The earlier book lays their methodological foundation in irony. The later essay explains them in retrospect as the work of divine Providence. That is what appears to be the case. Peter, however, was not sure. Jakop Peter Mynster, bishop of Sjaelland and primate of Denmark, read an abbreviated version of *The Point of View*, a cutting from the longer work, published by Kierkegaard himself in 1851. Concerning which Mynster told the author, "Yes, it is a clue [*Traad*, literally "thread"] to the whole thing, but spun later, but indeed you say no more yourself" (*Søren Kierkegaards Papirer*, X⁴ A 373).

The father's name was Michael Pedersen Kierkegaard.. There are lots of Peters in this story. And one that is not there.

I

The introduction to *The Point of View* identifies the occasion of the work. With the appearance of the second edition of *Either/Or*, Kierkegaard feels that he is permitted, indeed obliged, to break his long silence and explain the meaning of his work as a writer. The truth which he now can and must tell—wants to tell—is that he has always been a religious author, all his writings an explication of Christianity and a polemic against the illusions of Christendom.

The reader who "has the cause of Christianity at heart" is beseeched to read *The Point of View* "not curiously, but devoutly, as one would read a religious work" (*Point of View*, 6; hereinafter cited in this essay as PV).[1] The pseudonymous writings (Kierkegaard calls them "aesthetic") are one and all "an incognito and a deceit in the service of Christianity" (PV, 6). He who understands the aesthetic works, but not the religious meaning of the corpus as a whole, essentially misunderstands the author's intent. He who grasps the religious totality but fails to understand any of the pseudonymous writings lacks nothing essential. All that is a matter of indifference to the author.

---

1. I have occasionally altered Lowrie's translation, when I felt that a more literal rendering would be helpful. For the Danish text I have used *Søren Kierkegaard: Samlede Værker*, vol. 18. For two vastly different but equally interesting general comments on *The Point of View*, cf. Henning Fenger, *Kierkegaard, the Myths and Their Origins*, 26–31; and Sylviane Agacinski, *Aparté: Conceptions et Morts de Søren Kierkegaard*, 98–107. This book was written a year before the appearance of Christopher Norris's *The Deconstructive Turn*. I am pleased to note that his reading of Kierkegaard in general and of *The Point of View* in particular (his chapter 4) coincides at many points with my own.

The Point of View is written "for orientation." It is a "public attestation" (PV, 6). Søren is willing and eager and even duty-bound to set the record straight. But he will not defend himself nor offer an apology *pro libris suis*. That he could not do without forfeiting his integrity and abandoning the dialectical position he has always occupied. In any case the works and their author need no defense. This he knows "with God" (PV, 7), who has favored his undertaking.

Neither will *The Point of View* be an indictment of Søren's contemporaries. He would be justified in lodging an accusation against them. But while he might appear as the prosecutor of his age, he will not do so. This refusal to insist upon his rights is a necessary part of that overall self-denial in which he has chosen to serve the truth. It is his duty to do everything in his power to see to it that he is not "esteemed and idolized" (PV, 8).

There will be those who wonder whether the author's self-abnegation is authentic. They are advised to inspect their own motives:

> Only he who understands by himself what true self-denial is—only he can solve my puzzle and perceive that it is self-denial. He who does not understand this by himself must rather call my behavior self-love, pride, eccentricity, madness. I cannot consistently indict him for this, since I myself, in the service of true self-denial, contribute to the formation of his judgment. (PV, 8)

Søren has chosen to live and to work in such a way that none save the initiates of self-abnegation can know whether his comportment signifies pride or humility. This publicly undecidable disjunction—self-love/self-denial—is the cross on which he suffers. But he has elected this cross, and "all true Christian suffering . . . is voluntary" (PV, 8).

At least the author understands the truth (presumably the truth about Christianity) which he has delivered to his readers. And the contemporaries who misunderstand him now (those who interpret his humility as pride) will understand this truth "sometime," that is, beyond time "in eternity" (PV, 8), when they are at last delivered from the cares and troubles he has been spared even in time. Though he has suffered much from incomprehension—a misunderstanding he helped to create by making his life and work a perfectly ambiguous sign—he thanks God for the one thing that matters infinitely to him: that God has vouchsafed him an understanding of the truth (PV, 9).

"And then only one thing more" (PV, 9). (This is the first in a series of last words, though it is not exactly something more.)

> It goes without saying that I cannot wholly explain my work as an author; that is, in the purely personal inwardness in which I possess the explanation. . . . I cannot in this way make public my God-relationship; for it is neither more nor less than the common human inwardness, which every man can have, with no official distinction which it were a crime to conceal and a duty to proclaim, to which I could lay claim and plead as my justification. (PV, 9)

Even in this "direct communication" (the phrase appears on the title page), this "report to history" (ditto), Kierkegaard is still the ironist hiding behind a screen of equivocal signifiers that he himself has thrown up. Is his the irony of the elite? Or the catholic subjectivity without which no authentic human life is possible? Pride or humility? Is his work—and his life as part of his work—an instrument of self-assertion or a token of self-mortification? Because it concerns his private relationship to God, that is the essential secret. Essentially secret only insofar as it is in the public domain—an inward relation to God is available to all on the same terms—it may therefore not be adduced by Søren Kierkegaard as the official legitimation of his own enterprise. Though adepts of abjection may share his secret, his authorship remains—essentially—unauthorized.

The truth about Kierkegaard's life and work, direct report to history notwithstanding, is the mystery that shall not be revealed. At least not in time and not by the author; but only in eternity, when God at last shall come to judgment and once and forever disambiguate all the signs.

We have his word for it.

(The introduction to this book must be read together with the conclusion. At once. But not yet.)

II

Hard on the heels of this disclaimer we are offered (in part 1) an account of the problem and the key to its solution. (This text is not averse to contradicting itself.)

There is a duplicity in the corpus—is it aesthetic or is it religious?—answering to the ambiguity of the author's conduct. Søren is not embarrassed by this duplicity. On the contrary, since he intended it he comprehends it better than any reader could. It is in fact "the essential dialectical determination of the entire authorship, and therefore has a deeper ground" (PV, 10).

The duplicity is original. It dates from the almost simultaneous publication of *Either/Or* and *Two Edifying Discourses*. It is reasserted at the term of the authorship with the publication of *The Crisis and a Crisis in the Life of an Actress* along with the second edition of *Either/Or*. The ambiguity, in the work as in the life, is not an accident of the author's maturation: aesthetic in his youth, religious in his seniority. The truth is that he did not age at all. (As we are soon to be told, he was never young.) The duplicity is present from beginning to end, and dialectically defines the whole corpus. That is: defines it contradictorily.

Of course this end is not an end, nor this beginning a true origin. By authorial fiat the first work in the canon, *Either/Or* is preceded by (among others) *The Concept of Irony*. A book that evacuates the concept of origin by locating the source of authentic human existence in "infinite negativity."[2] Likewise the works of 1848 were not terminal; there were other writings, some of them pseudonymous. This particular false ending[3]—*The Point of View*, written in 1848—was postponed until after the end. Posterity, to whom the work was addressed, first brought it to light. Peter, the once offended brother, published it eleven years after it was written, four years after the death of the author. Peter, who with Søren did not expect to survive the father, who with Søren alone

---

2. For "infinite negativity", cf. *Concept of Irony*, 231, 238, 240, 271, 278; for irony as the source of authentic existence, cf. 336–42.

3. The *Concluding Unscientific Postscript* of 1846, which was meant to conclude the series of pseudonymous works, was an earlier false ending.

of all the children outlived him, spoke the eulogy at his brother's funeral. And (himself belated) delivered Søren's report to history. Departing from its destination, it alienates both origin and end. A roundabout way for a direct communication.

The duplicity of the works is essential. But the explanation (known to the author because he planned it all) is simple: Søren Kierkegaard is a religious writer, and his works one and all works of edification. In spite of appearances, which were designed to deceive. Just as his life was a regimen of self-denial in spite of his behavior.

This is not a plea that Kierkegaard enters on his own behalf. That he says he is a religious writer is not evidential. It must be sustantiated by an objective report, based on the texts themselves. Casting himself in the role [*Egenskap*: property] of third party, a mere reader, Søren proposes to render the decisive verdict on the meaning of his own works. "*Qua* writer it avails but little that I *qua* man protest that I have intended this or that" (PV, 15). *Qua* critic of his own writings, he will not commit the intentional fallacy by appealing to his own professions *qua* man. (What are we to make of *this* profession? In which of his roles (proprieties) does he offer this assurance?) There will be no protestations of purpose; though such might be permitted him (*qua* man) as a kind of lyrical self-gratification (remember that), and required of him (*qua* man) as a religious obligation.

For the reader-critic, the problem is this. If the duplicity is present first, last, and essentially in the texts themselves, then it cannot be explained but must be allowed to stand as is. (Unless we are willing to credit an affidavit from the author guaranteeing that his purpose was religious all along. But all such protests are disallowed.) No (Søren protests), that appears to be very acute [*skarpsindigt*], and is therefore really just sophistical [*spidsfindigt*] (PV, 16). There must be a better way out of this.

And is. The mystification perpetrated by Kierkegaard's writings was in the service of a serious purpose all along. The purpose was to obviate misunderstanding (of its purpose? of the truth? of Christianity?) and even more to forestall a too-previous understanding. (Of?) That purpose, and therefore the explanation of the mystery of the texts, is ready-to-hand and will be perceived by any reader who is sufficiently serious. (Do we have Søren's word that he, now performing in the role of reader, has the requisite gravity to understand his own works?) By analogy (what an analogy!) Christ's life on earth was altogether ambiguous, a genuine incognito (*Philosophical Fragments*, 39). Yet He was noticed and his secret divined by those serious enough to lay hold of it. The serious reader will read Kierkegaard's words as the faithful read the Incarnate Word. Like the God-man, the Kierkegaardian corpus is a sign of contradiction: a perfect duplicity. Piling analogy upon analogy, the would-be seducer will behave just like a man of honorable intentions. If appearances were not deceiving, mankind could not be saved nor women seduced. But "a woman's coyness has regard for the true lover, and yields when he appears" (PV, 17). A serious reader will know what Kierkegaard is up to, just as a woman identifies her true lover. Just as Peter (yet another Peter) recognized the Son of the living God. And we have his word for it (a direct communication) that Søren is a serious reader of his own works. So we have Jesus' own testimony that he is from the Father. So the true lover will swear to the honor of his suit.

A serious reader (a true lover or a knight of faith) will find the assumption that Kierkegaard was an aesthetic writer, suggested by his reading of *Either/Or*, breaking down when it encounters the two edifying discourses that accompanied it. On the contrary he will find the assumption that Kierkegaard was a religious writer verified by every new work that appears: it explains the corpus as a whole. The explanation itself will be given (not in this chapter entitled "The Explanation," but) in part 2 of *The Point of View*.

One might wonder: since the two series of works—pseudonymous and edifying—are almost perfectly parallel (for every aesthetic book a religious book and vice versa), why is this argument not perfectly symmetrical? Why doesn't the hypothesis that Kierkegaard is a religious writer fail when it meets *Either/Or*—supposing some serious reader to have opened *Two Edifying Discourses* first? Why isn't the assumption that he is an aesthetic writer the one that succeeds, the presupposition that explains the authorship as a whole? The privilege here awarded the religious reading does not appear to emerge inevitably from the mere perusal of the texts. Is the religious alone serious, the aesthetic frivolous? Is the seriousness perhaps supplied by the reader? Perhaps. "*Solche Werke sind Spiegel,*" after all. What you see in them—*Affe oder Apostel*—depends on who you are (*Stages on Life's Way*, 26). The assertion that they are essentially religious comes from the author himself. Which proves that they are religious. Or at least that he is a religious man. That is, sees himself as such in the mirror of his word.[4] Which proves that he is serious.

And so we get, once again, "only one thing more" (PV, 18, 9). What we get is the protestation we were denied before, the assurance Kierkegaard could not give. The claim, namely, that he has always been a religious writer. This he permits himself (*qua* man) as a lyrical satisfaction. This God exacts of him (*qua* man) as a religious duty.

Either/Or, he tells us, was a "poetical catharsis" (PV, 18). It was a purgation of the passions (a lyrical gratification and a religious service) which drove him away from the comforts of marriage and into the monastery, where, as Victor the Hermit, he wrote *Either/Or* and where, as Søren Kierkegaard, he constantly fed on devotional reading and monastic self-discipline.

And then, immediately after the publication of *Either/Or*, on his own birthday, he who had undertaken the death of the cloister published *Two Edifying Discourses* and dedicated them to his deceased father. Dedicated to the dead father, the discourses are addressed to "that *individual* whom with joy and gratitude I call *my* reader" (PV, 20). The formula is ritually repeated in the preface to every subsequent collection of edifying discourses. With the preface to the discourses of 1843, which "had and still has for me a very intimate and personal significance, such as it would hardly be possible for me to communicate" (PV, 20n.), he breaks with the public and speaks only to "the individual."

Regine, elsewhere described as the "one unnamed, who shall one day be named,"[5] appears here (in the discourses and in *The Point of View*) discreetly disguised. Coyly concealed from the world, she is revealed to her true lover as the comforting state of

---

4. On the Word as mirror, cf. *For Self-Examination and Judge for Yourselves!*, 33–74.

5. Kierkegaard's dedication to "Two Discourses at the Communion on Fridays," 1851, in ibid., 3.

matrimony Kierkegaard has denied himself and as the single one addressed by these works that issue from the crypt where, with the dead father, he lies buried. Beginning on his birthday: his birth as a writer, which is his true and second birth.

Kierkegaard's explanation of the duplicity of his writings is laced with strange correlatives: lyrical satisfaction/religious obligation, a woman's coyness/Christ's incognito, Regine rejected/ Michael Pedersen Kierkegaard dead. These are unusual couplings (duplicitous themselves), especially the conjunction of Regine and the dead father. His renunciation of Regine sends the author into the living burial of the cloister. Thence, as hermit and victor, in communion with the dead father, to whom he dedicates his religious work, he may communicate with the jilted bride, "that *individual* whom with joy and gratitude I call my reader." Regine effaced and disguised (the queen disowned, the abjured vagina) is the reality the alienation of which establishes the author's rapport with the absent God, whose negative presence is the death of the earthly father. "If I have no father upon earth, be Thou my father!" (*Fear and Trembling*, 27).[6]

Along this tangled trajectory of recuperation, Regine refused (equals the father dead equals the living God) restores him to the reality he has resigned. A reality now, by death and renunciation, made ghostly. That is: writing. The dead letter subserves the vivifying spirit.

But the name foretold ("to one unnamed, who shall one day be named") is never written. What is written is crypts and ciphers that repeatedly reveil without revealing. After his first wife had died childless, Michael Pedersen Kierkegaard began sleeping with her maidservant, Ane Sørensdatter Lund, whom he reluctantly married when he learned she was pregnant. She bore him

---

6. Henning Fenger calls attention to "Kierkegaard's cult of the father" (215) and adds that "it was precisely father figures such as Abraham and Job which exerted a magnetic attraction on Kierkegaard's imagination" (217). The reasons for his fascination with the father are clear enough from Kierkegaard's own accounts of his childhood and youth. Its effects on his conception of Christianity, his view of his activity as a writer, etc., are perhaps deeper and more extensive than is generally suspected.

seven children before she died in 1834. Five of them perished before the father's death four years later. By the time he was twenty-five, Søren knew the guilt that had driven his father into early retirement and lifelong penance: as a child (oppressed by his weary shepherd's life) he had cursed God, and as a man (sexually desperate after the death of his first wife) had carnal knowledge of Søren's mother before marriage. Shaken by this "earthquake" (*Søren Kierkegaard's Journals*, vol. 5, no. 5430: 140–41), and observing the rapid demise of their siblings, Søren and Peter formulated the melancholy hypothesis that Michael would survive all his children, standing alone at the last like a cross on the grave of his hopes (ibid.). After their father had confounded this theory, Peter assumed the paternal role in relation to his younger brother, a role he tried to play all his life. But Søren, who had been made in the image of the father, could not accept the paternity of Peter. It was necessary to make reparation for the father's crimes: because the mother had been violated, woman (read: Regine) must be left intact, and because his father had defied God, the son must practice a perfect submission. In obedience to God, he honors (at last) the promise made earlier to his father: he reads theology and passes his examination. One year later he takes his M.A. with a thesis on irony, and two years after that publishes *Either/Or*. . . .

Peter outlives his brother, preaches his funeral sermon (more apology than eulogy), and gives the world (indirectly) Søren's account of the meaning of his life and work. The triumph of the fatherhood of Peter: Peter, son of Pedersen, who possesses the patronymic more originally than the father. Yet Søren—son of Sørensdatter, who owns the patronymic more originally than the mother he never mentions—: Søren becomes the father. In him (dead) father Pedersen and brother Peter live. The always already deceased father of the never yet living mother (so rudely forced) becomes the father of the surviving father of the dead father. A strange ménage. Stranger still the family romance: an incestuous interlocking of the signifiers of identity and derivation whose issue is the knotted skein of the pseudonymous sons and supplements he (who?) calls his "literature."

To Regine he says, *Infandum me jubes Regina renovare dolorem* (*Søren Kierkegaard's Journals*, vol. 6, no. 6472: 191). Thou biddest me, O queen, renew an unspeakable grief. And of himself, *Perissem nisi periissem* (*Søren Kierkegaard's Journals*, vol. 6, no. 6154: 9). I had perished had I not perished. The writings are his repetition. Corpse become corpus, the repetition is repeated once more (and more than once) in *The Point of View*, and yet again (corpus once more become corpse), for posterity, by Peter. By posterity—by Peter the survivor. Peter, for his brother the negative image of the father, communicates Søren's last will and testament (that his sometime fiancée shall inherit all he leaves behind, just as if she were his widow) to his spiritual bride, Mrs. Fritz Schlegel, through her (earthly) husband (*Letters and Documents*, 33). Peter, when the Schlegels refuse the bequest, administers his brother's estate. Peter lives on and becomes the last author of *The Point of View for My Work as an Author*. Last, not final. As Søren was first, but not original. Peter had always regarded his brother's work with an uncomfortable mixture of respect and distaste, seasoned no doubt by the guilty suspicion that he was one of the official Christians Søren had denounced. Was his publication of *The Point of View* a vindication of his brother? Or a vindictive act vindicating Peter? Whose book is this? And what does it want to say?

III

Brought to its simplest terms, the structure of *The Point of View* comes to this:

Introduction
Part 1
Part 2 $\begin{cases} \text{I.} & \text{The works (the world)} \\ \text{II.} & \text{Personal existence (the self)} \\ \text{III.} & \text{Divine Providence (God)} \end{cases}$
Epilogue
Conclusion

Not knowing how to start and unable to conclude, *The Point of View* provides itself with two beginnings and two endings. Part 2, which makes up the bulk of the text, identifies the sources of the "literature." Its pattern—from the world through the self to

God—is perversely Augustinian.[7] Chapter 1 describes the author's rejection of the world, particularly that monster of bad faith which calls itself Christendom. The aesthetic writings constitute a deception, for its own good, of that world which *vult decipi*. Chapter 2 vindicates Søren's idiosyncratic way of arranging his personal life during the composition of his works. Chapter 3 ascribes the whole of his production—the life as well as the books—to divine Providence.

Christendom (chapter 1 informs us) is an illusion: the dissimulation of Christianity where none exists and the dissemblance of the paganism that goes about in the habiliments of Christian piety. To promote the love of wisdom among those who thought themselves already wise, Socrates had to strip away their conceit of knowledge and expose their fundamental folly. To introduce Christianity into Christendom, Kierkegaard had to deceive Christendom out of its self-deceit. He took the illusion of *soi-disant* believers and gave it back to them; whereupon he confronted them with a strict version of true Christianity. The effect of this strategy is first to get their attention and then to force their option. Christendom's judgment of the works will be the judgment of Christendom by the works, just as Socrates' contemporaries condemned themselves when they presumed to condemn him.

Paganism is immediacy. To introduce Christianity into paganism the apostles could use a direct and positive mode of communication. But Christianity is a product of reflection and Christendom a perversion. To introduce Christianity into Christendom one must be indirect and negative.

One must also (chapter 2) practice a more-than-Socratic self-effacement. This is the explanation and the justification of Søren's peculiar *modus vivendi* during the period of his pseudonymous

---

7. Augustinian structures are common in Kierkegaard's works, distorted as a rule by their passage through a Hegelian conception of reason and a radical Protestant conception of total depravity. Cf. the edifying discourse "To Acquire One's Soul in Patience" in *Edifying Discourses*, 1; 190–210. Cf. also *Philosophical Fragments*, chap. 3; and "A Ram in the Afternoon: Kierkegaard's Discourse of the Other," chapter 5 in this volume.

authorship. While producing the aesthetic works, he appeared to the world as "an idler, a dawdler, a *flâneur*, a frivolous bird, intelligent, perhaps brilliant, witty, etc." (PV, 50), but wholly lacking in seriousness. Inwardly and privately he lived as a monk and a penitent, suffering greatly and sustained only by the conviction that what he was doing was pleasing to God (PV, 48). While writing the religious works he was (at his own request) persecuted by *The Corsair*. This he regards as a gift of divine Providence and as proof of the truth of his religious teachings (PV, 59–60).

At the end of chapter 2, Kierkegaard adds (yet again: 68, 18, 9) "just one thing more":

> When some day my lover comes, he will easily perceive that at the time I was regarded as being ironical, the irony by no means was to be found where the highly esteemed cultured public thought. It lay—and this goes without saying, for my lover cannot possibly be so foolish as to assume that a public can understand irony, which is just as impossible as being an individual *en masse*—he will perceive that the irony lay in the fact that within this aesthetic author, under this appearance of worldliness, there was hidden a religious author, a religious author who at that very time was perhaps consuming for his own edification just as much religiousness as otherwise suffices an entire household. Moreover, my lover will see that irony is present again in the next period of my life, and precisely in that which the highly esteemed cultured public regarded as madness. In an ironic generation (that great aggregation of fools) there is nothing for the real ironist to do but to turn the whole relationship around and himself become the object of everyone's irony. My lover will see how it fit to a T, how my existence-relationship was altogether transformed in exact correspondence to the demand of the productivity. (PV, 62–63)

Who is this lover? When will he come? (It is *nota bene* a "he.") And where do the ironies stop?

At the beginning of chapter 3, Kierkegaard writes:

> This God-relationship of mine is the happy love of my life, which has been in many ways unhappy and troubled. And although this love story (if I dare call it such) has the essential marks of a true love story—that only one person can wholly understand it, and that there is only one to whom it is an absolute joy to tell it: the beloved, who in this case is also the Person by whom one is loved—still it is also pleasant to talk to others about it. (PV, 64–65)

God is Søren's lover. Having renounced Regine and lost his father, he regains them both in God, who is both "he" (the dead father) and lover/beloved (the rejected bride). God is Søren's lover?

God has done for him all the things a combination father and lover would do. He has protected Søren against the paralysis that might otherwise have been induced by his too great wealth of thoughts, for his pen could never keep pace with his ideas. God has prescribed his daily task of writing and (perhaps) told him what to write. Mastering him absolutely, God has defended him against his own strength, which was too much for him. God has been his confidant, the only one with whom he could be honest while he was deceiving the whole world. God has educated him in Christianity and used him as a spy in the service of the idea: a divinely commissioned *voyeur* and *agent provocateur*. Solitary occupations, both of them.

Is the "literature" itself to be ascribed to Søren Kierkegaard or to God?

> I have had more joy from my relation of obedience to God than from the thoughts I produced. It is easy to see that this is the expression of the fact that I have no immediate relationship with God to appeal to, that I cannot and dare not say that it is He who immediately implants the thoughts in me, but that my relationship to God is a relation of reflection, inwardness in reflection, as in general reflection is the distinguishing mark of my individuality, so that even in prayer my strength is in giving thanks. (PV, 68–69)

We are not yet done with irony. Not even here. In a reflective relationship to God—which to be sure rules out all prophecies, revelations, tongues, and other glimmerings of the inner light[8]—it is not clear (on the positive side) just who does what and to whom. And how does it follow from Kierkegaard's essential reflectiveness that his *forte* in prayer is thanksgiving?

> If I were to go right ahead and say that from the first moment on I had an overview of the whole dialectical structure of the whole of my work as an author, or that in every moment, step by step, I had exhausted the possibilities in reflection ahead of time, that subsequent reflection had taught me nothing, or at times something else, that what I had done was certainly right, but that now for the first time I rightly understood it myself: were I to do this, it would be a denial of God and dishonesty toward Him. No, in truth I must say: I cannot understand the whole, just because I can understand the whole down to the least insignificant detail; but what I cannot understand is that now I can understand it, and yet dare not by any means say that at the moment of beginning I understand it so exactly—and yet I am the one who carried it out and made every step with reflection. Idle chatter could easily explain this by saying, as indeed some have said of me, without having any notion of my literary work as a whole, that I was a genius of reflection. But just because I acknowledge the justice of calling me reflective—in truth I am much too reflective not to see that this juxtaposition of reflection and genius explains nothing. For insofar as one has genius he does not have reflection, and vice versa, since reflection is precisely the negation of immediacy. (PV, 72–73)

Søren understands his work—down to the smallest detail—and he does not understand it, the latter because of the former. He has planned and executed the whole, and yet he dares not say, on pain of offending God, that he understood it before he did it or that he understands it now that it is done. He is a genius

---

8. Kierkegaard's attitude toward "mysticism" of any sort is evident in, e.g., *On Authority and Revelation*, and in the scattered animadversions of Judge Wilhelm in *Either/Or*, vol. 2, and *Stages on Life's Way*.

(as he has elsewhere acknowledged),[9] and he is a paragon of reflection. Far from clarifying things, the contradictory relation of reflection and genius (immediacy) only renders the author's comprehension of his own work perfectly indeterminable. Does it also make this text—this final effort at self-understanding and self-explanation—undecidable?

> There is nothing meritorious [*fortjenstligt*] in this; I certainly do not build my salvation on it. Yet it delights me childishly that I have served [*tjent*] in this way, while in relation to God I offer this whole activity of mine with more diffidence than a child who gives its parents something the parents have given the child. O, but the parents are surely not so cruel that, instead of looking kindly upon the child and entering into its idea that this is a present, they take the present from the child and say, "This is our property [*Ejendom*]." So it is also with God; He is not so cruel when one brings Him as a gift . . . His own [*Eget*]. (PV, 89–90n.)

All property (propriety of ownership, proper ownership) is of God. And the whole of man's work—the whole of Søren's work as a writer—has been indulged by God as a charitable charade. A game of love between a loving child and a kindly Parent: whatever Søren has done is (properly) of God, who graciously accepts it as Søren's offering. The work is Søren's own, but only because he has first received it from God, to whom properly it belongs. That is the final resolution of the undecidability, that Søren (like all men, but (genius of reflection that he is) he knows this better than most) serves without deserving. So that (it is now clear why this must be so) all his prayers begin and end with thanksgiving.

By contrast with this idyllic picture of the doting heavenly Father and his trusting child, Søren's earthly father appears (reappears) in this account of divine governance as a melancholy old man who (moved by love) brought his child up in the craziest

---

9. Indirectly, of course, in the essay "Of the Difference between a Genius and an Apostle." Cf. *The Present Age*, 137–63.

way imaginable (PV, 76–83). Søren was sternly and seriously trained in Christianity by Michael, a doleful ancient who cruelly travestied a child as an old man and infected him with his own melancholy. The father, who is a metaphor of Christianity, and whom the child loved most deeply and unstintingly, made the child unhappy—out of love!—by treating him as a man.

A metaphor of Christianity:

> I loved Christianity in a way; to me it was venerable—it had, to be sure, humanly speaking, rendered me exceedingly unhappy. This corresponds to my relationship with my father, the person whom I loved most deeply. And what is the meaning of this? The point precisely is that he made me unhappy—but out of love. His error did not consist in lack of love, but in mistaking a child for an old man. . . . To love . . . him who out of love, though by a misunderstanding . . . made one unhappy—that is . . . the normal formula of reflection for what it is to love. (PV, 77)

As usual the metaphor says more (and less) than it means to. Like Søren's father, Christianity makes us unhappy—out of love. Did God, like Søren's father, mistake us (children) for old men? Kierkegaard's will-to-orthodoxy does not allow him to believe that God has loved us not wisely but too well.[10] But his language shapes a figure of reproach. God, like Michael Pedersen, loves us without understanding. Our task (in reflection) is to bear the misunderstanding . . . and return the love.

Perhaps we (read: Kierkegaard) are to understand God better than He has understood us. In any case, though he is persuaded

---

10. In *Philosophical Fragments*, especially chapters 1 and 2, which call attention to the "misunderstanding" between God and men, it is made clear that the fault is all on our side. Kierkegaard and his pseudonyms hold firmly to a traditional conception of God that rules out any imperfection of whatever sort. But in *The Point of View* Kierkegaard seems less in control of his language than he usually is, and in this passage his language belies him. In this book, in which he endeavors earnestly to define the correct view of his life and authorship, his powers of repression are diminished: in the process of donning his official costume, he inadvertently exposes himself to the public.

of the power of his own will, certain of his superiority to other men, and sure of success in whatever he undertakes, Søren is nonetheless convinced that he is good for nothing but works of penance, destined for frightful sufferings, singled out to be a sacrifice for his fellows.

The eventual death of the father explains the meaning of his upbringing and confirms its tragic effect:

> Then my father died. The powerful religious impressions of my childhood acquired a renewed power over me, in the milder form of ideality. Also I had now become so much older that I was better suited to my upbringing, which had just this misfortune, that it will first rightly do me some good when I get to be forty years old. [Søren was 35 when he wrote these words, 25 when his father died.] For my misfortune (almost from my birth, and completed by my upbringing) was this: not to be a man. But when one is a child—and the other children play or jest or whatever else they do: O, and when one is a youth—and the other young people make love or dance or whatever else they do—: then, although one is a child or a youth, then to be spirit! Fearful torment! Even more fearful if with the help of imagination one knows how to perform the trick of seeming to be the youngest of all. But this misfortune is already diminished when one is forty years old, and in eternity it does not exist. I have had no immediacy; in a strictly human sense, therefore, I have not lived. I began at once with reflection.... (PV, 80–81)

Treated from the beginning as an old man, Søren has never enjoyed the immediacy of childhood or youth. His task therefore is to recover something he has never lost: to begin with reflection and to regain, for the first time, a second immediacy. A new immediacy, which can exist only as a repetition of the first. He is required by his upbringing to create in himself an original repetition. Beginning with reflection, with which one cannot begin, he must recuperate a beginning from which he never began.

In this formidable undertaking he is assisted by the rejected bride. Regine, too, appears (reappears) in this chapter (PV, 83–84). This time disguised as a crucial "*factum*"—a word that means both "fact" (something done) and "fiction" (something made). As the immediacy always already rejected, Regine makes him a poet. As his own decisive rejection of immediacy, she pushes him beyond poetry into the new immediacy of religion. Thus the renounced Regine-God repairs/confirms the damage/good done by the absent father-God. A system of dualities recapitulated eternally in his reflective relationship with the living Father who writes/accepts his works.

Early in *The Point of View* (18) Kierkegaard says that *Either/Or* was a "poetical catharsis." The records of Frederiks Hospital for October and November 1855 show that he suffered almost daily from constipation during his terminal illness. The physician also notes that his patient had always had difficulty urinating when he thought he might be observed, though he passed water easily when alone. In the hospital he was inhibited by the ever-presence of the nurse. "He is almost constantly thinking about it. He even believes that this flaw has had a decided effect on his life and has made him an eccentric" (*Letters and Documents*, 30). Two days before his death he passes both urine and feces involuntarily. He could only live alone, and in solitude his works poured copiously and effortlessly from his pen—so much so that God had to step in and stop the flow (PV, 68).

Søren's dismissal of Regine is the act of self-abridgement by which he becomes (not a husband but) a writer. The symbolic precision of the phallus, by which he cuts himself off from society and social (sexual) production, releases the avalanche of signifiers. A dangerous supplementation. Those other formidable Christians who were obliged for one reason or another to "put away" their women, Aurelius Augustinus and Peter Abelard, confess the double sin of lust and language, from both of which they are saved by violent acts (and agencies) of God. Their castrations (real or symbolic) not only block access to woman, they also necessitate the sublimation of rhetoric and dialectic in prayer. Kierkegaard's gesture (recalling the drastic surgery of Origen) curtails the phallus in order to loosen the tongue and liberate the pen. Writing, which in Augustine and Abelard strives (against stupendous odds and with qualified success) to become a selfless commemoration of the Word, becomes in Kierkegaard the solitary vice of self-expression. A resurrection of/in the dead letter: neither a grateful *Confessions* nor a rueful *Calamitatum*, but a massively excogitated act of exculpation.

At least one of his commentators has believed that Kierkegaard's "thorn in the flesh,"[11] the secret torment from which he suffered throughout his life, was the "sin" of onanism (Geismar, 1: 48). Reality or fantasy (and onanism is both/neither), this is not inconsistent with his rodent melancholy, his morbid religiosity, the bizarre psychosexual configuration projected by his ruptured engagement ("Avec les femmes, il s'agit toujours, d'une façon ou d'une autre, de rupture" (Agacinski, 114)), and the erotic stoppage experienced by his characters. Not to mention his lifelong dread of public urination. His own excretions are all blocked, involuntary, or sinful.

A combination of prodigious productivity and feeble health obliges Søren to watch his diet: "the least dietetic indiscretion, and I am in mortal danger" (PV, 68). Embarrassed by his intellectual riches, he faces the dismal prospect of "starving in the midst of abundance" (PV, 70). But God intervenes and saves him from himself. As a result of his reflective and dialectical nature, his whole life—humanly and socially impoverished and miserable (a passion narrative)—is poured into his writings. God guides (has always already guided) his genius (immediacy) through reflection into writing. Under this divine pedagogy "a poetic and philosophic nature is put aside in order to become a Christian" (PV, 73). In his writings the poet is "got rid of" (PV, 74n.). This evacuation is essential if he is to actualize his religious potential.

That the "aesthetic" writings are a kind of excrement is frequently insinuated in *The Point of View*. "Well, obviously the poetical had to be evacuated. . . . The religious agreed to this elimination . . ." (PV, 84). "My intention was to evacuate as hastily as possible the poetical. . . ." As part of the discipline by which He governs him, God has put him on "a very spare diet" (PV, 86). The pseudonymous productions were "a necessary process of elimination" (PV, 86n., cf. 90). At the same time Kierkegaard was

---

11. Cf. *Søren Kierkegaard's Journals and Papers*, vol. 5, nos. 5913 and 6011: 334–36, 385–86; vol. 6, no. 6224: 37–38; also *The Journals of Søren Kierkegaard*, nos. 1252, 1271, and 1288: 462–64, 473–75, 486–87.

tortured by the thought that his "aesthetic" works were guilty ejaculations. The guilt, surreptitiously confessed by his extravagant essay in self-justification, would be that he had stained himself with self-ab/musing emissions instead of serving God. Søren often dreamed of becoming a pastor in a little rural parish, but some literary project always interposes itself and prevents his resolution. He liked to think that he had been set apart by God to be (Christwise) a sacrifice for many. But "le sacrifice ne s'écrit pas . . . , parce que écrire est une jouissance" (Agacinski, 106). As poet he littered the world with sterile disseminations when he should have been sowing the seed of the Word—and making Regine fruitful.

Not insignificantly, when he explains the technique of indirect communication by which he presents Christianity to his Christian contemporaries, his text is strewn with metaphors of money and of writing. The difference between explaining Christianity to pagans and explaining it to Christians is the "difference between writing on a blank sheet of paper and bringing to light by the application of a caustic fluid a text which is hidden under another text" (PV, 40). The subtext of Danish Christendom is the illusion by which people who are in fact pagans persuade themselves that they are Christian. To deceive them out of this self-deception, one accepts their illusion as "good money" (PV, 40), and by means of one's own counterfeit (which is the real thing in disguise) reveals that their currency is nothing but worthless paper falsely imprinted with the King's seal.

This language appears in a passage in which Kierkegaard is explaining that his "aesthetic" writings are not what they seem to be—dilettantish entertainments—but spiritual works of mercy prompted by faith in "the Lord Jesus Christ" (PV, 41). The metaphors of defecation occur in the veiled account of his renunciation of Regine and again in connection with the story of his education by Providence. Kierkegaard's upbringing—by father/Regine/God—was cathartic. Regine was a physic that consolidated the poet in him, flushed it out, and left him empty for God (PV, 83–84). The whole thing was an evacuation of his reality and a purification of his ideal resources in preparation for a final and spiritual replenishment. Such was the regimen of purgation by which his life and his work were ordered.

Unless, as his enemies think (who are they and where do they exist save in his own fears and fantasies?), the work and the life are nothing but masturbatory gestures aimed at self-gratification and ending in self-pollution.

For his epitaph Kierkegaard chose some verses by the Danish hymnodist, Hans Adolph Brorson:

> Det er en liden Tid
> Saa har jeg vunden,
> Saa er den ganske Strid
> Med Eet forsvunden,
> Saa kan jeg hvile mig
> I Rosensale
> Og uafladelig
> Min Jesum tale.
>
> (*Letters and Documents*, 27)[12]

His vision of eternity confirms and prolongs the course of his temporal life. His passion is never turned to action, but spilled and spent in . . . words.

But this was to be the story of a love affair: a "true love story" (PV, 64). When will the lover come (who is it?); who will fill the void left by this (salubrious or sinful?) kenosis? Though it pained him to talk about himself (why?), and though he would have preferred that his secret (what is it?) be buried with him, Kierkegaard is delighted to talk about his relationship with God. Though only he understands it, and though God—both lover and beloved—is the only one to whom he can speak of it with "absolute joy," yet "there is a joy also in talking about it to others" (PV, 64, 65). There is only one thing that has "more blessedness in finding than a lover in finding the beloved": the thought that finds its perfect expression in speech (PV, 67).

How shall the love of God find expression in the language of men? To love God "in a *Christian* way" (as opposed to "loving

---

12. In English: "In yet a little while / I shall have won; / Then the whole fight / Will all at once be done. / Then I may rest / In bowers of roses / And perpetually / Speak with my Jesus." Cf. in *Point of View*, 67, 103.

men") is to deny the ("Goetheo-Hegelian") claim that the inner is the outer and that truth is "'what the age demands.'" Kierkegaard has tried to express the thought that "in the eyes of the world the truth is a ludicrous exaggeration or an eccentric superfluity, and that the good must suffer" (PV, 88n.). Can Søren, who is still a man, express this thought without hubris? Can he express it at all in a language which is so "selfish" that it does not even suspect the incommensurable discrepancy between God and man? (*Philosophical Fragments*, 34–35). When his poet praises him for his "fidelity . . . to his first love" (PV, 102), he does not tell us who this "first love" is: Regine? the father? God? Could the poet, devoted to the "idea" and no respecter of persons, tell them apart? Maybe the poet himself (whose self?), who speaks as Søren's lover (for/as Søren?), is his first and only love, and all these others (Regine, father, God) merely masks. Whose masks?

"He is too much a poet to be a witness to the truth. He is a border line between them . . ." (PV, 134). *Ipse dixit*.

IV

At the beginning of his epilogue, Kierkegaard imagines a voice (whose is it?) asking him: don't you realize what you have lost in the eyes of the world by making public (not that he did, that was left for Peter) this explanation of your life and work? The answer is: I can no longer be regarded as interesting, crafty, an enigma. I know that I have lost that distinction. But I gain the satisfaction that the problem—how to become a Christian—is clearly formulated by this direct communication. Unless, he adds . . . unless the world becomes enraged at the fact that a mere man has presumed to be so . . . crafty (PV, 93).

Maybe the communication is not so direct after all. The craftiness remains. It is not undone, perhaps only exacerbated, by the revelation. The enigma is not resolved, the indirection not reversed by this direct report to history.

Can it be anything but disingenuous when Kierkegaard points to the "essential" ambiguity in his work and then, before the dust has settled, explains it all away? The duplicity is so carefully plotted, the explanation so breathlessly (hysterically?) offered. . . . To the charge that he began as an aesthete and ended, when older (senile?), in religion, Søren replies that he has barely aged at all, and adds that

> if this were the case, the author would not have written such a book as the present one, and surely would hardly have undertaken to give a survey of the whole work—least of all would he have chosen the moment which coincides with the republication of his first book. (PV, 11)

Unless, of course, he was lying—to his readers and/or to himself. The "explanation" is convertible without remainder. The whole course of his work—not just the publication of *The Crisis* (not to mention *A Literary Review*) after he was officially through with the "aesthetic", but also the planting of the *Edifying Discourses* early in the corpus—might be the cunningly contrived deceit of a poet who wanted to pass for religious. And when his readers were not fooled, he wrote *The Point of View* to tell them what they would not see for themselves. He is so perfectly dialectical—so wholly bereft by reflection of the last (or even the first) traces of his immediacy—that the "ambiguity or duplicity" in his authorship remains in spite of everything he says by way of clarification. Perfectly reflective is perfectly undecided. Who forgoes immediacy inhabits duplicity. Kierkegaard himself suspects that his disambiguation leaves the ambiguity in place, and what we are given sounds all too much like the "protestation" he knows to be of no avail (PV, 15–16).

The argument of part 2, chapter 1 (the explanation never quite forthcoming in part 1, B, "The Explanation") presupposes a hierarchy of motives in which the aesthetic is demeaned and the religious privileged: "the purely religious work . . . of course establishes the point of view" (PV, 42). But that order of values is exactly what is subverted in part 1 by Kierkegaard's insistence on the essential mystification of his writings. Religion is not posited from the first as the proper meaning of the whole, and the misunderstanding of his work—*Either/Or* praised, the *Discourses* ignored—is not due to his readers' imperception but to his own artistry. The irony required for the conception and execution of the canon proscribes any finite teleology, and the ambiguity inscribed in and by his texts has its source deep in that "personal existence" which Søren thinks he can distinguish from his writings. Deeper perhaps than he knows:

> Every religious author is *eo ipso* polemical; for the world is not so good that the religious man can assume that he has triumphed or is in the party of the majority. (PV, 59)

Yet he may (it appears) assume that the world is evil—so wicked that he is permitted (obligated?) to attack it. He assumes at any rate that *it* will attack *him* (in spite of appearances, a good and god-fearing man), and that it is his duty (v. the *Corsair* affair) to invite an assault on his person. He needs the credentials, and the world, which craves deception anyway, must be prompted to play its part in the script he has prepared for it. Søren offers his sufferings in evidence of his rectitude. What I say is true, and "I prove it by the fact that I am persecuted." But this "miraculous syllogism" (PV, 59)—his Christlike abjection—proves nothing. The "Magister of Irony" (PV, 57, 58) must know that not everyone who is derided is therefore a martyr and a witness for the truth: Christ himself was a "sign of contradiction" (*Training in Christianity*, 124–27; Kierkegaard is paraphrasing Luke 2: 34–35). It is only to be expected that the world will mistake his godly humility for arrogance. And it is hardly surprising that a man who, because he is "absolutely weak, and therefore . . . absolutely in need of God," isolates himself from human society and scorns the "indulgent judgment of 'a highly respected public'" (PV, 65n.) . . . will be thought proud.

Kierkegaard admits (PV, 72, 154) that the account of his work offered in *The Point of View* represents an understanding achieved after the fact. "From the beginning I could not thus survey what has been in fact my own development" (PV, 154). The pseudonymous corpus was a "Godfearing satire" flung against and exposed to the "profane satire" of the mob (PV, 161). But the pseudonyms have turned him every which way but loose, and even with the publication of *The Point of View* he has not lost "the interesting distinction of being an interesting possibility" (PV, 93). If anything he becomes even more interesting—the skein of possibilities even more intricately snarled—in this direct communication by which he inserts his final and definitive report in the record of history.

"Direct communication"? The pseudonymous works were an indirect communication designed to deceive people out of illusion into the truth for their own good. *The Point of View*, though it calls itself direct, is just as oblique as the rest. But who is deceived? And to what end? It has persuaded a lot of Kierkegaard's commentators to accept his own (retrospectively achieved) estimate of his life and work. Did it also deceive Søren?

Toward the end of the epilogue Kierkegaard allows that now the "benevolent reader . . . knows what kind of author I am" (PV, 98). But he adds, outside the text, that he himself possesses "a more exact and purely personal interpretation" of his life as a "matter of course" (PV, 98n.).

For all the direct communication, the secret is safe. Søren is confident that he belongs to history. He even knows what his place in history will be, though he's not telling. "What may betide me in the immediate future I do not know; how it will be in the following age when I have passed into history, that I know." But the historical future is of no moment compared to "that future which is nearest of all and at every instant equally near: eternity." In the historical future the author will be absent, and in eternity he shall have become—absolutely—"an absent one" (PV, 99).

Was he ever, even in the present, anything but the absent one? He admits that he has never had any immediacy: he has never been fully present in any period of his life, but always nowhere else in reflection. And is he not, even in/from this direct report . . . absent? Absent now, absent before, absent eternally. Søren is always already the absent one; absent first, last, and forever with the absent father, the absent bride, and the absent God. All one, and one and all gone.

In eternity, presumably, Søren's lover—all his lovers—will come at last. And the true love story will have a happy ending: "lived happily ever after."

Kierkegaard insists that his strictly religious works provide the point of view from which the others are to be understood. But the simple contradiction between the aesthetic and the religious writings does not by itself establish an ordering of the texts and an allocation of priorities. Of course we have Søren's word for it that he has always been a religious author. "Kierkegaard himself . . . was the first to provide the 'correct,' religious interpretation of his life" (Fenger, 213). But his privileging word only adds another to the series of religious works and therefore cannot legitimately ask to be taken as the transcendent perspective that unifies the canon. In a situation as equivocal as this, Kierkegaard's protestation sounds like the desperate *petitio* of a dialectician *in extremis*. He had outsmarted himself. The position he wanted earnestly and securely to occupy has been sabotaged by the methods he used to take it. The dialectic eats everything it throws up, and the mystifier becomes a mystery to himself.

Reflection divides but does not conquer: there is no such thing as "the corpus as a whole." The writings cannot constitute a totality. *The Concept of Irony* (among others) comes before the series of works designated as the "literature," but the point of view it defines is itself the interiority of the "literature." Irony, which undercuts every point of view, is the point of view from which all the works are written. *The Point of View* is (allegedly) written and (certainly) published after the last book in the corpus. Yet other books that do belong to the "literature" were published after it was written, and its own indirection *malgré soi* makes it legible as an iteration of its predecessors. Prologue and epilogue alike move in and out of the space of the "literature," so that the line that would demarcate the inside from the outside cannot be drawn. Like the line that would distinguish the two sides of the Möbius strip, the boundary of Kierkegaard's corpus ends, endlessly, with its own beginning. The canon contravenes itself.

In the little pamphlet "On My Work as an Author," which he himself published in 1851, Kierkegaard says, "All the earlier pseudonymity is lower than 'the edifying author'; the new pseudonym [Anti-Climacus] is a higher pseudonymity" (PV, 142n.). The quotation marks around "the edifying author," who is Søren Kierkegaard, are his own.

"Simultaneously," he says, "one surely cannot be older than oneself" (PV, 149n.). But Quidam is,[13] and so is the young man of *Repetition*. On his own showing ("I have never had any immediacy. . . . I began at once with reflection") Kierkegaard (him-

---

13. The melancholy author-hero of "Guilty? / Not Guilty?", the third part of *Stages on Life's Way*.

self) had always been older than himself. His upbringing, he tells us, does not "turn out completely to my advantage until I am forty years old" (PV, 80–81). This in 1848, when he is thirty-five. Already he speaks of himself in the past tense: "I also know *who* . . . I was" (PV, 98). Scarcely mature, but senile in reflection, he sums himself up and recalls his life as a thing foregone. To cap his retrospective he survives himself infinitely (as the poet, the "'absent one'") (PV, 100, 99) in the eternity of the imagination. Unable to overtake himself, Søren was never the same person. At most a free variable (an x), he is at last an absolute absence. A constant evanscence.

That Kierkegaard presumes his own integrity is not important. By itself that would be no more than a personal failing, a form of disingenuousness to which anyone might be tempted by circumstance. What is important is that he presupposes the *possibility* of an authenticity—a singleness of purpose and a coincidence of purpose and performance—against which his experience as the master of a whole troop of pseudonyms (not to mention his concept of irony) should have cautioned him. And this is not personal; it is an assumption necessary to the structure of *The Point of View*. But it is an assumption which can hardly be given sense, much less verity.

It is necessary to "regard the whole of Kierkegaard's life as a gigantic play in which Kierkegaard acted a profusion of roles, among them that of Søren Kierkegaard in countless versions" (Fenger, 147). He was a "poet who, as actor and prompter, every moment becomes so intensely a part of his role that he believes in it and in himself" (Fenger, 214). Peter was right: "Søren Kierkegaard" was one of the pseudonyms of Søren Kierkegaard. If a man writes three books, in the course of which he tries to develop a consistent point of view, and signs them all "Immanuel Kant," our invincible tendency as readers is to regard them as the work of one man and to identify the author as the historical person called by that name: 1724–1804, professor of logic at Königsberg, member of the Royal Academy of the Sciences in Berlin, etc. And even though the name be no more than shorthand for an authorial intention retrojected from the text, nevertheless the ascription is "just" in the only applicable sense of that word. But if a man writes two dozen works, outlining half a dozen incompatible positions, ascribes most of them to transparently fictive noms de plume, and signs the rest of them "Søren Kierkegaard" . . . the reader is (at least) put on guard.

There is perhaps never good reason (even in the "normal" case) to identify the "writer" with the "actual" person whose name he signs, though it is natural to do so. But in the latter the course of nature is blocked by the flagrant interposition of artifice. The irruption of artifice introduces the distinction between art and nature. The proliferation of artifice makes the distinction undecidable and the identity of the natural indeterminable. When a man fabricates as many masks to hide behind as Kierkegaard does, one cannot trust his (purportedly) direct asseverations. And when he signs his own name, it no longer has the effects of the signature.

Søren Kierkegaard was one of his own pseudonyms. Or perhaps all of them are God's pseudonyms. That is what Søren would have us believe.

In his conclusion Kierkegaard imagines what his poet will say when he comes. In this final work, his direct report to history, it is the poet—not the pseudonym "Søren Kierkegaard" but an anonymous poet—who gets the last word. Ironical to the very end. And the poet attributes all of the work to God. On behalf of Kierkegaard, who is now in the place of the hero:

> The dialectical structure he brought to completion . . . he could not ascribe to any man, least of all . . . to himself; if he were to ascribe it to anyone, it would be to Providence, to whom it was in fact ascribed, day after day and year after year by the author. . . . (PV, 103)

It is possible that no one wrote his books ("if he were to ascribe it to anyone"), and because his relationship to God is dialectical he cannot say with certainty just who wrote them. But "in fact" the corpus is ascribed [*tilegnet*: both "appropriated" and "dedicated"] to God.

Kierkegaard likes to remind us that he writes "without authority," and that he is not the author of his works but only their reader (PV, 155). The books which he appears to write are in fact a syllabus of readings prescribed for him by God as part of his training in Christianity. He himself is only an instrument (perhaps only an instrumentality) used maieutically by Providence to call the attention of others to what he has learned. It is to Providence, therefore, that he surrenders the authorship and the authority which he has renounced. It is divine Providence—this is the poet's view, and we have his word that it is also Søren's view—Who inscribed and to Whom are ascribed all of the so-called works of Søren Kierkegaard.

But if God wrote the Kierkegaardian "literature," who wrote this report to history that provides the definitive point of view on the work as a whole? That detotalized whole, of which *The Point of View* both is and is not a part? "In conclusion I will let another speak, my poet . . ." (PV, 100). It is the poet—repressed and rejected—who wraps it all up. His encomium is fenced off by quotation marks. To the members of his divided self Kierkegaard assigns the roles of (religious) hero and (aesthetic) poet.[14] The poet is sacrificed to the man of faith . . . and surviving him composes the panegyric that assures his immortality. Etc. The process of supplementation and relocation, like any product of reflection, goes on and on and on. . . . Once quotation marks demand to appear, they don't know where to stop. That's a quotation.

In the course of explaining the role played by divine Providence in the production of his works, Kierkegaard writes, "Away from 'the poet' . . . , away from speculation . . . to becoming a Christian. The movement is [this is italicized]: *back*" (PV, 74–75). "On My Work as an Author" glosses this "back":

> And this is also (*in reflection*, as in fact it was originally) the *Christian movement*. In the Christian sense simplicity is not the point of departure from which one goes on to become interesting, witty, profound, poet, philosopher, etc. No, quite the contrary. One begins *here* [with the interesting, etc.] and then becomes simpler and simpler; one *arrives at* simplicity. This, in "Christendom," is the *Christian* move-

---

14. Cf. the discussion of the relation of hero and poet in *Fear and Trembling*, 30–31. Cf. also the discussion of this and other passages in Reed, *Meditations on the Hero*, chap. 2.

ment of reflection; one does not reflect oneself into Christianity, but one reflects oneself out of something else and becomes, more and more simply, a Christian. (PV, 144)

This far from simple pronouncement sounds like the fantasy of an autobiography. A life that did not begin with the simplicity of the immediate and proceed to reflection, but rather began with reflection—always already lost in the maze of dialectic—and moved toward achieving simplicity. A new *acquired* immediacy repeating an originality that never had been.

To become a Christian is to leave behind the illusions of "the interesting," in which one has always already been entrapped, and to progress toward the recovery of a simplicity and integrity one has never enjoyed. Is that possible? "That things go round and again go round / Has rather a classical sound" (Stevens, *Collected Poems*, 150). There *are* pleasures in merely circulating. But dialectic is a maze without an exit. Without so much as the satisfaction of a minotaur at the center. Without, for that matter, a center.

Simplicity? Surely the Master of Irony knows that reflection is incurable and irreversible and that the thought of attaining simplicity is incoherent, so that to reflect oneself out of reflection is an absurd project. But perhaps . . . by virtue of the absurd . . . it is possible to arrive at a simplicity that is not possible. By virtue of the absurd. A direct way through the maze of reflection. And survival beyond it. There is (absurdly) Ariadne's thread. And Scheherazade's neck. Things hold together somehow.

Peter was punctilious in his choice of articles. This book is not *the* point of view for his work as an author. It is only *a* point of view. Another point of view in a series from each of which the texts that compose the corpus regroup themselves. A plurality of wholes and no totality. There is no such thing as the point of view for Kierkegaard's work: no superintendent signified that organizes, finally, its inscriptions. There is just another perspective, and then another, and then. . . . The death of the author, who "historically died of a mortal disease but poetically died of longing for eternity" (so his poet) (PV, 103), is only the fortuitous disappearance from the scene of the last of the pseudonyms. Søren himself had always been, absolutely, absent.

Did he know this? In this book he doesn't want to know it. But in spite of himself, his negative capability was almost perfect. Almost:

> The neutral and not neutrality, the neutral beyond dialectical contradiction and all opposition: such would be the possibility of a "narrative," a *"récit,"* that would no longer be simply a form, a genre, or a literary *mode*, and that goes, that is borne, beyond the system of philosophical oppositions. The neutral cannot be governed by any of the terms involved in an opposition within philosophical language and natural language. And yet it is not outside of language: it is, for example, narrative voice. Despite the negative form that it takes on in grammar (*ne-uter*, neither-nor) and that betrays it, it surpasses negativity. It is linked rather to the double affirmation (yes, yes, come, come) that requotes [*ré-cite*] itself and becomes involved in the *récit*. (Derrida, "Living On: Border Lines," 106–7)

"Not everything has yet happened" ("Living On: Border Lines," 145). The infinitude of the dialectic is (may be) an infinite openness. If it's a trap, it's a trap in which there is always another trapdoor. The neutral surpasses neutrality and negativity. We survive ourselves. Under erasure, marked by the sign of the cross, we live on. Survival, at and through the still point of the dialectic—the placeless place and the present beyond presence and absence—the point at which all oppositions are neutered: is that the always already impossibly given new immediacy? The Other that eludes dialectical alternation and recuperation? The reality of grace? Do we—did he—await an advent that has always already taken place?

That would be (yes, yes) a double affirmation. Surely I come. Amen. Even so, come.

Shortly before his death St. Thomas Aquinas experienced rapture. Called to work again by his secretary, he said, "I can do no more. Such things have been revealed to me that all that I have written seems to me as so much straw" (Maritain, *St. Thomas Aquinas*, 54). To which Jacques Maritain adds: he could say that, he had written it (*Art and Scholasticism*, 145).

Karl Barth once reported the following dream. I dreamed, he

said, that I had died and gone to heaven. I presented myself at the gates of pearl with copies of all my theological works held tightly in my arms. I showed them to St. Peter and identified myself as Professor Karl Barth, author of the *Kirchliche Dogmatik*. St. Peter gave me a little red child's wagon to carry my books and summoned an angel to take me to my destination. I followed the angel down a street paved with gold, tugging the wagonload of books behind me. The street was lined on both sides with high hedgerows, and from beyond the hedgerows I heard a great noise, like the sound of many waters. After a while I could resist the temptation no longer. I climbed upon the volumes of the *Kirchliche Dogmatik* stacked in my wagon and looked over the hedges. There I saw all the numberless multitude of the heavenly host, together with the whole company of saints . . . laughing.

Brother Thomas and Professor Barth had attained, perhaps, the only possible point of view for their work as authors. The case of Magister Kierkegaard is not so clear.

Bibliography

Agacinski, Sylviane. *Aparté: Conceptions et Morts de Søren Kierkegaard*. Paris: Aubier-Flammarion, 1977.
Auerbach, Erich. *Mimesis*. Princeton: Princeton University Press, 1953.
Bloom, Harold, et al. *Deconstruction and Criticism*. New York: Seabury Press, 1979.
Booth, Wayne C. *A Rhetoric of Irony*. Chicago: University of Chicago Press, 1974.
Capel, Lee. Translator's historical introduction to Søren Kierkegaard. *The Concept of Irony: With Constant Reference to Socrates*, q.v.
Danske Sange. Edited by Bo Bramsen and Else Larsen. Copenhagen: Politikens Forlag, 1954.
Delaney, Samuel R. *Tales of Nevèrÿon*. New York: Bantam Books, 1979.
Derrida, Jacques. *Dissemination*. Translated by Barbara Johnson. Chicago: University of Chicago Press, 1981.

———. "Living On: Border Lines." In Harold Bloom et al., *Deconstruction and Criticism*, q.v.

———. "Of an Apocalyptic Tone Recently Adopted in Philosophy." *Semeia*, no. 23 (1982): 63–97.

———. *Of Grammatology*. Translated by Gayatri Spivak. Baltimore: Johns Hopkins University Press, 1976.

———. "Structure, Sign and Play in the Discourse of the Human Sciences." In Jacques Derrida, *Writing and Difference*, q.v.

———. *Writing and Difference*. Translated by Alan Bass. Chicago: University of Chicago Press, 1978.

Doescher, W.O. "Kant's Postulate of Practical Freedom." In *The Heritage of Kant*, edited by G.T. Whitney and D.F. Bowers. Princeton: Princeton University Press, 1939.

Fenger, Henning. *Kierkegaard, the Myths and Their Origins*. New Haven: Yale University Press, 1980.

Geismar, Eduard. *Søren Kierkegaard: Hans Livsudvikling og Forfattervirksomhed*. Copenhagen: G.E.C. Gads, 1926.

Gray, J. Glenn, ed. *G.W.F. Hegel on Art, Religion, Philosophy*. New York: Harper and Row, 1970.

Kant, Immanuel. *Kant's Critique of Practical Reason and Other Writings in Moral Philosophy*. Edited and translated by L.W. Beck. Chicago: University of Chicago Press, 1949.

Kelly, Walt. *Ten Ever-Lovin' Blue-Eyed Years with Pogo*. New York: Simon and Schuster, 1972.

Kierkegaard, Søren. *Christian Discourses*. Translated by Walter Lowrie. London: Oxford University Press, 1940.

———. *The Concept of Anxiety*. Translated by Reidar Thomte and Albert B. Anderson. Princeton: Princeton University Press, 1980.

———. *The Concept of Dread*. 2d ed. Translated by Walter Lowrie. Princeton: Princeton University Press, 1957.

———. *The Concept of Irony: With Constant Reference to Socrates*. Translated by Lee M. Capel. New York: Harper and Row, 1965.

———. *Concluding Unscientific Postscript*. Translated by David F. Swenson and Walter Lowrie. Princeton: Princeton University Press, 1941.

———. *Edifying Discourses*. Translated by David F. Swenson and Lillian Marvin Swenson. Minneapolis: Augsburg Publishing House, 1962.

---. *Either/Or*. Translated by David F. Swenson and Lillian Marvin Swenson. Revisions and foreword by Howard A. Johnson. Garden City, N.Y.: Doubleday, 1959.

---. *Fear and Tembling*. In Søren Kierkegaard, *Fear and Trembling* and *The Sickness Unto Death* (in one volume), q.v.

---. *Fear and Trembling* and *Repetition*. Translated and edited (in one volume) by Howard V. Hong and Edna H. Hong. Princeton University Press, 1983.

---. *Fear and Trembling* and *The Sickness Unto Death*. Translated (in one volume) by Walter Lowrie. Princeton: Princeton University Press, 1968.

---. *For Self-Examination* and *Judge for Yourselves!* Translated (in one volume) by Walter Lowrie. Princeton: Princeton University Press, 1944.

---. *The Gospel of Suffering*. Translated by David F. Swenson and Lillian Marvin Swenson. Minneapolis: Augsburg Publishing House, 1948.

---. *Johannes Climacus or, De omnibus dubitandum est*. Translated by T. H. Croxall. Stanford: Stanford University Press, 1958.

---. *The Journals of Søren Kierkegaard*. Translated and edited by Alexander Dru. London: Oxford University Press, 1938.

---. *Letters and Documents*. Translated by Henrik Rosenmeier. Princeton: Princeton University Press, 1978.

---. "Man's Need of God Constitutes His Highest Perfection." In Søren Kierkegaard, *Edifying Discourses*, q.v.

---. *On Authority and Revelation*. Translated by Walter Lowrie. Princeton: Princeton University Press, 1955.

---. *Philosophical Fragments*. 2d ed. Translated by David F. Swenson and Howard V. Hong. Introduction and commentary by Niels Thulstrup. Princeton: Princeton University Press, 1962.

---. *The Point of View for my Work as an Author*. 2d ed. Translated by Walter Lowrie. New York: Harper and Row, 1962.

---. *The Present Age*. Translated by Alexander Dru and Walter Lowrie. London: Oxford University Press, 1940.

---. *Purity of Heart*. New York: Harper and Brothers, 1948.

---. *Repetition*. Translated by Walter Lowrie. New York: Harper and Row, 1964.

———. *Samlede Vaerker*. 3d ed. Edited by A. B. Drachmann, J. L. Heiberg, H. O. Lange. Revised and updated by Peter P. Rohde. Copenhagen: Gyldendal, 1962–64.

———. *The Sickness unto Death*. In Søren Kierkegaard, *Fear and Trembling* and *The Sickness Unto Death* (in one volume), q.v.

———. *Søren Kierkegaard's Journals and Papers*. Translated by Howard V. Hong and Edna H. Hong. Bloomington: Indiana University Press, 1978.

———. *Søren Kierkegaards Papirer*. 2d ed. Enlarged by Niels Thulstrup. Copenhagen: Gyldendal, 1968–78.

———. *Stages on Life's Way*. Translated by Walter Lowrie. Princeton: Princeton University Press, 1940.

———. "To Acquire One's Soul in Patience." In Søren Kierkegaard, *Edifying Discourses*, q.v.

———. *Training in Christianity*. Translated by Walter Lowrie. Princeton: Princeton University Press, 1947.

———. "Two Discourses at the Communion on Fridays." In Søren Kierkegaard, *For Self-Examination* and *Judge for Yourselves!* (in one volume), q.v.

Lacan, Jacques. *Écrits*. New York: W. W. Norton, 1977.

Lewis, C. S. *Essays Presented to Charles Williams*. Grand Rapids: William B. Eerdmans Publishing Co., 1974.

Lønning, Per. "Samtidighedens Situation." Oslo: Forlaget Land og Kirke, 1954.

Mackey, Louis. *Kierkegaard: A Kind of Poet*. Philadelphia: University of Pennsylvania Press, 1971.

———. "Kierkegaard's Lyric of Faith: A Look at *Fear and Trembling*." *Rice Institute Pamphlet* 47, no. 2 (July 1960): 30–47.

Maritain, Jacques. *Art and Scholasticism*. New York: Charles Scribner's Sons, 1962.

———. *St. Thomas Aquinas*. New York: Meridian Books, 1958.

Nietzsche, Friedrich. *Beyond Good and Evil*. Translated by Walter Kaufmann. New York: Vintage Books, 1966.

Percy, Walker. *The Last Gentleman*. New York: Avon Books, 1978.

Pynchon, Thomas. *The Crying of Lot 49*. New York: Bantam Books, 1967.

———. *Gravity's Rainbow*. New York: Viking Press, 1973.

Reed, Walter L. *Meditations on the Hero*. New Haven: Yale University Press, 1974.

Said, Edward. *Beginnings: Intention and Method*. New York: Basic Books, 1975.
Stevens, Wallace. *The Collected Poems*. New York: Alfred A. Knopf, 1954.
———. *Opus Posthumous*. New York: Alfred A. Knopf, 1957.
Wilde, Alan. *Horizons of Assent*. Baltimore: Johns Hopkins University Press, 1981.

Index

Abelard, Peter, 178
Abraham: as the hero of faith, 45; as higher than the universal, 54–56; irony of, 59–60; and knight of resignation, 50–51; as not needing a poet, 46; as paradigm of faith, 63; as paradox, 49; as unmediatable, 8; as winning the temporal, 46
Absence: S.K. as, 185, 187, 190–91
Absolute Spirit: as its own estrangement and recuperation, xix
Absurd, by virtue of: defined, 51; as making possible repetition, 91; and making the religious movement, 82
Accidental, the: Christ as, 97; as metaphor in *Repetition*, 76–77, 97
Acosmism: irrelevance of for S.K., 144, 148, 152; problem of in the *Postscript*, 143; result of S.K.'s rhetoric, 157–58; and rhetoric, 142
Actuality: as category of being, 126–27; and conjunction of certainty and uncertainty, 128; and essence, 126–27; of existence, 146; Kant's view of, 146–47; of past, 123; of self, 146–47
Agacinski, Sylvianne, xiii, 161n, 179, 180
Alterity: as the limit of language, 102; as the suppressed language of the West, 124–25; as theme of *Philosophical Fragments*, 102
Analogy: absence of logic of in Hegel and S.K., 156
Androgyne: Constantin as, 82–83; the young man as, 83
Apocalyptic: S.K.'s texts as, xiii
Aquinas, Thomas, 191
Aristotle: on being and essence, 126; and freedom and history, 127
Auerbach, Erich, 40n
Augustine, 36–39; and the reality of the world, 152; and the structure of S.K.'s works, 170–71; and writing, 178
Augustinus Aurelius, 178

Barth, Karl, 191–92
Beginning: of *The Point of View*, 170; and repetition, 16, 35
Being: and essence, 125–27; as gift, 101; as grace, 101; as repeated, 101; and thinking, 143; and thought, 101
Belief: as affirming becoming, 128; and certainty, 128–29; and dialectic, 190–91; as noncognitive, 128; as object of faith, 129
Book: as attempted rape of reality, 98; defined, 95; and *Repetition*, 95–96
Borderline: the girl in *Repetition*, 84, 88; humor as borderline of faith, 96; of the interesting, 74; Job as, 87–88; S.K. as, 182; of S.K.'s writings, 186; of transcendence, 90

Castration: as the violence of writing, 98
Christendom: as illusion and dissimulation, 171; S.K.'s relation to, 171; as self-deceiving, 171
Christianity: and absolute knowledge, 114; and the death of philosophy, xxi; as decentering sexuality, 99; and despair, 61; as dissimulated by Christendom, 171; and *Fragments*, *Postscript*, 20; and the irrationality of history, 132; as man different from God, 113–14; metaphor of, 176–77; and paganism, 171; and the possibility of irrationality, 120; as reality of history, 96–97; and reason, 109–10; and the relation of history to the eternal, 120–23; as repeating paganism, 99; as subject of *Fragments*, 102; as transforming religious consciousness, 34n; as unthinkable, 113–14; view of history, 129; view of time and eternity, 108
Clement of Alexandria, 92
Conscience: the Good's accusation of as the eternal, 31; as inefficacy of self-discipline, 32–33
Constantius, Constantin: as androgyne, 82–83; as mad, 83, 85
Contemporaneity, 121–22

Derrida, ix, x, xviii n
Descartes, René, 3
Dialectician: and the absurdity of faith, 53–54; and silence, 49; vs. the lyricist, 47
Difference: as absolute, 111–12; and the absolute paradox, 123; as indistinguishable from the same, 112–13; the introduction of Christianity that undoes philosophy, xx–xxi; as irreducible to identity, xx; and life and death, 116; as the subject of thought, 115–16; a unmediatable, xx
Direct communication: of *Point of View*, 163, 183–85; vs. indirect communication, 134–35

Essence: and being, 125–27
Essential Secret: God as S.K.'s, 163; S.K.'s as onanism, 179; as never revealed, 163
Eternal, the: Christian view of, 108; as coming into being in the Moment, 105–6; as demanding the whole of time, 24–25; and faith, 121; as the Good accusing conscience, 31; the historicity of, 120–21; and history, 127; and human forgetfulness, 28; and the intelligibility of the eternal, 71; and the object of faith, 129; and the temporal, 46; as transcendent signified, 107
Ethical Reality: as isolation of individual, 152, 154; of subject as only reality, 143, 148
Ethics: as defined by the eternal, 24–25; and despair, 30; and faith, 54, 60; and the Good, 30–31; impasse of, 23, 39; S.K.'s discussion of as unique, 24; S.K.'s as lacking concern for metaphysical basis, 141; S.K.'s need for metaphysical basis, 142–43; as making itself impossible, 27–28; reality of subject, 143; as referred to by actuality, 147–48; relationship with religion, 23, 49; and repentance, 64–65; and silence, 60–61; and sin, 65–66; situation of as religious, 28–29; strategy of S.K., 141–42
Exception, the: and breaking with the universal, 92; as collision of the ethical and the religious, 88–89; Job as, 88; and the poet, 92; the religious exception, 93

Faith: Abraham as hero of, 45; Abraham as paradigm of, 63; absurdity of and ethics, 54; as being of God, 53; as the happy passion, 121; as noncognitive, 121; object of, 129; as the relation of history to the eternal, 120–21; silence of and ethics, 60–61; silence of and poetry, 88; unintelligibility of, 122–23; as union of the finite and the infinite, 53; vs. despair, 61, 71

Farce: as the accidental securing the essential, 80–81; and the book, 95; characters and situations of as types, 80; Christ as, 97; as comical repetition, 81; and the mature person, 79; as transcendence intruding into reflection, 84; as transgressive, 95

Fenger, Henning, 161 n, 168 n, 185–86, 187

Freedom: as generating its own possibilities, 155–56; and guilt, 37; and history, 127, 150–51; as infinitized, 154–55; as postulate, 27; and reality, 149–51; as *sine qua non* of ethics, 149–50

Geismar, Eduard, 179

Genius: contradictory relation of to reflection, 175; S.K.'s as directed by God, 179

God: as absolute fact, 34; as existential possibility, 34; and faith, 53; as the Good, 23, 31, 33; as guiding S.K. in his writing, 188; as indemonstrable, 109; as indulging S.K., 175; as S.K.'s lover, 173; S.K. as pseudonym, 183; S.K.'s writings as ascribed to, 188; as the knight of resignation, 50; and natural theology, 154; and need of the Good, 37; as negatively present, 153–54; as owning the Kierkegaardian *corpus*, 175; as prescribing S.K.'s writings, 173, 188–89; relationship with man as absolute surprise, xx; as revealed by guilt, 83–84; and transcendence, 90; as the transcendent, 93; as using S.K. as a spy, 173

God-man, the: as sign of contradiction, 168, 184

Good, the: as absolutely different than man, 33; as defined in terms of its acquisition, 29; and ethics, 30–31; exposition of, 30; as God, 23, 31, 33; and guilt, 31, 33; and the individual, 24; and the moral task, 25–26; and need of, 34, 37; as nonexclusive, 30; as nonfinite, 29; as problem of being, not values, 25

Grace: of being, 101

Guilt: as accused by the Good, 31; acknowledgment of as difference from God, 33; and consciousness of obligation, 26; as fundamental moral phenomenon, 26–27; and the Good, 33; as highest expression of the religious, 64–65; and S.K.'s alleged onanism, 180; of S.K. and his father, 169; and S.K.'s writings, 179–80; as need of the Good, 37; and penitence, 28–29; as purity of heart, 31; as revealing reality of God, 33–34; and sin, 65

Hegel, G. W. F.: and absolute spirit, xix; and *The Concept of Irony*, 1; and concept of nothing, negation, 19; as erasing the thing-in-itself, 147; and existential dialectic, 34; and indistinguishability of identity and difference, 156; S.K.'s relation to, xix; as mastering irony, 12, 15; mendaciousness of, 147; and relation of time to the eternal, 122; view of history, 129

Hero, the: of doubt, 45–46; and the poet, 44–47; as relinquishing the world, 52

History: Christian view of, 108; Christianity as reality of, 96–97; as conjunction of time and eternity, 18; defined, 17–18; and faith, 121; as intercourse of irony, 18; and irony, repetition, 21; as irrational, 132; S.K.'s place in, 185; and reality, 150–51; in relation to the eternal, 120–21, 127; Socratic view of, 108

Humor: as place of faith, 96

Hymen, 99

Idea, 3–5

Indirect Communication: as confusing connotation, 136; and ethics, 24; as existential address, 24; as intro-

Indirect Communication (*continued*) ducing Christianity into Christendom, 171–72; as ironic, 134, 137; as obviating reference, 135–36; as resulting in acosmism, 157–58; rhetoric of, 141–42, 153–54; as self-defeating, 156–57; a sign vs. referent, 136–37; as undercutting itself, 138; unique hermeneutical problem of, 141–42; vs. direct communication, 134–35

"Individual, that": as both Michael Pedersen Kierkegaard and Regine Olsen, 168; as Michael Pedersen Kierkegaard, 167; as ritually repeated, 167

Individual, the: as higher than the universal, 54–56; as *inter-esse* between thinking and being, 143; as third category between ethics and selfishness, 58

Interesting, the: and the absurd, 101; and becoming a Christian, 190; as borderline between the actual and the ideal, 74, 88; as interruption of the ideal by the actual, 77; metaphysics as, 71; as sexual, 74; as unrepeatable, 74; woman as saving us from, 97–98

Irony: of Abraham, 59–60; as beyond surprising, 99; as a case of allegory, 13–14; as anomaly of the absolute, 134; as autotelic, 14–15; as beginning, 9–10; defined, 133; defined as infinite freedom, 9; as defining the essence of subjectivity, 16, 20; as diremption of subject and object, etc., 8, 13, 20; and doubt, 2; as estranged from existence, 15; as guaranteeing the other-than-discourse, 7; as Hegelian negative, 15; and history, 17–18; as indeterminable naysaying, xx; irony *an sich*, 12; as the Kierkegaardian *corpus*, 173–74; and the magnanimity of woman/being, 101; as mastered by Hegel, 12; and mediation, 130–32; as necessary condition of repetition, 99; as neither affirmative nor negative, 16; as never a result, as saying and meaning nothing, 20; as originating concept of the modern age, 2–3; as opposed to the concepts of nothing and negation, 19; and the other, 5; as penance of language, 100; and poetry, 16–17; principle of, 133–34; as recovery of authenticity, 17, 21; Socrates, 37; as suspending existence, 14; as technique of concealment, 14; and transcendence, 132–33; as using up reality, 99

Job. See *Job*

Job: as addressed by the Other, 93; as bait and wager of God, 85; at the confines of poetry and the limits of faith, 87–88; as exception, 88; language of and transcendence, 86–87, 90; as nonrepresentable, 88; as restructuring human discourse, 87; and silence, 88; and thunderstorm, 76, 89; and the transcendent, 87, 89, 93; as unquotable, 88; and the young man, 85–87

Kant, Immanuel: and actual experience, 146; and the categorical imperative, 26; doctrine of autonomy, 31–32; doctrine of immortality, 35; as impossible in antiquity, 38–39; as opposed by S.K., 23; and Plato on ethics, 34–35; and the problematic of the Good, 35; and skepticism, 146, 148; view of actuality, 147; view of moral autonomy, 153; view of self, 146–47

Kenosis: and S.K.'s love, 181

Kierkegaard, Michael Pedersen, 98; and Ane Sørensdatter Lund, 168–69; death of, 177; as metaphor of Christianity, 175; as not understanding S.K., 176; as raising S.K., 175–76; and Regine Olsen, 168; as replaced by God, 173

Kierkegaard, Peter Christian: as assuming paternal role in relation to S.K., 169; and *The Point of View*, 170; as uncomfortable with S.K.'s works, 170

Kierkegaardian *Corpus*, the: as ascribed to God, 188; the Augustinian structure of, 170–71; authorial claim of, 166–67; authorial explanation of, 171–72; authorial explanation of duplicity of, 166–67; as both understood and not understood by

S.K., 174–75; and Christendom, 171; as contradictory, 164; duplicity of, 164–67, 182–83; as indulged by God, 175; as a kind of excrement, 179–80; and metaphors of money and writing, 180; parallelism of, 166–67; and Peter Christian Kierkegaard, 170; as prescribed by God, 173; as the product of S.K.'s whole life, 179; as received and owned by God, 175; and Regine Olsen, 169–70; as sign of contradiction, 166; no single point of view for, 190; uncertainty of authorship, 188; and woman, 166

Lacan, Jacques, xiii, 98 n
Language: as actuality of reflection, 71–72; as alienating reality, 93; and alterity, 102; and being in love, 72–73; against the boundary of transcendence, 90; everything about S.K. is, 72; of God, 87–98; impotence of, 100, 139; of Job, 86–88; and S.K.'s inquisition of, xviii; and the limits of, 102; and its other, 7–8, 87, 102; as pure self-transcendence, 108; as self-love, xvii; violence of as turning on itself, 100; and woman, 74; and the young man in *Repetition*, 86–87
Leap: defined, 111
Luke, 57, 184
Lund, Ane Sørensdatter: and Michael Petersen Kierkegaard, 168–69; as daughter of S.K., 169

Maritain, Jacques, 191
Møller, Paul, 98
Moment, the: and the absolute paradox, 119; as the coming into being of the eternal, 105; of learning, 106; as second birth, 106

Name: of the author, 187–88; and the girl in *Repetition*, 96; loss of, 85–86, 168; as never written, 168; only in farce in *Repetition*, 96; patronymic, 169; and the young man in *Repetition*, 85–86
Negation, Radical: as freedom, xx; as unmediatable, xx
New Critics, xv–xvi, xvii

Nietzsche, F., xiii, 4–5; and the moral man, 32; truth as unsuccessful seduction, 4–5
Norris, Christopher, 161 n
Novelty, 106

Obligation: and freedom, 155–56; and other realities, 151–52
Offense: and absolute paradox, 118–19; as acoustic illusion, 119; nature of, 118–19; as passive, 119
Olsen, Regine, 5, 72, 98, 182; as beneficiary of S.K.'s will, 170; and defecation, 180; as discreetly disguised, 167–68; as establishing S.K.'s rapport with God, 168; as *factum*, 177–78; as grace of *Repetition*, 101; and S.K.'s writings, 169–70; as making S.K. a poet, 178; and Michael Pedersen Kierkegaard, 168; preservation of her virginity, 169; refused, 168; as replaced by God, 173
Onanism: as both/neither reality and fantasy, 179; as S.K.'s secret torment, 179–80
Origen, 178
Other: as crucial to S.K.'s concept of irony, 5; and its indistinguishability from reason, 112; as invading the subject deconstructively, xvi; as irrationality, 87; of language, 100, 102, 139; as nonconstructible, xvi; as other than same, xix–xx; as source of language, 102; transcendence as irruption of, 84, 86–87

Paradox: and difference, 112, 115–16; of faith, 121; and the historicity of the eternal, 120–21, 123; indistinguishability from reason, 112; and the Moment, 119; and the offense, 118–19; as paradoxical, 121; of reason, 110–12; and self-concealment of God, 154; and signification, 122–23; and the text, 115
Parody: as "copying backwards," 75, 119
Parson, the: and Abraham, 47–48; vs. the dialectician, 47–48
Passion: as defining man, 53; of infinite resignation, 53; of reason, 109; vs. reason, 52–53
Paul, 40
Philosophy: death of, xxi–xxii; as

Philosophy (*continued*)
  going beyond faith, 48–49; S.K. opposed to, xviii; as older than history, 5–6; as other than history, 6; and repetition, 76; as undone by Christian difference, xx
Philostratus the Elder, 99
Plato: and Kant on ethics, 34–35; and the problematic of evil, 34
Poet, the: as anonymous, 188–89; as an exception, 92–93; and the hero, 44–47; and the magnanimity of woman, 91–92
Poetry: as different from religion, 93–94; of faith, its failure, 43; and faith, silence, 88; and the hero, 44–45; as ironic diremption of subject and object, etc., 16–17; reflection and being in love, 72–73
Pontius Pilate, 100
Possibility: and actuality, 125–26; as annulled by the past, 128; as category of being, 126–27; defined, 148; and essence, 126–27; essential as object of thought, 147; as higher than reality for the aesthete, 148–49; reality as higher than for the ethical, 149; relation to reality, 147
Preface: author of as both editor and author, xii; as irreducibly duplicitous, x–xi; irresponsible sanctuary of, xv
Pynchon, Thomas, xxiii

Questioning: and doctrine of recollection, 104; presupposition of, 104, 106; and truth, 104

Realism: S.K.'s classical realism, 144–45, 157; as necessarily presupposed, 147
Reality: and the farce, 80–81; and freedom, 149–51; as higher than possibility for the ethical, 149; and history, 150–51; of individual as interest, 143; as *inter-esse* between the actual and the ideal, 97; S.K. restored to by Regine refused, 168; possibility as higher than for the aesthete, 148–49; as related to subject externally, 149, 151; and repetition, 70, 76; of the subject as ethical, 143; subject's possibility-relation, 148; as unmotivated in relation to reason, 97; as woman, 68, 73, 91–92, 93, 97; of world as irrelevant for S.K., 143
Reason: and its absolute other, 112–13, 118; and Christianity, 110; and difference, 115–16; and the finite, 52; fulfillment of as its own undoing, 109; and God, 109; and the irrational, 119–20; and the leap, 111; and reality, 97; reality of, 110; and the unknown, 109; as untrustworthy, 119–20; vs. passion, 52–53
Recollection: doctrine of as necessary, 106; eternal recollection of guilt, 65; and hope, 69; and lack of presence, 72–73; and the love of the young man in *Repetition*, 72–73; and modern philosophy, 70; presumption of doctrine of, 103; as reality, 70; as relationship of temporality and the eternal, 7; Socratic doctrine of, 103; as unhappy, 70
Reed, Walter L., 189n
Reflection: and being in love, 72–73; contradictory relation of to genius, 175; and farce and transcendence, 84; the impossibility of halting itself by means of itself, 137; of the Kierkegaardian *corpus*, 173–75; and new immediacy for S.K., 177, 190; and woman, 72, 93
Religion: and the Good, 23; relationship with ethics, 23, 28–29, 49; and religious poetry, 93–94; as transformed by Christianity, 34n
Remorse and Penitence: defined, 29; as exposition of the Good, 3; and the Good, 23, 29–30, 33; and the moral situation, 28–29; as the moral situation, 33; and the reality of God, 37
Repetition: as absolute surprise, 99; and beginning, 16; cannot be written, 99–100; defined, 69, 71; and the exhaustion of human possibility, 91; and farce, 80–81; and immediacy, 76; and impotence of language, 100; impossibility of principle of, 75–76; as interest of metaphysics, 88; and irony, 21; irony as necessary condition of, 99; as not in any text, 99; as origin of beginning, 85; as reality, 70, 76; as

relationship of temporality to the eternal, 71–72; required by S.K., 177–78; the Resurrection as, 100; as transcendence, defined, 84; only viable meaning of, 81

St. Augustine. *See* Augustine
St. Luke. *See* Luke
St. Paul. *See* Paul
Seduction: and the Kierkegaardian text, 166; as nonrepeatable, 77; and woman, 76
Self-denial: of S.K., 162
Sexuality: and Christianity, 99
Signification: and the absolute paradox, 122–23; and Christianity, 122; and faith, 121; and Hegel, 122; as pure self-transcendence, 108; and relation of time to eternity, 108, 122; as true subject of *Philosophical Fragments*, 107; as unmediatable, 122
Silentio, Johannes de: as almost brought to silence, 44, 55; and the cul-de-sac of dialectics, 50; irony of, 66–67; as lyricist and dialectician, 47, 49; meaning of name, 41–42; and the paradoxicality of faith, 53–54; and the poetry of faith, 43
Sin: as beyond ethics, 65–66; as obverse of guilt, 65
Skepticism: as irresoluble, 148; and Kant, 146
Socrates: as akin to S.K., 37–39; and the concept of irony, 6–8; as dead end, 20–21; death of as consummate irony, 10, 16; his doctrine of recollection, 107–8; as infinite negativity, 9, 11; as irony *an sich*, 12; irony and ignorance of, 15–16, 37; and S.K.'s relation to Christendom, 171; view of history, 129; view of signification, 107–8
Sophists, the, 8–9
Stevens, Wallace, xxiii, 116
Surprise: impossibility of, 104–5; and irony, 99; relationship of God with man as, xx; and repetition, 99

Teacher, the: as divine, 105; as more than an occasion, 105; the Socratic view of, 103–4
Temporality: intelligible only in relation to the eternal, 71; and Job, 89; as rhetoric of death, 77

Temptation: and freedom, 155–56; and other realities, 151–52
Text: absolute paradox of, 115; and being as the excess of, 96; and the beyond-the-text, 115; defined, 95; meaning of, 112; nothing outside of, 115; and repetition, 99; as transgressed by farce, 96
Theater: and the cryptic personality, 78–79
Theology: S.K. as opposed to, xviii, xxi; and philosophy, 49
Thought: and difference, 115–16; and existence, 114–15; and the unthinkable, 114–15
Time: Christian view of, 108; its conjunction with the eternal, 18; and the eternal, 24–25; and the eternal reconciled in it, 89; Hegel vs. Christianity's view of, 122–23; and object of faith, 129; as paradoxical, 122–23; and signification, 108, 122; its unmediatable relation to eternity, 122; as unreal, 128
Tolkien, J. R. R., 100
Transcendence: defined, 84; God as, 93; and Job, 86–87, 93; and language broken against, 90
Transcendent, the: God as, 93; as irrupting into the world, 87; and Job, 87, 89, 93
Truth: and the learner as untruth, 105; Socratic view of, 103–4

Unintelligibility: and Christianity, 113–14; as self-verifying, 106–7

Woman: and the grace of God, 98; as incapable of the ideal, 90; and the Kierkegaardian *corpus*, 166; magnanimity of and the poet, 72, 74, 91; magnanimity of as an ironic inversion, 101; as reality, 68, 73, 91–92, 93, 97; and reflection, 72; as saving *Repetition*, 101; as saving us from the interesting, 97–98; and seduction, 74; as subject of *Repetition*, 68
Wilde, Alan, xxii n
Writing: and author, 187–88; and castration, 178; God and S.K.'s, 173; as not constituting totality, 186; and phallogocentrism, 96; and the phallus, 178; violence of, 95, 98, 100

32465648 908